PLURALISM IN PHILOSOPHY: CHANGING THE SUBJECT

OTHER BOOKS BY JOHN KEKES

A Justification of Rationality

The Nature of Philosophy

The Examined Life

Moral Tradition and Individuality

Facing Evil

The Morality of Pluralism

Moral Wisdom and Good Lives

Against Liberalism

A Case for Conservatism

Pluralism in Philosophy: Changing the Subject

JOHN KEKES

Cornell University Press

Ithaca and London

First published 2000 by Cornell University Press

Printed in the United States of America

Library of Congress Cataloging-in-Publication Data

Kekes, John.
   Pluralism in philosophy : changing the subject / John Kekes.
     p. cm.
   Includes bibliographical references and index.
   ISBN 0-8014-3805-5 (alk. paper)
   1. Life. 2. Pluralism. I. Title
BD435 .K37 2000
147'.4--dc21   00-009351

Cornell University Press strives to use environmentally responsible
suppliers and materials to the fullest extent possible in the publishing
of its books. Such materials include vegetable-based, low-VOC inks
and acid-free papers that are either recycled, totally chlorine-free, or partly
composed of nonwood fibers. Books that bear the logo of the FSC
(Forest Stewardship Council) use paper taken from forests that have
been inspected and certified as meeting the highest standards for
environmental and social responsibility. For further information, visit
our website at www.cornellpress.cornell.edu.

Cloth printing   10 9 8 7 6 5 4 3 2 1

FSC FSC Trademark © 1996 Forest Stewardship Council A.C.
SW-COC-098   ® GCU

For J. Y. K.

Contents

Acknowledgments

Many people gave generously of their time and attention to help make this book better. Graeme Hunter, James Kellenberger, and Wallace Matson have read and commented on the entire manuscript. Joseph Carcasole, Rachel Cohon, Eric Fried, Joel Kupperman, Jonathan Mandle, and Daniel Thero did the same with parts of it. I thank them for their criticisms. They have made the resulting work better, often very much better. All of them disagree more or less strongly with its general argument. It is much the more noteworthy that they helped to make it less inadequate.

Much of the material in Chapter 5 has been published as "The Meaning of Life" in *Midwest Studies in Philosophy* 24 (2000). The permission of the journal and of Blackwell Publishers to make use of this material is gratefully acknowledged.

Roger Haydon has been, for the fourth time, my editor at Cornell University Press. I could not wish for a more sympathetic, helpful, and reliable editor than he has been over the years. He is a beacon in the treacherous waters of academic publishing, and I have been guided by him again and again. I can only hope that the end product will justify his support of it.

The book is dedicated with love and gratitude to my wife, who makes all manner of things not only possible but also better.

JOHN KEKES

ITHAKA
Charlton, New York

PLURALISM IN PHILOSOPHY: CHANGING THE SUBJECT

Introduction: At a Turning Point

> By a turning point I mean a transformation of outlook. This is
> something different from the kind of change that occurs when
> a discovery, even one of crucial importance, solves even the
> most central and tormenting questions. A solution to a ques-
> tion, set in terms of that question, does not necessarily alter the
> categories and concepts in terms of which the question pre-
> sented itself. . . . By a turning point I mean . . . a radical change
> in the entire conceptual framework within which the questions
> had been posed; new ideas, new words, new relationships in
> terms of which the old problems are not so much solved as
> made to look remote, obsolete, and, at times, unintelligible, so
> that the agonising problems and doubts of the past seem queer
> ways of thought, or confusions that belong to a world which
> has gone.
>
> ISAIAH BERLIN, *The Sense of Reality*

The aim of this book is to change philosophical think-
ing about good lives. This is bound to appear as a grandiose ambition motivated by hubris. It may be accepted as a mitigating factor, however, that the
aim is not to propose yet another generalization about what must be done to
make lives good, but to suggest that philosophical thinking about good lives
should no longer aim to satisfy the craving for generality that has characterized the history of this subject. The thinking should recognize instead the
plurality of reasonable conceptions of a good life, it should eschew the general in favor of the particular. The change may even be welcomed if it is
borne in mind that philosophical thinking in the past has led to familiar and
intractable problems. Perhaps the change from the general to the particular
will result in an approach that resolves some philosophical problems. It is
that possibility, rather than hubris, that partly motivates the argument.

Another part of the motivation is that some of the philosophical problems that have proved so intractable in the past are obstacles to living good lives. These problems, therefore, are not intellectual puzzles invented by minds addicted to abstraction, but real practical difficulties. Philosophy used to be thought of as holding the key to good lives. Doubts have been growing on this score because the keys philosophers have dangled have seemed to open doors that led not to good lives but only to other doors. A strong reason for trying to change the subject is to restore the fading reputation of philosophy as the home of the best that has been thought about living good lives.

The aim of the book dictates its approach. Changing a subject calls for a new way of thinking, a break with old patterns of thought. These patterns have not been successful in the 2,500-year history of the subject, so it is not unreasonable to suppose that it would be fruitless to make yet another attempt to think more carefully, painstakingly, precisely in the old ways. The failure of the old ways is a failure not of technique but of orientation. The reorientation envisaged in this book opens up possibilities; it proposes a new way of approaching old problems. Its approach, therefore, is exploratory. The intent of the book is not to say the last word on any of the problems it treats but to show how their treatment can avoid the endless arguments that have grown ever more arcane and distant from the pressing predicaments that prompted them.

This approach does not constitute a radical break with the past. On the contrary, it grows out of past ways of thinking by presenting an alternative to them. Understanding what it is and why it is needed requires understanding what it is an alternative to and why its predecessors have reached the impasses so painfully familiar in the history of philosophy. The proposed approach, therefore, must begin with an explanation of the nature of philosophical problems and the reasons for the failure to resolve them. Only against that background will the need for a new approach become apparent. The reason for following it, however, is not just that it is needed but also that it actually does better at resolving the problems than the alternatives. And that must be—and will be—shown.

There is a time for exploration, and there is a time for consolidation. The book is written in the belief that ours is a time for exploration because we have reached a historical turning point. During the last hundred years or so, deep changes have disrupted the customary patterns of everyday life. The exponential growth of scientific knowledge and technological expertise has created countless new possibilities and dangers; revolutions in communication, warfare, sexual and reproductive practices, medicine, travel, and agriculture have been transforming the traditional ways of engaging in these activities; empires have risen and fallen; secularization, universal franchise, decolonization, population explosion, and urbanization have been changing long-standing political arrangements; DNA research, space exploration, computerization, and atomic energy have been producing incalculable consequences; great wars have been fought and great massacres have occurred. We reflect on these changes, as we must, in order to understand them, control them when possible, and adjust to them when it is not.

It is a distinctive characteristic of our times, however, that there is a deep change also in the nature of the reflection by means of which we aim to understand, control, and adjust to these changes. It is thus not only the external conditions of our lives that are changing, but also the internal ones: our standards, expectations, sensibility, and values. The changes within us, of course, are intimately connected with the changes outside us. We are changing because the disruptions of our lives require it. But it is a consequence of the changes in us that how we cope and what we hope to gain from it are also changing.

The combination of these external and internal changes has brought us to a turning point in our history. Turning points are rare but not unprecedented. They have occurred also in Athens in the fifth century B.C., in the Roman world during the rise of Christianity, and in Europe as the joint product of the Renaissance and the Enlightenment. The external conditions on these past occasions were, of course, very different from each other and from our own. What is not different, however, is that a profound change occurred then and is occurring now in the form that reflection on the world takes. The world has begun to look different, not just because of changes in it, but because we have come to reflect on it in a different way. As a result, there is a gradual but undeniable turning away from older ways of seeing and responding to the world and a turning toward a new way.

We are turning away from the traditional certainty that reality is permeated by a beneficial design and that the key to a good life is to live in conformity to it. We have come to doubt that the scheme of things is conducive to our welfare, that reality and human existence have a plot or a purpose, and that the goodness of our lives depends on anything other than how successful we are in coping with the conditions in which we find ourselves. The conviction is growing that since many of these conditions are adverse, it is not merely the deficiencies of our reason and will that stand in the way of good lives. There is widespread doubt about the absolutist way of looking at the world that the great religions, metaphysical systems, poetic visions, and other overarching, all-inclusive world views share—whose articulation our predecessors took to be the object of reflection.

These doubts are subversive and dangerous because they foster a distrust of time-honored beliefs about what is true and good. The combination of beliefs in human fallibility and in the absence of a beneficial design leads to predictable, destructive, and by now familiar consequences: to nihilism that claims that if there is no God, then everything is permitted; to fideism that celebrates faith and spurns reason; to romanticism that places its hope in great men who heroically struggle against overwhelming odds while trampling on the lowly lives of common humanity; to ideologies that unmask all convictions, except their own, as disguised symptoms of domination, exploitation, false consciousness, anxiety, and so on; to irony that regards human concerns with the bemused detachment of an impartial spectator; and to hedonism that prefers the mindless pursuit of immediate pleasure to self-control and planning for the future. To these attitudes others could easily be added. What unites them is the relativistic view that our traditional beliefs have no reasonable grounding. If relativism in one of its many forms were true, then the turning point that we are experiencing would present an extremely serious threat to our efforts to live good lives. If we are to avoid this threat, we must go beyond the denial that there is a beneficial design permeating reality. We must restore confidence in our capacity to arrive at reasonable beliefs about what is true and good. This is the great challenge that faces those who recognize what is happening to us, who are turning away from absolutist certainties, and who recognize the need to avoid relativistic arbitrariness. It is to the meeting of this challenge that the present book is intended as a contribution.

An alternative to absolutism and relativism is pluralism. Pluralism, like the alternatives to it, has different versions. It may be ontological, having to do with the ultimate constituents of reality; epistemological, concerning the standards of reasonable belief; axiological, pertaining to the values that make lives good; anthropological, regarding the cultural forms that human lives may take; or political, advocating arrangements that recognize the legitimacy of many conceptions of a good life. In all its versions, pluralism is committed to there being reasonable beliefs about the true and the good, but it insists that they have a plurality of forms. Pluralism is thus not absolutist, because it denies that the truth of beliefs and the goodness of lives are determined by absolute standards. But it is not relativistic either, because it denies that the rejection of absolute standards makes it ultimately arbitrary what beliefs are true and what lives are good.

The version of pluralism defended here (simply "pluralism" from now on) is a mixture of epistemological and axiological components. Its epistemological component is the claim that reflection on our lives, circumstances, and the disruptions that we face occurs in an irreducible plurality of modes, which include the scientific, historical, religious, moral, aesthetic, and subjective. The axiological component of pluralism is the claim that each of these modes of reflection provides a perspective that is believed to make an important contribution to good lives. One central claim of pluralism is that it follows from the plurality of modes of reflection that good lives may take a plurality of forms. The turning point that we are experiencing may then be characterized as a turning away from absolutism and a turning toward pluralism, but it is a pluralism that stops short of relativism.

Pluralism attempts to break fresh ground by proposing a new way of understanding the nature of the internal changes we face. It begins with the fact that modes of reflection often yield conflicting conclusions. Since one main purpose of reflection is to cope with changes in the world, and since different modes of reflection often lead to incompatible suggestions about how we should cope, it is essential to resolve conflicts among them. If these conflicts were the result of disagreements about what the facts are, then their resolution would present no theoretical difficulty. We would merely have to ascertain what the facts really are, and then accept or reject the conclusions of particular modes of reflection on that basis. But the conflicts between modes of reflection turn not on what the facts are but on how we should understand the significance of the relevant facts. The conflicts concern not how the world is but the significance that we attribute to how the world is. The disagreements are about the right mode in which we should reflect on the significance of the facts. The conflicts produced by such disagreements do present serious theoretical difficulties, because there are intractable problems with the traditional absolutist approach to resolving them.

We cannot just follow the absolutist strategy and assign precedence to a favored mode of reflection, because doing so would relegate rival modes to an inferior status that their defenders would rightly reject as arbitrary. It requires a reasoned argument to assign preference to one mode of reflection over the others. Such an argument cannot appeal to the overriding significance of the favored mode of reflection because that is what needs to be established. Nor can it appeal to any external fact in the world, because the other modes of reflection dispute not the facts but their significance. Nor does it help to claim that one mode of reflection leads to better ways of coping with disruptions than the others because what is taken to be a better way also depends on the standards of the mode of reflection that has been accepted. Pluralists conclude therefore that absolutist strategies of coping with conflicts between modes of reflection result in an intractable impasse.

The evidence for the existence and intractability of this impasse emerges from reflection on five familiar problems that perennially recur in serious thought about good lives: the meaning of life, the possibility of free action, the place of morality in good lives, the art of life, and the nature of human self-understanding. These are traditional philosophical problems, but that is not what is interesting about them. What is interesting is that they are unavoidable once it is recognized that there is a plurality of modes that reflection on the significance of facts may take and that reflection in these modes leads to incompatible conclusions. The scientific, historical, religious, moral, aesthetic, and subjective modes of reflection are alternative ways of making sense of our lives and circumstances. The conflicts they produce occur among and within us as we reflect in these conflicting modes, each of which we believe we have reason to value. We are naturally unwilling, therefore, to resolve the conflicts by abandoning the modes of reflection that we value, even though we recognize them as the sources of our conflicts. But if we continue to reflect in these ways, we inevitably encounter serious problems that stand in the way of our attempts to live good lives.

The remedy proposed here is to change the subject. The subject is complex. It includes: *ourselves*, who are to be changed by changing the nature of our reflection on how we should live; *philosophy*, which is to be changed by making it more pluralistic and less absolutist than it has traditionally been; and the five perennial *problems* that form part of the subject matter of philosophy, which are to be changed by understanding and coping with them in a new way.

The argument in support of these proposed changes falls into two parts. The first contains chapters 1–4. Its aim is to construct a theory that explains the nature of one type of philosophical problem. These chapters deal with the disruptions of everyday life that call for modes of reflection, with the nature of these modes, with the perennial philosophical problems that are caused by conflicts among them, and with the pluralistic approach to resolving these problems. The second part contains chapters 5–9. It applies the theory constructed in the preceding part and proposes a resolution of each of the five perennial problems mentioned above. A concluding chapter sums up the argument.

The two parts of the argument are logically independent. The theory may be correct even if its particular applications are failures; and the theory may be wrong even if all or some of the proposed resolutions of the five problems are successful. But, of course, the two parts are meant to reinforce each other. The successful resolution of a problem is meant to serve as evidence for the theory that is being applied, and the theory is meant to explain why a proposed resolution is successful.

PART ONE

The Theory

PREAMBLE

The aim of the theory is to explain the nature of one type of philosophical problem and to propose an approach to resolving it. The explanation is needed because of the failure of assiduous and highly sophisticated attempts to find solutions that carry general conviction. The explanation is that the failure of the attempted solutions is the result of a mistaken absolutist approach. The proposed alternative approach is pluralistic.

The philosophical problems that concern us here have their origin in some disruption of everyday life that seriously interferes with our attempts to live good lives. Science, history, religion, aesthetics, morality, and subjectivity are particular attempts to cope with these disruptions. But these attempts often conflict with one another because they propose incompatible ways of coping. The absolutist approach to resolving these conflicts is to formulate a general outlook derived from one of these attempts and then assign it precedence over other general outlooks. A mode of reflection then is a general outlook that aims to understand the true significance of the relevant facts. This approach will not resolve the conflicts, however, because the defenders of each mode of reflection claim that precedence should be assigned to the mode that is based on the particular attempt at coping with the disruption that they favor. Each mode of reflection proposes a particular way of understanding the significance of the relevant facts, but the generality of each mode makes the proposed understandings of significance just as conflicting as the original attempts were. There will, therefore, be endless controversies over whether the true significance of the relevant facts is revealed by scientific, historical, religious, aesthetic, moral, or subjective reflection.

The theory claims that it is these controversies that make intractable the philosophical problems that we identify as the meaning of life, the possibility of free action, the place of morality in good lives, the art of life, and the nature of human self-understanding. These problems have been intractable because of the absolutist assumption that one mode of reflection must be assigned precedence—an assumption that inevitably gives rise to endless arguments about which mode leads to the true significance of the relevant facts and should therefore be assigned precedence.

The theory claims, furthermore, that success in resolving the problems and coping with the disruptions depends on abandoning the absolutist approach in favor of a pluralistic one. According to the pluralistic approach, there is no such thing as the true significance of the facts; no mode of reflection ought always to be assigned precedence over the others. This, however, does not lead to relativism because there are good reasons for assigning precedence to particular modes of reflection; but these reasons will always be particular, holding in specific contexts only. The theory explains how reasons can be good even if they are not general.

1

Everyday Life

> It is so difficult to find the *beginning*. Or, better: it is difficult to begin at the beginning. And not try to go further back.
>
> LUDWIG WITTGENSTEIN, *On Certainty*

I

We live and we think. Thinking is part of living, but living comes first, thinking second. We need to think because we encounter problems, doubts, incapacities, despair, misfortune, conflicts, injustice, and they disrupt our lives. If thinking goes well, it enables us to cope with disruptions and it restores the smooth flow of life. But it may not go well, because it may be misguided, misdirected, or defective in other ways, and because the disruptions may be too severe even for exemplary thinking. We need to understand these disruptions and how to think well about them. Everyday life is the background against which both the disruptions and the thinking occur, and it is with it that we must begin.

Most of our lives are spent in familiar activities. We sleep, wash, dress, eat, go to work, work, shop, relax, balance the checkbook, clean house, do the laundry, have the car serviced, chat, pay bills, worry about this or that, and take small pleasure in small things. We do all this as we mature, age, and die, have children and lose our parents, graduate, find a job, get married and divorced, fall in and out of love, set up house, succeed at some things and fail at others, make friends and have fights, move house, change jobs, get fired or promoted, fall ill and recover, save for retirement and retire. So life goes for just about everybody in our society. These activities constitute everyday life. Life is mostly everyday. In other societies the details are different, but they affect only the forms everyday life takes, not their all-pervasive familiarity, nor the fact that they occupy a very large part of everyone's life.

The advantage of beginning with these truisms is that they are true. The disadvantage is that they seem jejune. That they are not becomes apparent if the alternatives they exclude are borne in mind. They exclude beginning with Cartesian ideas whose clarity and distinctness render them indubitable, or with a Platonic transcendental world that the appearances of everyday life imperfectly reflect, or with some deep structure buried in the natural world or in the human mind that causes our experiences to be what they are. The beginning is thus not Darwinian evolution, Hegelian history, Marxist sociology, Freudian psychology, nor the Kantian categories that ordain how we must think. The beginning is the familiar world of everyday life that one can hardly fail to know, and the knowing of which requires no research, no arcane knowledge or skill, no higher education. Knowing it takes only minimal intelligence and the opportunity to employ it by participating in some recognizably human forms of life, whose details naturally vary with historical, cultural, and individual circumstances.[1]

The first thing that must be said about everyday life is that it is *social*. Our lives need not be social: they could be merely biological, persisting in virtual isolation from other human beings, like the lives of feral children or hermits. Such lives, however, are only marginally human. They provide very little scope for the development of characteristically human potentialities. They are without communication, division of labor, companionship, affection, reciprocity, trust, or the possibility of improving one's opinions by way of comparison with those of others.

Social life, of course, involves strife, animosity, adventure, competition, and risk taking. But everyday life, though part of social life, lacks these excitements. Everyday life is *routine*. It provides order and predictability. It is the safe haven from which we venture out to do our battles, make our discoveries, enrich ourselves with real or metaphorical treasures, and to which we return to enjoy our gains, lick our wounds, recharge our batteries, tell our tales, and plan the next forays. Everyday life is the background of social life. To be that, however, it must be *conventional*. It must have familiar forms that are widely known, recognized, and practiced by a very large majority of those who live in that context.

The conventions that sustain everyday life are authenticated by a pervasive conformity to them. Hume called them "a kind of lesser morality,"[2] and Jane Austen referred to them as "the civilities, the lesser duties of life."[3] Offense against them is a breach of civility. Frequent violations of a particular convention may occur, of course. When they do, they indicate that everyday life is changing in that respect. Such changes are inevitable and often salutary because they are responses to the changing conditions of a particular society. But frequent violations of the bulk of the conventions of everyday life are serious matters because they indicate the disintegration of a society. They disrupt order and predictability; they make the previously safe haven fraught with controversy, anxiety, and uncertainty. It is as if what is happening to our conventions regarding sexual relations were to happen also and simultaneously to our conventions regarding education, commerce, sports, eating and drinking, travel, entertainment, music, and humor; to our expressions of grief, sympathy, respect, admiration, and congratulation; to our styles of dressing, furnishing, and lovemaking; to how we argue, fight, make amends, lay blame, and celebrate. If all this, and more, were changing at once, we could not count on continuity, on not being misunderstood, on having the comfort of not having to explain and justify ourselves all the time, and "we would all go out of our minds."[4]

There is, of course, much more to the evaluative dimension of life than the familiar everyday conventions. Morality, politics, aesthetics, and the law raise hard and complex questions to which the unreflective, spontaneous responses of everyday life do not provide adequate answers. Everyday life is not the last word on anything, but it is the first one on many things. Its simplicities form the background against which complexities are recognized. The complexities call for thought, and they unavoidably force going beyond everyday life. This makes apparent another feature of everyday life: it is *practical* rather than theoretical. Its primary concern is with acting, not with thinking about acting. Everyday life is not thoughtless, but it is not thoughtful either. Following its conventions is usually simple enough not to require much thought and certainly no theory. The comfort—and the danger—of the conventional activities of everyday life is that one need not think about them.

Participation in everyday life, however, involves not merely habitual conformity to conventions but also having particular motives for doing so and sharing those motives with fellow participants. These motives derive from a shared view about the basic conditions required for living a recognizably human life. But everyday life is much more than just a conventional outlook. It also guides action, inspires emotions, and provides a framework of interpretation and judgment. Everyday life does all this because it is *evaluative* and its evaluations have pervasive *emotive* significance for its participants.

The evaluative dimension of everyday life involves familiarity with the discriminations, nuances, judgments of importance and priority, and the sources of conflict and tension that partly form its texture. Participants in this dimension know not merely which person is admirable or contemptible but also what makes them so, why one is better or worse, more or less culpable or praiseworthy, weaker or stronger, more capable of improvement or more hopelessly corrupt than another person in similar circumstances. They know what is outrageous, shocking, offensive; what is a sophomoric attempt to provoke, a cry for help, or an assertion of independence, and whether it is premature, timely, or overdue; they know the distinctions between what should be encouraged, tolerated, forbidden, and respected; they know what is shameful, dishonorable, forgivable, or a sign of weakness or wickedness; they know how to tell what is significant or banal and what lies in between.

Through immersion in everyday life participants know these and thousands of similar things in a particular manner. They do not know them as an umpire knows the rules. They do not normally ponder and then carefully select the appropriate conventions that best fit the case on hand. Knowing the conventions has become second nature to them. Making the distinctions, noticing the nuances, being alive to the conflicts, priorities, pitfalls, and temptations no longer requires much thought. Just as an accomplished violinist knows how to play an adagio and a rock climber knows how to manage an overhang, so participants in everyday life know about elementary conventional matters. There are times, of course, when they have to stop and think. But that happens only in difficult cases. They can normally handle the flow of life spontaneously.

Nor is the required knowledge like that of anthropologists observing another society. The crucial difference is that anthropologists are outsiders. They may privately approve or disapprove of what they observe; they may feel sympathy, revulsion, or indifference; and they may compare it favorably or unfavorably to customs in other societies. Participants in everyday life are necessarily insiders. They can observe social behavior perhaps as accurately as any anthropologist, but they cannot be indifferent. They are not bound to judge their own conventions superior to others. Their basic judgments, however, are made in terms their conventions provide. Participation in everyday life means that they answer many evaluative questions in customary ways.

This could not be otherwise. For everyday life largely forms people's view of the basic conditions whose enjoyment makes life worth living; of virtuous and admirable personal characteristics; of the proper ways to treat people; of the acceptable forms of personal relationships; of coping with misfortune, adversity, and the prospect of failure; and of the duties and privileges of the various positions in life their society affords. These constitute the shared basic level of their lives and inform the sensibility through which they evaluate the significance of whatever happens. Indifference would mean the loss of an indispensable part of the evaluative dimension of their lives.

Everyday life thus leaves its imprint on its participants. It shapes how they think and feel about their lives and how they interpret the disclosures of their experiences. But by being so shaped, individuals come to belong to a community whose members share an outlook and sensibility. Everyday life unites fellow participants by providing them with common ways of interpreting and responding to the world. It thus confers the rudiments of *identity* on its participants. This is something that both unifies them and makes them the individuals they are. The basis of their shared identity is not that they know, love, or even like one another. There need be no fundamental principle to which they all subscribe, no overarching ideal whose inspirational force motivates them. Their solidarity may be real and strong without having a unitary base. There is a largely spontaneous, unreflective, customary conduct, and an unarticulated feeling of ease in one another's company. These guarantee that there is much that need not be said, and that when something needs to be done, they know how to do it.

II

If everyday life is understood as social, routine, conventional, practical, evaluative, emotive, and identity-conferring, if it is seen as the background against which other activities occur, if it is recognized as involving activities basic to our humanity, then it will be apparent that in some sense everyday life is necessary. It must be made clear now what it is necessary *for* and what *kind* of necessity it has. It is necessary for *good* lives and its necessity is *conditional*.

To begin with good lives, everyday life is a necessary but not sufficient condition for them. To have a good life is more than having a biological life in which such basic physiological needs as nutrition, shelter, rest, and the like are satisfied. Human beings also have basic psychological and social needs. We must make a living, cooperate with others, have some freedom, hope for an acceptable future, attend to our sick and dead, have some relief from drudgery, defend ourselves against external and internal attacks, be free from terror, raise our children, and so on. We cannot do all this alone, so we must live in a society that has division of labor, rules that are generally observed and enforced, a distinction between the private (where we are left alone) and the public (where matters affecting our society are settled), and so forth. In good lives, these basic needs are also satisfied. But good lives also depend on what happens beyond the satisfaction of the basic physiological, psychological, and social needs. Good lives are similar because human beings are alike in having these basic needs. But good lives are also different partly because there are great differences among societies in how they go about meeting basic needs. The everyday life of a society is the framework within which these needs are addressed. That is why everyday life is necessary for good lives.

This necessity is *conditional*. A negative characterization of it is that it is neither logical nor natural. There is nothing in logic that dictates that life must go well enough to be called good. And there is no law of nature to the effect that our lives could not be entirely occupied with securing biological subsistence. A positive characterization of the necessity being conditional is that *if* we are to go beyond mere biological subsistence and live good lives in which not only basic physiological but also basic psychological and social needs are met, *then* there must be widely accepted conventions in our society regarding how these needs are to be met, and most of our relevant activities must by and large conform to these conventions. Everyday life is necessary if our lives are to be good because everyday life is the system of conventions and activities that makes our lives good. Its necessity, however, is conditional in two different ways.

One is that it is a contingent fact whether a society has the material resources that allow it to meet basic needs and whether it is successful in creating and maintaining the necessary conventions. Societies vary widely in both respects, and even in societies where the material resources and the necessary conventions are present, there is still great variety in the distribution of the benefits they provide. This variety ranges from an arrangement in which the benefits are distributed according to the recipients' position in a hierarchy, through various intermediate stages, to an egalitarian one in which the benefits are distributed equally among all the recipients. As a result, everyday life is necessary, on the condition that life in a society is good. But it may not be good, and even if it is for some members of the society, it may not be for all.[5]

The other way in which the necessity of everyday life is conditional follows from the conventions that govern how basic needs are met. Each basic need, be it physiological, psychological, or social, may be met differently in different cultural and historical contexts. As a result, there are many different conventions, and one is not prima facie superior to the others. Nutrition is necessary, but whether calories are consumed cooked or raw, ceremoniously or expediently, come from cattle or pigs, fish or fowl, is contingent. Children have to be raised, but it can be done by parents, grandparents, nurseries, nannies, extended families, and so forth. Security must be maintained by some authority, but it may be the police, priests, the elders, the king, and so forth. None of these conventions is individually necessary. What is necessary for good lives is that at any given time in a society there be a system of conventions that governs how basic needs are met. Yet the necessity of this system is conditional on the identity of the conventions that constitute it, and there is no reason why the individual conventions, and thus the system, could not change in response to the changing conditions of the society. The system— everyday life—must, however, endure, if the participants are to live good lives.[6]

Part of the reason for dwelling on the necessity of everyday life is to support the claim for it being the beginning from which disruptions are best approached. This claim will be further strengthened by distinguishing between everyday life and some cognate notions that may be confused with it. If by "the given" the collection of immediately experienced sense data is meant, then everyday life is not the given. Everyday life has a wider scope than the given because of its social, practical, evaluative, emotive, and identity-conferring features, whereas the given is purely epistemological. Moreover, the given is supposed to be the indubitable—or at least the indefeasible—foundation of empirical knowledge, but no such claim is made for everyday life, which is fallible, open to criticism, and often changing.

For similar reasons, everyday life should not be confused with the common-sense view of the world either. The latter is supposed to comprise true beliefs known with certainty, whereas everyday life contains beliefs that are not known with certainty, includes much more than beliefs, and is recognized to be historically and culturally variable. Nor is everyday life the life-world (*Lebenswelt*) of phenomenology. The life-world is subjective, intuitive, and in its essential features universal, whereas the everyday life of a society is social, learned, and shaped by the variable conditions that prevail in a particular context. Everyday life is richer and more revisable than the system of simple impressions of classical empiricism, the protocol sentences of logical positivism, the basic or observation statements of logical empiricism, or the atomic propositions of Wittgenstein's *Tractatus*. It is fallible, not certain or indubitable; practical, not just perceptual; evaluative and emotive, not just epistemological; social and public, not individual and private; and variable and changing, not constant and universal. These conditional features notwithstanding, everyday life is necessary for good lives because it provides the conventions that make the satisfaction of basic needs possible.

III

The reasons for thinking that everyday life is necessary for good lives are also reasons for denying that it is sufficient. Everyday life is constantly beset by disruptions, but it lacks the resources for coping with them. The disruptions that first come to mind are *physical dangers* that threaten the satisfaction of basic needs: epidemics, scarcity of natural resources, crop failures, disasters, and so forth. Science and technology have been remarkably successful in coping with these dangers. It is perhaps for this reason that there is a widespread tendency to assimilate other types of disruptions to those amenable to scientific or technological treatment. This tendency should be resisted, however, because it leads us to look at the wrong place for ways of coping with many of them.

A case in point are disruptions caused by *conflicts* among the conventions of everyday life. Justice and benevolence, prosperity and equality, friendship and impartiality, the need to earn a living and the desire to pursue individual projects, social responsibility and private life, freedom and order, and so on are parts of everyday life that often exist in a state of tension. It is not the remediable scarcity of resources but the very nature of conventions necessary for good lives that is responsible for such conflicts. The social aspect of morality attempts to cope with these disruptions.

Another type of disruption that often assails us is the *drabness* that results from following the familiar routines of everyday life. We grow tired of utilitarian pursuits, even if we are successful at them, and we want some relief, joy, and beauty in our lives. We want to be taken out of our routines and see the world with fresh eyes. We want to do, have, admire, or learn about things, not because of the practical benefits they may yield, but because we find them worthwhile in themselves. We want what aesthetics makes possible: the enjoyment of beautiful, delightful, and interesting objects for themselves alone.

Yet a further form that disruptions may take are the *novelties* for which the conventions of everyday life have not prepared us. The world intrudes, interferes with our routines, and presents us with situations to which we must respond, but for which our conventions provide inadequate guidance. These unexpected situations may be technological, like the sudden availability of life-sustaining medical apparatus; social, like the sexual revolution; political, like the implications of greater racial and gender equality; aesthetic, like nonrepresentational art; demographic, like the effects of increased life expectancy on employment patterns; personal, like the ready availability of recreational drugs, and so on. The very success of our conventions often produces unforeseen and unintended consequences that disrupt other areas of life.

There are also disruptions that occur on a subjective level. Few lives are so fortunate as to escape serious disappointment, injustice, grief, accident, illness, or failure. Such misfortunes may make us wonder about the point of participating in conventional activities, especially since the bad thing that has happened prevents us from doing so successfully. Even if our lives are good enough because our basic needs are satisfied, we may still find them devoid of meaning. We may just see our lives as a long sequence of ultimately pointless activities that terminate only in death. In this way, we may be assailed by the *meaninglessness* of life and turn to religion, mysticism, art, philosophy, or literature for consolation or hope. Or we may turn inward, cultivate our subjective resources, and try to give meaning to our lives by pursuing private projects that may have significance only for us.

The last kind of disruption that will be mentioned here takes the form of *challenges* to the prevailing conventions. They may be external to the society and come from its enemies, critics, or colonizers, who assert the superiority of their own conventions. Much harm has been done in this way, although it must also be acknowledged that external challenges to wretched societies may be perfectly justified. Some conventions stand in the way of good lives, and it is right to challenge them. Slavery, female circumcision, child prostitution, repression of dissent, religious intolerance, and blood feuds are examples that come to mind. External challenges, however, need not be explicit; they may be implied by the mere existence of a society whose relevant conventions are obviously better. It does not need to be shouted from the rooftops that Canadians are better at handling their ethnic conflicts than the citizens of what used to be Yugoslavia, that the English attitude to political dissent is preferable to that of the Chinese, or that North Korean central planning is not a patch on the South Korean market economy. The challenges may also be internal, mounted by homegrown dissatisfactions and doubts. They may be issued because the conventions seem arbitrary, overly restrictive, pointless, obsolete, or discriminatory. A society may or may not be able to meet these challenges. One time-honored way of trying to meet them is historical. It consists in explaining how the prevailing conventions arose, what needs they were meant to serve, and what conditions peculiar to the society have shaped them, and thus to look to the past for justification.

This list of disruptions is meant to be merely illustrative, not systematic or exhaustive. Its purpose is to call attention to their nature and variety and to the need to recognize that a society must have at its disposal many different ways of coping with them. Part of the importance of science, history, morality, aesthetics, religion, and subjectivity is that they are approaches that aim to cope with the disruptions caused by physical dangers, challenges, conflicts, drabness, novelties, and meaninglessness that beset everyday life and thus endanger good lives. There are, of course, also other approaches, such as philosophy, literature, magic, and mysticism, but we shall concentrate on the first examples because their connections with the disruptions of everyday life has already emerged.

IV

These approaches represent different ways of describing, interpreting, and coping with the disruptions of everyday life. This is not, of course, all they do, but it is an important part of it. Science seeks to explain the occurrence of events in terms of law-governed regularities. Its explanations aim to exhibit the connection between causes and effects. The regularities it formulates predict that if a specifiable event—the cause—occurs in specifiable conditions, then another specifiable event—the effect— will always follow. These events are located in space and time. They either are observable by the unaided senses and scientific instruments or have observable signs, traces, or consequences. Scientific explanations, then, may be said to aim at fitting events into a space-time-causal network. The scientific understanding of the disruptions of everyday life depends then on locating them in this network and thereby exhibiting their connections with other events.

History intends to make the past intelligible by focusing on human beings and institutions. It is concerned with nonhuman events only insofar as they influence human affairs. It aims to make it understandable why people at times and circumstances different from ours have acted as they did. But the understanding history aims at is not primarily biographical. Its interest is not in individuals as such but in individuals who have, for better or worse, exerted a formative influence on the course of events or who were representative products of a past society, institution, or mentality. The historical approach to the disruptions of everyday life is to understand them as the intended or unintended products of human agents and institutions.

Religion tries to comprehend the natural world of which human beings are a part in terms of a transcendental order that explains the origin, sets the purpose, and provides the meaning of human lives. Religion aims to guide human lives and actions so that they will conform to this order, whose ultimate nature is assumed to be rational and benign. For knowledge of the transcendental order, religions rely on sacred texts, prophets, and revelations through special events and experiences. The disruptions of everyday life are seen from the religious point of view as signs of deviation from the rational and benign order that permeates reality.

Morality is the human approach to trying to make our lives better. Its aim is to create a social framework that guarantees the conditions required by human beings to live good lives. It formulates the principles that guide the evaluations of individual lives and actions and of social institutions as right or wrong, or good or bad, from the point of view of their bearing on the goodness of human lives. It involves our attempts to shape a world that is not particularly hospitable to our endeavors, to adjust our endeavors to what is unchangeable in this world, and to harmonize our often conflicting individual endeavors so that we can pursue them with minimal interference from one another. The moral understanding of the disruptions of everyday life is evaluative, and the evaluations are guided by the influence of the disruptions on human lives.

The aesthetic approach is also evaluative, but the focus of its evaluations is the appreciation of the form of its objects and the delight, inspiration, or illumination they give to those who attend to them. These objects are often works of art, but they may also be landscapes, natural events, bodies, or human lives. Aesthetic appreciation is frequently derived from objects that are deliberately created in order to produce certain effects, so that aesthetics is closely connected with the arts and crafts. This connection, however, is not necessary because natural objects may also be appreciated, and the effects that merit appreciation may be unintended even if the objects are created. From the aesthetic point of view, the disruptions of everyday life are interruptions of creative efforts, of disinterested attempts to take delight in certain aspects of the world, and of the appreciation of objects for what they are in themselves, independently of the uses to which they may be put.

Subjectivity leads agents to view the world from the perspective of their needs, interests, sensibility, and projects. It is not to be confused with selfishness or self-centeredness because the subjective concerns of agents may be intimately connected with their deep concern for other people, institutions, and social, political, and cultural matters. Nevertheless, subjectivity approaches the world from the agent's point of view, regardless of how inclusive or exclusive that may be. The disruptions of everyday life, then, are interferences with the agent's needs, interests, projects, and sensibility.

From these approaches follow various ways of coping with the disruptions of everyday life. Take, for instance, AIDS. We cannot just ignore it. We need to make sense of the deaths, the changes of sexual habits, the connection with homosexuality, the suffering and the dangers associated with it. We can approach it scientifically, looking for its cause and cure; religiously, trying to fit it into a transcendental order; historically, as a result of social change brought about by secularization and the sexual revolution; morally, as people getting or not getting what they deserve; aesthetically, as a variation on the dramatic theme of the dangerous consequences of greater freedom; or subjectively, as it affects one's sensibility, relationships, and conduct. But we do not start with any of these approaches. We start with noticing that many people are slowly dying of a sexually transmitted disease. Then we feel that we must understand why it is happening and what we can do about it. And after that we look to the various approaches that may help us to do so.

The thought then is that living a good life requires participation in everyday life. Everyday life is disrupted in various ways and it often lacks the resources to cope with these disruptions. This is the point at which the various approaches become important. The argument in favor of beginning with everyday life must not, therefore, be taken as a denial of the importance of these approaches. At the beginning, everyday life is important and the approaches are not. As disruptions occur, the approaches to coping with them become important and everyday life recedes into the background. At the threshold between these two contexts are the disruptions themselves.

The very success of these approaches in coping with the disruptions, however, will prompt the question, Why should not they, or one of them, replace everyday life as the beginning of the attempt to live good lives? After all, everyday life is constantly beset by disruptions and we are consequently forced to look beyond it for help in coping, the successful approaches avoid the disruptions that beset everyday life and have the means to cope with others. It may be granted that everyday life has been the unavoidable beginning in the cognitive infancy of humanity, but now that we are maturing, it may be supposed, we should leave childish things behind.

V

This thought is an ever-present temptation, but there are three reasons for resisting it. First, science, religion, history, aesthetics, morality, and subjectivity, in their different ways, all go beyond the facts of everyday life and suggest ways of understanding our lives and circumstances. Their suggestions may be true or false, but even true ones require evidence to support them. Such evidence must be either that a particular way of understanding makes better sense of the facts than competing understandings or that from a favored way of understanding it is possible to derive successful predictions about how facts will turn out. In this way, both the understanding and the predictions appeal to facts to support the approach from whose context they are derived. The various approaches thus presuppose the facts of everyday life. They cannot, therefore, be alternatives to beginning with them.

This is not to deny, of course, that an approach could cast doubt on the reliability of some beliefs in everyday life about the facts. Any such belief about any fact may turn out to be mistaken, and an approach could be appealed to in order to explain how the mistake came to be made. The sun does not rise; it is the earth that moves, but it is too big, moves too slowly, and we do not feel it. The explanations that show that a particular belief is mistaken presuppose, however, that other beliefs in everyday life are true, namely, those that are involved in the construction and calibration of the instruments utilized for the explanation, in the observations made by the instruments, and in the collection and collocation of the data on which the explanations are based. Just because a particular approach strongly suggests that some everyday beliefs are mistaken, it does not follow that all everyday beliefs could be mistaken. For all approaches unavoidably depend on some everyday beliefs whose truth they cannot be simultaneously used to question. The first reason, then, why science, history, and so forth cannot be genuine alternatives to beginning with the facts of everyday life is that these approaches *presuppose* everyday facts as their observational data, explicandum, evidence, and even as a means of criticism.

The second reason emerges in answer to the question of how defenders of everyday life could be reasonable in beginning with its supposed facts if any belief about these facts *may* be mistaken and if the various approaches to coping with its disruptions have often been successful in showing that many everyday beliefs actually *are* mistaken. The question rests on an implicit assumption, which, once made explicit, proves to be untenable. The assumption is that everyday life and the various approaches are rival systems of beliefs. If one rival can be used successfully to criticize the beliefs of another, the assumption is, then that one is shown to be preferable to the other. Now, quite apart from the fact that everyday life is not a rival of any approach to coping with its disruptions because, as we have just seen, the approaches presuppose everyday life even in the course of criticizing some of its beliefs, it is a bad misunderstanding of everyday life to take it to be a system of beliefs. To be sure, everyday life involves many beliefs, but there is much more to it than these beliefs.

Everyday life is above all practical. It is the framework of routine and conventional *activities*. Engagement in them certainly implies that the agents hold various beliefs, but the beliefs are incidental by-products, usually unarticulated, and the agents are not normally aware of holding them. The point of the activities is not to prove, disprove, or test the agents' beliefs, but to get along in life. If I am driving to work, I believe that I am holding the steering wheel, the car has an engine, there are highways, I know how to drive, and so on. But the immediate reason why I am driving is to get to work, and the more remote reason is to earn a living. Everyday life is made up of such activities, and its ultimate purpose is to satisfy the participants' basic needs in whatever happen to be the conventional ways of a particular society. Most people living in a society must participate in these activities, otherwise their lives could not be good. If the odd billionaire and recluse are free of this necessity, it is only because in one way or another their basic needs are met by those who participate in their stead. And even the most iconoclastic rebel can challenge only some of the prevailing conventions, for conformity to very many of the others is the indispensable means to living the sort of life in which rebelling is a possibility.

The salient fact is that the vast majority who participate in the conventional activities of everyday life champion various approaches as alternatives to beginning with everyday life. Scientists, historians, theologians, moralists, aesthetes, and subjectivists who propose different understandings of what lies behind the facts of everyday life are in the same position as the rebel. They must shop for groceries, balance their checkbooks, have their hair cut, eat meals, pay taxes, dress after waking up, and generally participate in everyday life in countless ways. Reliance on everyday life enables them to call into question some of the beliefs of everyday life. But they cannot consistently propose alternatives to all of them because everyday life is a condition of their living the kind of life in which they can propose anything. As Freud memorably remarked, a cigar sometimes just is a cigar—especially when he smoked it.

Holding that a certain approach is a better beginning than everyday life involves an inconsistency between beliefs and actions. No one can reasonably believe that the facts of everyday life are mistaken, and that a given approach reveals how things really are, if one's actions outside the context of that approach take for granted the truth of other beliefs. There is, of course, no inconsistency in believing that some beliefs are mistaken, but believing that, as we have seen, presupposes the truth of other beliefs. Science, history, and so forth can be used to criticize and correct aspects of everyday life, but they cannot be used to dislodge it from its position as the beginning from which activities, beliefs, and conventions can be criticized and corrected. To suppose otherwise is *inconsistent*.

The third reason for beginning with everyday life to understand its disruptions is an argument that G. E. Moore gave in defending the commonsense view of the world. There are good reasons, as we have seen, for not identifying everyday life with the common sense view, but Moore's argument for the latter can, with some small changes, be adapted to defend the former. Moore, in his inimitable manner, held up his finger and said to his audience: "This, after all, you know, really is a finger: there is no doubt about it: I know it and you all know it. And I think we may safely challenge any philosopher to bring forward any argument in favour either of the proposition that we do not know it, or of the proposition that it is not true, which does not at some point, rest upon some premise which is, beyond comparison, less certain than is the proposition which it is designed to attack."[7]

As it stands, Moore's argument is open to the familiar skeptical objection based on the possibility of phantom limb sensations, optical illusions, hypnotic suggestion, and the like. So let us change the argument by adding the qualification that both the owner of the finger and the audience that beholds it have carefully examined it, thought about the context, found nothing that would warrant distrusting the appearances, and are unanimous in believing that it is indeed a finger. And let us broaden Moore's challenge to philosophers to include scientists, cubists, psychoanalysts, theologians, ethnographers, sociologists, and ideologues who see false consciousness clouding everyone's judgment but their own.

Notice, furthermore, what the argument does not claim and what it does. It does not claim that the belief, given the amended circumstances, is certainly true and could not be false. For it could be false. We could be deceived by an evil demon, we could be brains in a vat, we could be dreaming, and so forth. What the argument claims is that we believe that it is true and that we have better reasons for doing so than we have for believing the familiar skeptical hypotheses. Moore was quite clear in holding that there is no evidence in favor of any of the skeptical hypotheses. They are logical possibilities; they should be acknowledged as such; but there is no reason to regard them as more than that. Moore, however, was less clear on the question of why the belief he adduced as an example is not just another hypothesis on a par with the skeptical ones. Moore did not say what the reasons were *for* believing it, apart from a strong subjective sense of certainty. But it is not difficult to supply these reasons on the basis of what has already been said about everyday life.

To begin with, everyday beliefs, of which Moore's example is one, are not held in isolation from other everyday beliefs. They continually and reciprocally confirm one another. Saying to the audience that "This is a finger" goes with the beliefs that one can talk, be understood, hear and understand responses; that one has a hand to which the finger is attached, as the hand is attached to the arm, and the arm to the body; that one can move the finger, the hand, the arm, and the body; that one remembers how to talk; that one stands before the audience properly dressed, rather than in the nude; that the building is not burning down, and so on and on for an untold number of congruent beliefs that one holds, even if one is not aware of holding them. Obvious as this is, it is still not enough support for the argument because idealists, Marxists, fundamentalists, and astrologers may make the same claim for the coherence and reciprocal evidential support of their beliefs as has just been made for everyday ones.

It is necessary to emphasize once again, therefore, not just that everyday life is a system of beliefs, but that it is primarily practical. Its beliefs are unintended and usually unarticulated conclusions derived from successful conventional engagement in the familiar activities of everyday life. One main type of reason for these beliefs is that they are continually tested and confirmed by the successful activities of the agents who hold them. That this is so is often overlooked because the activities, like breathing, are normally taken for granted, and because the associated beliefs, such as having a head, are so obvious that it is hard to imagine a context in which there would be a need to articulate them. Moreover, these beliefs are acted on, and thus tested and confirmed, not just by people who take everyday life for granted, nor only by those who regard everyday life as the right beginning for approaching its disruptions, but also by those who champion science, history, and so

forth as a better beginning. For no one living in a society can avoid participating in everyday life, performing its routine activities, and holding
condign beliefs because the satisfaction of their basic needs depends on it.
The third reason, then, for beginning with everyday life is that it is *reasonable* to do so and that it would be unreasonable to begin with any of the approaches to coping with its disruptions. To this third reason, there may be
added, by way of reminder, the preceding two: the various approaches *presuppose* everyday life as a beginning, and the failure to acknowledge it as a beginning results in an *inconsistency* between the avowed beliefs and the actual
activities of the agent.

This is not to say that everyday life is important and the approaches to
coping with its disruptions are not, nor that the first is more important than
the second. Both are necessary for living good lives, so both are important.
The aim of this chapter has been to show how everyday life bears on living
good lives, how disruptions require going beyond everyday life, and how that
involves reliance on science, history, morality, aesthetics, religion, and subjectivity. The aim of the next chapter is to understand better the difficulties
that require going beyond both everyday life and these approaches.

2

Modes of Reflection

Every person who is actually absorbed in any given form of experience is by this very absorption committed to the opinion that no other form is valid, that his form is the only one adequate to the comprehension of reality. Hence arises discord; for when artists and scientists, who do after all inhabit a common world of fact, meet and discuss their aims, each is apt to accuse the other of wasting his life on a world of illusions. The "ancient quarrel between poetry and philosophy" is only one of a whole series of such quarrels in a ceaseless international war in which every country on the map is eternally embroiled with every other.

ROBIN G. COLLINGWOOD,
Speculum Mentis or the Map of Knowledge

I

The disruptions of everyday life motivate participation in science, history, religion, aesthetics, morality, and subjectivity. Each of these approaches to coping with the disruptions has traditions, conventions, and methods, notable successes and failures, strengths and deficiencies, and they endure because they command the allegiances of countless participants. Many books have been written to provide a detailed examination of these approaches, but this book has a different purpose. It is to concentrate on a particular development that occurs if the participants do not merely engage in the activities proper to one of these approaches, but also reflect on the nature and implications of the approach itself. Although such reflection is not unavoidable, two reasons make its occurrence likely. One is internal, the other external to the approaches.

The internal reason is that the appropriate methods, conventions, and aims of each approach are almost always a controversial matter among the participants.[1] They may agree about what counts as an exemplary achievement in the past, but they often disagree about what made it exemplary—genius, a new method, synthesis of the works of others, the reformulation of a problem, discovery of new facts, and so forth—and what guidance the achievement suggests for the future of the approach. They also typically disagree about whether current practices should be continued or changed, which new developments are worth exploring, what problems are basic, where the important issues lie, and whose ideas are promising. These internal controversies force participants to reflect on what they are doing and why, and how the past, present, and the future of their shared approach ought to be interpreted and related.

The external reason that invites reflection is that people normally participate in not one but many of these approaches. Since part of what motivates their participation is coping with the disruptions of everyday life, the question of which approach is the best for coping with the particular disruption they face naturally arises. A scientist may be morally concerned, have a keen aesthetic sense, and be a religious believer. We all respond to the world in the light of subjective considerations, such as our needs, interests, sensibility, and projects, but that may go hand in hand with seeking historical understanding, being a creative artist, or living a life in science. People are in some sense obviously conscious of their participation in these approaches, otherwise it would be inexplicable why they respond appropriately in their respective contexts. They do not go to church to conduct experiments, listen to music to gain historical perspective, or champion human rights to cope with their fear of snakes. Each approach has methods, standards, conventions, principles, goals, and so forth peculiar to it. Moderately well educated people know what these are, and they routinely act on their knowledge. This knowledge, however, is of how to proceed once it has been decided what approach is appropriate. Reflection is needed because making that decision is often difficult.

The central claim of this chapter is that from each of these approaches it is possible to derive a particular mode of reflection, that modes of reflection conflict with one another, and that the five philosophical problems that concern us here have their source in these conflicts. Making good on this claim requires understanding modes of reflection.[2]

II

Modes of reflection must be sharply distinguished from the various approaches to coping with the disruptions of everyday life. A mode of reflection is derived from one of these approaches, and its purpose is to provide an understanding of the world from its point of view. A mode of reflection, therefore, generalizes the particular features of one of these approaches and proposes to understand the world in those generalized terms. There is, thus, science, history, religion, aesthetics, morality, and subjectivity, on the one hand, and scientific, historical, religious, aesthetic, moral, and subjective reflection, on the other. This distinction is crucial to the argument. It will be marked by referring to the various approaches as science, history, and so forth, whereas the modes of reflection derived from them will be referred to as scientific reflection, historical reflection, and so forth.

Modes of reflection are parasitic on the approaches from which they are derived. If it turns out that a particular approach is basically defective, which may of course happen, then the mode of reflection that is derived from it becomes indefensible. But the transmission of defects does not work in the other direction. It may be that scientific, historical, or other reflection is indefensible, but that may not call into question the defensibility of the approach from which the indefensible mode of reflection is derived. For the source of the defect may be the generalization of what ought not to be generalized. Science, history, and so forth, may work fine in their appropriate domain, but it may nevertheless be mistaken to suppose that the world in its totality should be understood scientifically, historically, or in the terms of any of the other modes of reflection. So the rational evaluation of science, history, religion, aesthetics, morality, and subjectivity is one thing, and the rational evaluation of scientific, historical, religious, aesthetic, moral, and subjective reflection is another. The argument will have much to say about the rational evaluation of modes of reflection, but next to nothing about the rational evaluation of the particular approaches from which modes of reflection are derived.

A mode of reflection, then, is a general outlook whose aim is to understand the world. Part of the reason why this is important is that understanding the world is necessary for coping with the disruptions of everyday life, but, of course, there are also other much less immediately pressing reasons for seeking understanding, such as searching for truth, improving the human condition, alleviating misery, seeking meaning in life, and so forth. "General outlook," however, is as vague and imprecise an expression as "mode of reflection," so much more needs to be said to make its meaning clear.

The general outlook that a mode of reflection provides is the disposition to understand the world in a particular way. It is the tendency to try to make sense of it from a scientific, historical, religious, moral, aesthetic, or subjective point of view. A mode of reflection, therefore, generalizes the understanding that is characteristic of a particular approach. The world is to be understood in terms of a space-time-causal nomological network, or in terms of historical influences, or in terms of objects whose form, beauty, and illumination merit appreciation, or in terms of a transcendental order, or in terms of its effects on the goodness of human lives, or in terms of the projects of the agent.

The reason for trying to understand the world in one of these ways is because it is thought that that is how the significance of the facts is to be found. This is the object of the understanding that modes of reflection seek. It needs now to be made clear what that understanding is supposed to involve. This will be done by identifying three levels of increasing complexity through which the understanding must pass in order to provide the desired account of the significance of the facts.

The first level, *description*, occurs largely in the context of everyday life. The descriptions it provides are based on simple observation of ordinary objects like tables, dogs, mountains, and stars; of events and actions like sunsets, floods, divorces, and wars; and of difficulties, successes, and failures like lacking a cure for cancer, setting a world record, or not meeting a deadline. The observed facts described in this simple way are uncontroversial, publicly available, and accessible to anyone with moderate intelligence and no handicap. These facts are part of the raw data that all approaches to understanding must either accommodate or explain why it is justified to disregard them.

On the second level, *interpretation* involves placing the described facts in the framework of a particular approach. The aim is to understand the relevant facts from the point of view of science, history, and so forth. Such understanding may or may not involve explanation. To understand Beethoven's late quartets, the dangers of lack of self-control, the parable of the Good Samaritan, or the corrupting effects of a lucrative public relations job is to explain nothing—although, of course, what has been understood can often be explained to others, so that they can also understand it. The understanding that science, history, and religion yield often involve explanation; the understanding that aesthetics, morality, and subjectivity provide often do not. And even when understanding does involve explanation, it may be essential to it to provide more than that. Explanation is typically the most important feature of the understanding science or history provides. But moral understanding does not merely explain why an act is bad, it also involves strengthening the motivation to avoid it. Similarly, aesthetic understanding may include the explanation of the imagery of a poem, but unless it is accompanied by a critical appreciation of it, the understanding is incomplete.

Interpretation, therefore, involves understanding some set of facts from the point of view of science, history, religion, aesthetics, morality, or subjectivity. Its aim is to understand the facts either in terms of their place in the nomological network; or as products of past social, cultural, or institutional influences; or as manifestations of a transcendental order; or as objects whose form, beauty, and illumination enrich life; or as causes that affect human lives for the better or worse; or as forces that help or hinder the agent's pursuit of personal projects. Such understanding is achieved by expressing the facts in the vocabulary of a particular approach, by evaluating them as important or unimportant, reliable or dubious, novel or banal, suggestive or commonplace, and so forth in the light of the standards of that approach, and by judging whether and how the facts fit into the kind of understanding that it is the goal of that approach to provide.

The characteristic activity on the third level is *reflection*. It is on this level that modes of reflection become important. Modes of reflection are general in the sense that they are committed to understanding not just some particular set of facts, but the whole world scientifically, historically, religiously, aesthetically, morally, or subjectively. Each mode of reflection claims to be the primary, the deepest, the most basic, or the most important way of understanding the world. Each mode of reflection, therefore, has a constructive and a critical task. The constructive one is to work out the details of the general outlook that it champions. It is to construct a framework in which the descriptions and the interpretations reached at the first and second levels can be accommodated in a coherent system. The critical task is to recognize that other modes of reflection also construct frameworks of understanding, that these alternative frameworks are incompatible with one another, and to explain why its own framework is preferable to the others.

Suppose, for the moment, that a particular mode of reflection has successfully completed both the constructive and the critical tasks. It has then provided a general way of understanding the world. Such an understanding accommodates the descriptions of everyday life, the interpretations of the various approaches, and it comes to terms, in some manner, with the alternative understandings of competing modes of reflection. If a mode of reflection has accomplished all this, then it may be said to have understood the significance of the facts. The purpose of modes of reflection is to reach such an understanding, and their justification depends on having done so. Facts, therefore, acquire what is here called their significance from their position in the general outlook of a particular mode of reflection.

The distinction between appearance and reality is a central part of each mode of reflection. Each leaves open the possibility that what appears to be the case is not. Each mode of reflection, therefore, recognizes the possibility of error. And errors may occur on each of the levels: in description, in interpretation, and in reflection. Errors of description occur when illusion, unfavorable external conditions, or some other kind of misperception leads observers to regard something as a fact when it is not. A mode of reflection consequently may attribute the wrong significance to some fact because of misdescription.

Errors of interpretation occur when accurately described facts are misinterpreted. The fact may be subsumed under the wrong scientific law; a historical event may be more or less influential than it is supposed; a work of art may be too complex, obscure, or iconoclastic and defeat conventional attempts at appreciation; a religious text or a prophet may point in a direction quite different from what the faithful suppose; a value may be ascribed the wrong importance because it is viewed in isolation from other values with which it may conflict; and a subjective experience may be falsified as a result of self-deception, stupidity, inattention, or lack of self-knowledge. A mode of reflection thus may go wrong by way of misinterpretation.

Errors of reflection occur when the wrong significance is attributed to correctly described and interpreted facts. Reflection may conclude that some fact has been accommodated in a general outlook or that it is anomalous, that it is relevant or irrelevant, or that it presents a theoretical problem that must be dealt with or merely a practical one that can be safely set aside. Such reflection may be mistaken in either the constructive or the critical aspect of a mode of reflection. In the first case, its defenders suppose that some fact does not present a serious difficulty for their general outlook when it actually does. In the second case, they suppose that it does present such a difficulty for another mode of reflection, which they regard, for that reason, as faulty, but their supposition is false. A mode of reflection, consequently, may be vitiated by erroneous reflection.

The importance of the distinction between appearance and reality, and of the recognition of the resulting possibility of error, is that each mode of reflection is committed to evaluating claims as being true or false, reasonable or unreasonable. These notions of cognitive appraisal are routinely used to evaluate the significance that is attributed to some fact by a particular mode of reflection.

Although each mode of reflection aims to understand the significance of the relevant facts, the actual significance they attribute to them are radically different. Nomological explanation, historical reconstruction, religious belief, aesthetic appreciation, subjective judgment, and moral evaluation may all reflect the true significance of their subjects and yet express fundamentally different general outlooks. There is, therefore, truth and falsehood in scientific, historical, religious, aesthetic, moral, and subjective reflection. In all of them, truth depends on accurate description, interpretation, and reflection; but the nature of truth and what constitutes accuracy vary from one to another. Analogously, there is rationality and irrationality in each mode of reflection, and in all of them rationality depends on aiming at the truth and trying to avoid falsehood; but how to do that systematically varies. In none of these modes of reflection is the attribution of significance arbitrary. Each has, and the participants of each aim to conform to, familiar epistemological standards. But when the standards are applied within different modes of reflection, they come to different things.[3]

This way of thinking about modes of reflection is incompatible with some forms of relativism with which it may be mistakenly confused. Truth and rationality are attainable and valuable in each mode of reflection. The form of relativism that denies this is mistaken. Furthermore, truth and rationality are not internal notions, dependent on the context of each mode of reflection, because in each mode they are connected with the real state of affairs that exists apart from any mode of reflection. The form of relativism that denies this is also mistaken. Nor is it the case that each mode of reflection is self-validating. It is possible that not just particular attributions of significance but an entire mode of reflection is mistaken. If for some reason nomological accounts, historical reconstructions, aesthetic appreciation, transcendental explanations, moral evaluations, or subjective judgments are impossible or unjustifiable, then the mode of reflection that seeks to attribute significance on that basis is mistaken in its totality. Again, the form of relativism that denies that this may happen is mistaken.

There nevertheless may still remain the suspicion that there is a form of relativism that is compatible with everything that has been said up to this point. This form involves the denial that any mode of reflection could result in the attribution of the true significance to any fact on the ground that a mode of reflection can express, at best, only the partial significance of anything. True significance would be the overall significance that is the joint product of the conjunction of all the various kinds of partial significance. That, however, cannot be had. It will emerge from the argument that the denial of the possibility of finding overall significance is right. It will also emerge that this lends no support whatsoever to any view that deserves to be regarded as relativistic because there are also independent standards to which adequate modes of reflection must conform. Showing why this is so will go a long way toward clarifying further the nature of modes of reflection.

III

One identifying characteristic of modes of reflection is their generality. They are the most general ways in which the significance of facts may be understood. All facts can be understood as effects that stand in a lawful nexus to their causes, as the products of a historical process, as manifestations of a transcendental order, as objects whose form, beauty, and illumination enrich life, as conditions that bear on the goodness of human lives, or as influences that affect one's projects. The generality of modes of reflection means that they should be capable, in one way or another, of accommodating all facts in their terms. It does not, however, mean that all facts are accommodated by them. Their generality should be understood in terms of a distinction between facts whose significance is discernible in their terms, facts that are unimportant from their points of view, and facts that present problems for them.

To begin with the last, scientific reflection has trouble with coincidences and anomalies, religious reflection with evil, historical reflection with senseless, irrational acts, aesthetic reflection with repulsive works of art, moral reflection with contingency that affects the moral capacities of agents, and subjective reflection with impartiality. Moreover, for each mode of reflection there is likely to be a range of clearly relevant facts whose significance is not understood because of certain limitations. The strategy for coping with these problems is to claim either that only practical, nontheoretical obstacles prevent their accommodation in a particular mode, or that they are not problematic but unimportant from its point of view. Such ways of dealing with problems often look suspiciously ad hoc, but even ad hoc solutions may turn out to be justified. The salient point is that the presence of such problems is normal for all modes of reflection. The problems present objections to the modes only if they are numerous and if serious attempts to cope with them fail repeatedly. This may happen, of course, and then the mode of reflection ought to go the same way as magic, numerology, and astrology have gone. The existence of this possibility reinforces the point made earlier that the recognition of the plurality of modes of reflection is compatible with the rejection of relativism.

Turning now to the second part of the distinction, for each mode of reflection there is a range of facts that is unimportant from its point of view. No significance has been attributed to some facts because, from a particular perspective, they have none. There is no reason why a scientific account should be given of the distribution of fallen leaves, why history should be concerned with lullabies, why religion should be interested in the smell of garlic, why mass-produced nails should be objects of aesthetic appreciation, why geological rock formations should elicit moral concern, or why Kurdish courting customs should have a bearing on one's projects. It is conceivable, of course, that such matters may become relevant. But, barring improbabilities, each mode of reflection may be justifiably disinterested in very many facts. What it cannot justifiably do is to regard facts that present difficulties for it as unimportant.

The generality of modes of reflection, therefore, does not amount to comprehensiveness. A mode of reflection is not deficient if it does not attribute significance to all facts, for some facts are insignificant, irrelevant, routine, or presently unaccounted for as a result of practical obstacles. Nevertheless, although modes of reflection are not comprehensive, they are still the most general ways of seeking to understand the significance of facts. Their generality is always a matter of degree because the range of facts that is unimportant or problematic for them may be wider or narrower. To say that modes of reflection are the most general approaches to the significance of facts, therefore, is to say that the range of facts that they reasonably regard as unimportant or problematic is narrower than the ranges of other points of view whose more limited interests disqualify them from being modes of reflection. The importance of commerce, medicine, and jurisprudence is great, but, because the range of facts to which trading, health, or legality is irrelevant is very wide, they are not general enough to qualify as modes of reflection.

There may, of course, be modes of reflection in addition to the ones we have been discussing—philosophy, economics, and literature, perhaps—but the argument does not depend on having a complete list of all modes of reflection. The important point is that modes of reflection are distinguished from other ways of thinking about the significance of facts on the basis of their generality, and that their degree of generality depends on the range of facts that is unimportant or problematic for them being comparatively narrower than the ranges of other ways of thinking.

The generality of modes of reflection yields a special kind of understanding: that of the significance of facts. To have this kind of understanding is to grasp meaning, make sense, comprehend, realize importance, or appreciate. As we have seen, this may or may not involve explanation. It is important, therefore, to avoid identifying modes of reflection with attempts to provide explanations. The temptation to make this mistake comes from setting up the scientific mode of reflection as a model that all modes of reflection ought to imitate.[4]

A similar mistake is the failure to realize that while all modes of reflection have both a theoretical and a practical aspect, they combine them in different ways and proportions. In scientific and historical reflection, the theoretical aspect dominates over the practical. In aesthetic and subjective reflection, it is the other way around. In religious and moral reflection, they are fairly evenly mixed. Modes of reflection are also modes of activity, even if the respective importance of theory and practice varies in each. This is part of the reason why it is much too simple to think of modes of reflection as alternative approaches to understanding, and then point to the great success of science and claim for it superiority over other modes of reflection.

Modes of reflection aim at different kinds of understanding, so they are not different ways of doing the same thing. They are different ways of doing different things.

We may sum up then the identifying characteristics of modes of reflection that have emerged so far. First, they aim to understand the significance of facts. Second, they do so partly in order to cope with the disruptions of everyday life. Third, they arise out of science, history, religion, aesthetics, subjectivity, and morality by way of generalizing their approaches and forming a general outlook, in the sense just explained, that aims to understand the significance of facts from its point of view. Fourth, for each mode of reflection, the distinction between appearance and reality, and consequently between truth and falsehood, rationality and irrationality, can be drawn. But in each case the distinction is drawn differently.

It must be emphasized that the just completed account of modes of reflection is only an initial one. Each mode will be discussed further in subsequent chapters in which the philosophical problems that concern us here will be shown to result from conflicts between modes of reflection. Enough has already been said about them, however, to draw attention to some implications of the account in order to clarify further the nature of modes of reflection. To begin with, modes of reflection are *systematic*. Their concern is not with individual facts as such but with finding a way in which the significance of facts can be generally understood. They are interested in fitting facts into a pattern rather than in finding facts that form a pattern. Next, they are *reflective*. The facts that constitute their subject matter are given to them by the descriptions of everyday life and the interpretations of the various approaches out of which they have arisen, so that their aim is not to discover relevant facts, but to find the significance of already discovered facts. They may be said, therefore, to be second-order reflections, as opposed to first-order inquiries.[5] Moreover, they are *evaluative*. Each has both external and internal standards of evaluation. The internal ones include the epistemological criteria of truth and rationality by which achievement is traditionally measured in their respective contexts. The external ones are their success in coping with the disruptions of everyday life. There is yet a further implication that needs to be considered, but, because of its central importance for the argument, it requires a more extended treatment.

IV

If modes of reflection are the most general ways of understanding the significance of facts, then each mode of reflection should be able to accommodate the other modes of reflection in its own terms. It is obviously a significant fact about human beings that their attempts to understand the significance of facts are scientific, historical, religious, aesthetic, moral, and subjective, so that an adequate mode of reflection must accommodate the significance of that fact. It may seem at first sight that this is a simple matter. There seems to be no reason in principle why a scientific account could not be given of historical, religious, aesthetic, moral, and subjective reflections. In each case, their aims, methods, conventions, and practices can be viewed as the effects of causes, and the causes and effects can be fitted into the nomological network of science. The same seems to be true of historical reflection: for every mode of reflection, including the scientific, it is possible to reconstruct the past influences whose understanding would make intelligible the activities of the participants. Religious reflection can also regard different modes of reflection as so many attempts to understand the human significance of the transcendental order. Likewise, all modes of reflection can be evaluated morally by asking about their effects on the goodness of human lives. The same can be done by viewing all modes of reflection aesthetically as attempts to appreciate aspects of the world by imposing beautiful or illuminating form on them. And it is no less obvious that all modes of reflection can be seen subjectively as various ways in which one's projects are affected by them. Each mode of reflection, therefore, appears to have the capacity to treat other modes of reflection as special cases within its domain. If a mode of reflection were to fail in this respect, it would fail to accommodate the significance of highly relevant facts, which would be a serious objection to its adequacy.

Contrary to first appearances, however, all modes of reflection are open to this objection. The favorable initial appearance is the result of the capacity of modes of reflection to accommodate the descriptions and interpretations of the *facts* that are also accommodated by other modes of reflection. Modes of reflection face no logical difficulty in this respect. But they do face a logical difficulty in accommodating the *significance* that reflection in the various modes attributes to the facts. It is a central concern of each mode of reflection to provide a general understanding of the significance of the facts. If it cannot accommodate in its own terms the accounts of the significance of facts that other modes of reflection provide, then it is basically flawed. But why could not modes of reflection do this?

Consider as an example a work of art: *The Tragedy* from Picasso's blue period. Three enigmatic and devastated figures stand on the shore. They are barefooted and their eyes are cast down, looking away from one another. Something bad has happened, but there is no clue as to what—a drowning? a parting? terrible news? a hitherto buried secret spoken? We do not know. Enigma and doom permeate the picture. We feel what we feel when dark times are upon us, but we feel it vicariously, with relief that it is not for real, with sympathy for the painted figures, and with admiration, once we catch our breath, for the artistry with which it is communicated to us. It is a disturbing, haunting picture—there is nothing but different shades of blue in it. All of this comes to us in the aesthetic mode of reflection.

We can step out of that mode. We can reflect on the picture scientifically in terms of the geometry of perspective, the evolutionary function of blue, the human visual apparatus, the causes that made Picasso a painter and the painter of that picture, and so forth. Let us suppose that scientific reflection yields a complete account in which no fact is left unaccounted for. Something is still missing, but what? Not how the painting affects us aesthetically, because if all the facts are accounted for, then that one will be among them. What is missing is that in scientific reflection the significance of facts depends on their place in the nomological network, but in aesthetic appreciation their significance depends on the form, beauty, and illumination of the painting. We focus on the enigmatic doom and what it means for human existence, but unless we are critics or connoisseurs we do not care much about how it was produced, what went into Picasso's artistry, or whether light is really like that at dawn or sunset in the Mediterranean, if that is where it is. From the point of view of aesthetic reflection, the painting has a particular significance, but from the point of view of scientific reflection its significance is quite different. If the account that scientific reflection provides is complete, part of it will be that we find certain features aesthetically significant. But to give a nomological explanation and to predict accurately what will be found to be aesthetically significant is not the same as finding it aesthetically significant. To know and predict that music composed in a minor key will sound sad is not to be sad. And, of course, those who reflect from the scientific point of view can themselves understand the aesthetic significance of a work of art, but when they do so they are no longer reflecting on it scientifically and have begun to reflect on it aesthetically.

But why could they not do both? Of course they could, but not simultaneously. If their reflection is scientific, they want to fit the painting into the nomological network. It does not matter then that it is a masterpiece; Jackson Pollock's dribbles would do just as well. If their reflection is aesthetic, they appreciate the form, beauty, and illumination of the painting, but then it does not matter whether or not the evolutionary account of the function of blue is correct. The point of saying this is not to take scientific reflection down a peg. An analogous account could be given of the failure of the attempt to understand the significance of a scientific theory by way of aesthetic reflection. Of course it is possible to look at a scientific theory as a work of art. But then it is of no significance whether it happens to be true or false, whereas from the scientific point of view that is what is significant about it. Picasso's painting can also be seen as having historical, religious, moral, or subjective significance. But as it is understood in the terms of a particular mode of reflection, so the significance that is attributed to it in other modes must be excluded. In that case, however, all modes of reflection are inadequate because they fail to accommodate the significance of some highly important facts.

Let us now introduce two unsatisfactory responses to this difficulty: the absolutist and the relativist. The argument will return to them again and again to explain and amplify the reasons for rejecting them. The absolutist response is to acknowledge the failure and to attempt to overcome it by insisting that one mode of reflection overrides all the others. The overriding mode of reflection alone attributes the true significance to the facts. Other modes of reflection are more or less mistaken, depending on how closely they approximate the standard set by the overriding mode. The incompatibility of the overriding mode with the others is not a defect but the virtue truth has of excluding falsehood. Positivistic scientism, Marxist historicism, Old Testament moralism, romantic aestheticism, Protestant fundamentalism, and egoistic subjectivism are all fallacies of absolutism, committed when other modes of reflection are evaluated by the standard of a favored mode. The true core, and the attraction, of these various forms of absolutism is that their favored mode of reflection can accommodate the relevant facts. Their mistake is the result of the false supposition that all that an adequate mode of reflection has to do is to accommodate the description and the interpretation of the relevant facts. What this leaves out is the equally important requirement to accommodate the significance that reflection in other modes attributes to the facts.

It is a mark of civilized minds that they recognize that the same facts may have quite different significance when viewed from the perspectives of different modes of reflection and that this enriches life by opening up new possibilities of understanding. The absolutist response that calls for epistemological reduction in order to eliminate the messy plurality of modes of reflection is a symptom of the failure to appreciate the richness of life. It comes from a self-imposed confinement to a particular mind-set and a lack of imagination or willingness to recognize that there are others that also accommodate all the facts, but in a different way.

The other response is the relativist one. Unlike absolutism, it recognizes the plurality of modes of reflection and it values the richness that the resulting recognition of different kinds of significance makes possible. It acknowledges that each mode of reflection fails to accommodate the significance that other modes attribute to the facts, but it denies that this presents a difficulty. A mode of reflection is a particular way of understanding the significance of facts. Each mode has its own aims, methods, conventions, and practices. It is only to be expected that each will turn out to have its own way of attributing significance to facts. This makes the significance of the facts relative to modes of reflection. Relativists see no difficulty here. Modes of reflection are general in aiming to accommodate the description and interpretation of all the relevant facts. They are not general in sharing with each other their reflection on the significance of the facts. But why should they? There is no reason why an understanding of the significance of the facts could not be attempted from the points of view of several modes of reflection, provided it is not attempted simultaneously. The analogy that comes to mind is with being multilingual. It enriches life, increases one's understanding and possibilities, provided one does not try to speak the languages simultaneously.

The problem with this response is that the analogy between languages and modes of reflection breaks down because modes of reflection, unlike languages, conflict with one another. They attribute not just different but incompatible significances to the same facts. That is the reason why the significance of the facts cannot be understood from the points of view of different modes of reflection, regardless of whether the attempt is made simultaneously or serially. We need now to show that this is indeed the case.

That the same proposition cannot be expressed simultaneously in, say, English, French, and German is a contingent fact about individual language users; it has no bearing on the truth of the proposition. Three language users could express the same proposition simultaneously in three different languages, or the proposition could be printed in three languages side by side on a page. All these expressions of the proposition could be true concurrently. It is otherwise with the significance that modes of reflection attribute to facts. The significance of the same facts can be understood individually in a scientific, historical, religious, aesthetic, moral, or subjective mode, but it cannot be understood collectively regardless of whether the attempt is made simultaneously or serially by one person or by several. This is because the impossibility is logical, not contingent. All the modes of reflection that attribute different kinds of significance to the facts are incompatible with one another because the attribution of one kind of significance excludes the attribution of other kinds.[6]

The reason for this incompatibility follows from the generality of modes of reflection. Each mode is an attempt to understand the world in its totality. To accomplish this, it constructs a framework in which all the relevant facts are accommodated, and from which reasons for regarding facts as irrelevant are derived. The significance of facts, then, depends on understanding their place in this framework. The existence of alternative modes of reflection, of alternative attempts to understand the world in its totality, must be recognized as a relevant fact by all defensible modes of reflection. Each mode of reflection, therefore, must provide an understanding of why the totality of the world appears as it does to another mode of reflection, why that appearance is, at best, only a partial understanding of the world, and why its own understanding succeeds in overcoming the partiality of other modes of reflection. In other words, each mode must either provide a reason for being truer, deeper, or more general than other modes or give up the claim to have provided a general way of understanding all the relevant facts. Each mode of reflection must regard its own account of the significance of the facts as true and the accounts of the other modes as partial. Because modes of reflection aim to be general, and because the significance of facts depends on their place in the general framework that each mode provides, no mode can accept the possibility that there may be equally reasonable but alternative accounts of significance. If there is a true understanding of the world in its totality, then there can be only one true account of the significance of the facts. And if there is no true understanding of the world in its totality, then there can be no defensible mode of reflection.

This is a far-reaching general claim that will be supported by the rest of the book. As a beginning, it will be useful to show how it holds in the specific conflicts between particular modes of reflection that give rise to the five philosophical problems that concern us.

V

The first case in point is the conflict between the religious and the moral modes of reflection regarding the meaning of life. The problem originates in the context of everyday life. If life goes well enough for some people so that their basic needs are satisfied, and they have sufficient resources and leisure, they may stand back and survey their lives and wonder about the point of it all. They may ask themselves why they should continue to be engaged in the endless routines that constitute their lives, why they should struggle, compete, discipline themselves, and why they should conform to the standards of success that happen to prevail in their society.

Their reflections may carry them in one of two directions. They may seek answers to their questions within the context of their lives or outside it. If they look within, they will be led to the moral mode of reflection that tells them that it is they who have to give meaning to their lives, that meaning is made, not found, and that it is made by constructing a reasonable conception of a good life and living according to it. If they look outside this context, their reflections often take a religious form. They will be led to think that there is a benign order permeating reality and that the meaning of their lives derives from that order. Having a meaningful life depends on understanding that order and living according to it. Meaning has to be found, not made.

These two modes of reflection thus give conflicting accounts of the meaning of life. One locates the significance of the relevant facts in the shape that people give to their own lives. The other locates it in living in conformity to an order that exists independently of humanity, one that is unalterable by human effort. Moral reflection will object to the religious answer by acknowledging that conformity to an external order may be a prudential necessity, but it will deny that such conformity could give life meaning, since it is but yet another standard imposed on people against their will. Religious reflection will object to the moral answer by pointing out that conceptions of a good life that are the products of the agents' will must be reasonable and cannot be arbitrary. And what makes them reasonable is that they conform to an order external to them. Moral reflection assigns primary significance to the contribution people make to the meaningfulness of their lives. Religious reflection assigns primary significance to the external order that alone makes lives meaningful.

The direction in which true significance is thought to lie has, of course, a profound effect on how people satisfy their need for meaning in their lives. Reflective people are often in the grip of both of these modes of reflection. They insist that they are the ultimate arbiters of the meaningfulness of their own lives. But they also acknowledge that meaning depends on conditions that exist independently of their arbitration, conditions that are not subject to their will. The meaning of life is thus a problem that will occur to many reflective people, and they will find it formidably difficult.

The second case is the conflict between the scientific and the subjective modes of reflection concerning the possibility of free actions. The disruption of everyday life that is the ultimate source of this conflict is the widespread experience of countless people that they have insufficient control over their lives. They often and rightly feel that their actions are the result of external influences of which they may not even be aware, and that if they knew what these influences were, they would prefer not to be subject to them. As they understand this, so they will see the area over which they have control shrink. It is a natural step to begin to wonder whether they have any control at all, whether they are not always subject to influences of which they are unaware.

Scientific reflection strengthens this suspicion because it holds that there is a nomological explanation of everything. The significance of the facts is how they fit into the network of laws. Human actions, of course, are among these facts. If we think in this mode, we shall understand human actions as the effects of physical, biochemical, physiological, and psychological causes. Part of the significance of human actions is that our ignorance of the structure and workings of the brain prevents us from having a full scientific account of their causes. Human actions, however, include our own actions. When we reflect on them in the subjective mode, we unavoidably believe that many of our actions are the results of choices and that it is up to us whether or not we perform them. Part of the significance of chosen actions is that they demonstrate that we have at least some control over our lives.

Human actions thus have a particular significance in the scientific mode of reflection and an incompatible significance in the subjective mode of reflection. The first tells us that the truth about human actions is that they are the effects of causes and that if the causes are present, then the effects will occur. The second tells us that the truth about many human actions is that they are the results of choices and that we often choose the actions we take after we have evaluated the causes that influence us. If we believe one, we cannot believe the other. We cannot abandon the view that human actions have causes because the thought that there are uncaused actions is incoherent. Nor can we abandon the conviction that we are making choices all the time, because we are more sure of that than of any scientific theory. Thus arise the familiar problem of the possibility of free action and the associated problems of self-control, responsibility, and autonomy as scientific and subjective reflection conflict.

The third case is the conflict between moral and subjective reflection about the place of morality in good lives. It is agreed by all concerned that good lives must include both reasonable personal satisfactions and adherence to moral requirements. It is also agreed that these components of good lives often conflict because reasonable personal satisfactions may be morally unacceptable and what would be morally acceptable may be contrary to reasonable personal satisfactions. The problem arises because moral and subjective reflection provide incompatible answers to the question of how such conflicts should be resolved. According to moral reflection, if reasonable personal satisfaction conflicts with moral requirements, the latter should override the former. Good lives are moral lives. Reasonable personal satisfactions matter, of course, but they have a place in good lives only if they conform to the requirements of morality. According to subjective reflection, if reasonable personal satisfaction conflicts with moral requirements, the former should override the latter. Good lives are satisfying lives. Meeting moral requirements is important, but only if they are so designed as to increase the reasonable personal satisfactions of the agents.

Moral and subjective reflection thus provide incompatible accounts of the significance of morality in good lives. The first subordinates the agents' reasonable personal satisfactions to moral requirements; the second does the opposite. Moral reflection sees the requirements of morality as holding universally. No individual has a privileged position, consequently the satisfactions of any one person have no greater or lesser importance than the satisfactions of any other. From the point of view moral reflection, subjective reflection is mistaken in privileging the agent's satisfactions. Subjective reflection insists that the justification of moral requirements must be that conformity to them will make the agents' lives more rather than less satisfying. If moral requirements meet this condition, they are reasonable, otherwise they are arbitrary.

The conflict between personal satisfactions and moral requirements is a ubiquitous disruption of everyday life. But since reflection prompts incompatible responses to this disruption, the place of morality in good lives appears to be an intractable problem. We are unwilling to regard morality as merely a means to increasing personal satisfactions. Yet we are no less unwilling to suppose that a life can be good if moral requirements continually take precedence over the agent's reasonable personal satisfactions.

The fourth case is closely connected to the previous three. Even if there were authoritative answers to the questions about the meaning of life, the possibility of free actions, and the place of morality in good lives, the practical question would still remain: How to bring these answers to bear on one's life? It is one thing to know that good lives must be meaningful, free, and moral, and quite another to know how to achieve these desirable goals. The art of life is the skill whose possession enables people to achieve them. But the nature of the art of life is just as problematic as the nature of the goals that may be achieved by its means. For clearly the moral and the aesthetic modes of reflection give incompatible accounts of the art of life.

According to moral reflection, the art of life is a moral art. It involves the application of knowledge of good and evil to the often complex situations in which people find themselves. Those who possess the art of life are practically wise. They know how to live moral lives in the midst of the requirements and temptations of personal satisfaction, political realities, economic conditions, loyalties to family and friends, and religious commitments. According to aesthetic reflection, the art of life is a genuinely creative art. Its medium, however, is the agent's own life. The possession of this art makes it possible to create out of the raw material of the agent's genetic inheritance, education, experience, talents, and resources a uniquely individual character and way of life that at once exemplifies and enlarges human possibilities. According to moral reflection, the essential character trait that the art of life requires is good judgment. According to aesthetic reflection, the required essential trait is creativity. On the first view, the art of life is to navigate well in troubled, poorly mapped waters. On the second view, the art is that of a pioneer who blazes the trail that others may follow. On the first view, life is fraught with dangers and the art consists in avoiding them. On the second view, life is full of possibilities and the art consists in making the most of them. The first is classical, the second is romantic.

These two modes of reflection provide incompatible accounts of the significance of the same set of facts. Their accounts lead to understanding the significance of meaning, freedom, and morality in incompatible ways. They both seek a good life and regard the art of life as the key to achieving it, but they disagree about the nature of good lives and about the nature of that art. Their disagreement hinges on whether the significance attributed to the facts should be primarily moral or aesthetic. Neither needs to exclude the other, but each attributes primary significance to its own mode of reflection and, at best, only secondary significance to the other mode. How this conflict is resolved in one's own life will have a formative influence on how one lives. It is unclear, however, whether the conflict lends itself to a reasonable resolution, especially because reasonable people will see the attractions of both modes of reflection.

The fifth case is the conflict between scientific and historical reflection regarding the form human self-understanding should take. This conflict, of course, is inseparable from the previous four, for part of human self-understanding is to find the place of meaning, free actions, morality, and the art of life in everyday life. The problem is that the scientific and historical modes of reflection provide incompatible accounts of what needs to be done to achieve an understanding of the human situation in the world.

Scientific reflection seeks to understand humanity and its place in the world from the outside, from the perspective of the world. It views human beings as natural entities who are as subject to the laws of nature as any other natural entity. The key to human self-understanding is understanding the laws of nature that explain the way we are, our beliefs, and our actions. That it is we who seek to understand ourselves is an incidental matter that has no effect whatsoever on what genuine understanding reveals. Historical reflection, on the contrary, seeks human self-understanding from the inside, from the perspective of humanity. It accepts that we are natural entities subject to the laws of nature, but it denies that that is what is significant about us. What is significant is that we are the kinds of beings who can view critically their own beliefs, form intentions on the basis of their beliefs, and execute their intentions in actions that they judge to be appropriate. Scientific reflection, therefore, understands human lives as the lawful effects of natural causes. Historical reflection, by contrast, understands human lives as the products of societies whose institutions and conventions are designed to achieve greater control over our lives. The two modes of reflection need have no disagreement about the facts, but they have a deep disagreement about the significance of the facts.

The ideal scientific reflection seeks to approximate is to see humanity *sub specie aeternitatis*, as God would see it. From that perspective, our beliefs, intentions, actions, and the values that inform our lives are just further facts about us. Historical reflection seeks to understand humanity *sub specie humanitatis*; it aims to understand how we live as a reflection of how we think it would be good for us to live. And it views human history as the record of the successes and failures of our attempts to live according to the various socially conditioned values that we have developed over the ages. From the perspective of historical reflection, our beliefs, intentions, actions, and the values that motivate us are essential features of our humanity, and understanding ourselves depends on understanding what it is like to be the kinds of beings who are motivated by the particular values that have historically motivated us. These two modes of reflection are incompatible because one mode seeks to understand the significance of human concerns by viewing them from the outside, whereas the other looks for their significance through the imaginative reconstruction of human concerns by viewing them from the inside, as the agents whose concerns they were viewed them.

These five problems—the meaning of life, the possibility of free action, the place of morality in good lives, the art of life, and the nature of human self-understanding—are meant to support the claim that different modes of reflection attribute incompatible significance to the same set of facts. The brief accounts that have just been given of these problems are merely introductory. Each problem and its proposed resolution will be discussed in much greater detail in a subsequent chapter.

VI

All five of these problems are, of course, philosophical. This is the conclusion that the argument of this chapter was intended to reach. These philosophical problems occur because we try to understand the significance of the same facts in terms of two modes of reflection. The problems are difficult, to put it gently, because such understanding does not seem to be possible.[7] Should we not conclude, then, that since these philosophical problems occur when we try to reconcile incompatible modes of reflection, we should stop trying to do the impossible? If we stopped, the philosophical problems would soon cease to bother us.

This is the voice of prudence, but in this case it should not be heeded. The attempt to understand the significance of facts is not motivated by a foolish or perverse flirtation with overcoming unavoidable logical limitations. It is forced on us if we carry our reflection beyond a certain point. Why not, then, avoid these philosophical problems by giving up one or another of the modes of reflection whose conflict produces them? Because these modes of reflection are not luxuries that we may enjoy if we have leisure and a reflective bent. They are forced on us by our need to respond to the disruptions of everyday life. If we start reflecting on them, we will realize that their significance can be understood by way of scientific, historical, religious, aesthetic, moral, or subjective reflection, and that if we leave out one of these modes, we fail to ask and try to answer questions that the disruptions of everyday life continually force on us.[8]

The fact remains, however, that we can, and many people do, refrain from trying to understand the significance of facts in terms of nomological explanations, past influences, a transcendental order, appreciation of their form, beauty, and illumination, the goodness of human lives, or private projects. But to refrain from doing any of these, to teach ourselves not to be alive to these matters, to refuse to face the questions that will occur to most of us, or to cease trying to answer them is to impoverish ourselves deliberately. If we do reflect in these ways, however, then we shall come to hold incompatible views of the significance of the facts.

If the significance of facts is understood in a certain way, then that is taken to be a truth about them. If it is understood in other ways, then those are taken to be truths about them. If we are interested in *the* truth about them, in the real significance of the facts, if reflection has forced us to seek their significance in different modes, if additional reflection merely strengthens our commitment to these modes, and if these efforts result in our coming to hold incompatible beliefs about the truth or the real significance of the facts, then we encounter some of the apparently intractable problems that we have learned to call philosophical.[9]

Perhaps then those are right who teach themselves not to feel the force of these philosophical problems because they do not much care about the true significance of the facts, because they are satisfied with the understanding one mode of reflection provides, or because they are reluctant to push their reflections far enough. People who have the capacity, opportunity, and education for reflection can adopt this attitude only by opting for intellectual dishonesty, nurturing a false sense of comfort, keeping busy with trivia, hoping that if they ignore the deep problems they will not have to cope with them, or allowing faith in some form to quiet the disturbances of their intellect. That some people can sustain this attitude is obvious because many do sustain it.

But they do so only because of the efforts of others who struggle to cope with the disruptions of everyday life whose symptoms these problems are.

The five philosophical problems that have been introduced arise when modes of reflection conflict. But modes of reflection will conflict because they arise out of science, history, religion, aesthetics, subjectivity, and morality. They will arise because difficulties—internal doubts about how to carry on these activities and external questions raised by the choices we must make about which of them we should participate in and when—will force reflection on us. The disruptions of everyday life will force us to make choices about participating in them and to try to resolve their internal difficulties. These philosophical problems are therefore unavoidable.[10] The effort to solve them is necessary because they stand in the way of coping with the disruptions of everyday life and because the failure to cope with them endangers the basic conditions that enable us to live good lives. If the argument of this chapter is correct, however, then the prospect of solving these philosophical problems is poor. The argument in the next chapter will deepen the explanation of why the problems are intractable and prepare the ground for a proposal about changing the subject so as to improve the prospect.

3

Philosophical Problems

> Philosophical questions . . . arise because some kind of crossing
> of intellectual lines has occurred—some kind of collision, at
> times on a grand, paralysing scale, of the traffic of ideas. Philo-
> sophical questions have a certain desperateness about them, are
> accompanied by a degree of emotional pressure, a craving for
> an answer whose very nature is not clear, a sense at once of ur-
> gency and insolubility which indicates not a quest for facts . . .
> but rather that there is a conflict—some inner conflict of ideas,
> of concepts or ways of thought . . . a head-on crash, a confusion
> and interreaction of entire conceptual systems, of whole meth-
> ods of looking at the world and of describing it, which leads to
> the so-called "perennial" problems.
>
> ISAIAH BERLIN, "Philosophy and
> Government Repression"

I

Questions about the meaning of life, the possibility of free
action, the place of morality in good lives, the art of life, and the nature of
human self-understanding cannot be answered by empirical research that
leads to the discovery of new facts or by the construction of more sophisticated axiomatic systems.[1] The facts relevant to these philosophical problems
are readily available to all who care to look, and new formalisms merely lead
to the restatement of the familiar problems in an unfamiliar idiom. But if
these philosophical problems are not factual or formal, then what kind of
problems are they?

The answer given in the preceding chapter is that they are problems
about the significance of facts. Their significance is problematic because
different modes of reflection give conflicting accounts of it. These conflicts
are deep and serious because reflective agents believe themselves to have

good reasons to carry on their reflections in both of the modes of reflection from which the incompatible accounts of significance follow. They cannot resolve the conflicts by reducing one mode of reflection to another because the reduction would leave out an essential aspect of the to-be-reduced mode of reflection, namely, its understanding of the significance of the facts. Nor can they resolve the conflicts by accepting that different modes of reflection provide different accounts of the significance of the facts because their accounts are incompatible. This is the result of reflection that occurs on the third level of understanding, not on the first level of description or on the second level of interpretation. Different modes of reflection typically agree about the basic, everyday description of the relevant facts. They can also agree that the interpretations of these facts by science, history, religion, aesthetics, morality, and subjectivity are alternatives that may coexist without conflict. But given their absolutist assumption, they cannot agree that the same is true of the results of reflection. They assume that the aim of a mode of reflection is to arrive at a general understanding of the true significance of the facts. Such understandings, however, are by their very nature incompatible. For if a mode of reflection allowed alternative understandings, then it would fail in its generality, since it set out to understand the true significance of the facts and the presence of alternatives shows that it has failed. The very existence of alternatives to a mode of reflection thus constitutes an objection that implies the inadequacy of that mode of reflection.

The remaining option, simply to ignore the conflicts, is not open to reflective agents because they have been forced to reflect, both by disruptions that threaten the conditions of good lives and by internal and external questions that arise over the various approaches to coping with disruptions. It seems, therefore, that the philosophical problems that concern us here can be neither ignored nor solved.[2]

This chapter expands the previous account of why philosophical problems appear to be intractable by examining further the absolutist and the relativist ways of trying to cope with them and by understanding why both are unsuccessful.

II

It is a notorious embarrassment to philosophers that their subject appears to make no progress. Many of the problems that Plato and Aristotle dealt with are by and large the problems of Aquinas and the scholastics, of the rationalists and the empiricists, of Kant and Hegel, and of contemporary philosophers. Science and history are cumulative, there is growth of knowledge in them, but it seems to be otherwise in philosophy. We are no closer now to having a widely accepted account of the meaning of life, the possibility of free action, the place of morality in good lives, the art of life, or the nature of human self-understanding than we were when they were first recognized as problems. If these philosophical problems are solvable, why have they not been solved? One way of responding to this embarrassing question is to present solutions to them and explain why so many people have not accepted them.

The absolutist approach to this double task is to begin with the situation of reflective agents who are in the grip of a philosophical problem. They understand that there is a plurality of modes of reflection and that they provide incompatible accounts of the significance of the same set of facts. They participate in and accept the accounts provided by at least two modes. The minds of such agents are, therefore, divided because they understand the significance of facts in incompatible ways. This is how they experience philosophical problems. How, according to absolutists, should they cope with this division in their minds?

A step toward an answer follows from the observation that while it is true that the minds of reflective agents are typically divided, it is only rarely and exceptionally true that they are evenly divided. Most reflective agents feel the force of one mode of reflection more strongly than the pull of others. This may be expressed by saying that in their minds one mode of reflection is dominant and the others are recessive. Their dominant mode of reflection is, say, scientific, and although they appreciate the attractions of the others, if they come into conflict the scientific one prevails. The philosophical problems that concern us are thus solved by giving precedence to one of the modes of reflection whose conflict causes the problems.

This may be a psychologically accurate description of how reflective agents actually cope with their divided minds and philosophical problems, but its accuracy leaves it open whether the agents are reasonable in giving precedence to one mode of reflection. The assigned precedence may just be a result of their prejudices, their upbringing, a bias they learned from their teachers, their neuroses, class interests, indoctrination, or other social, economic, or political influences that color their judgments—or they may also have good reasons for them. Defenders of absolutism, of course, hold that the assignment of precedence ought to be based on good reasons. What might these good reasons be? Absolutists assume that good reasons are general; that is, they are not just reasons for a particular agent in a particular situation but reasons that hold for all agents in all situations of that type. This assumption will be rejected in the next chapter, and its rejection is a crucial step in the argument; for the time being, however, let us suppose that it holds. The general reason absolutists need, then, for assigning precedence to a particular mode of reflection is that its account of the significance of the facts is better than the account of the mode of reflection that conflicts with it.

The absolutist claim is not merely that the precedence of a mode of reflection holds in a particular context but that it holds generally in all contexts. If it did not, the reason would be particular, not general. So the absolutist claim is not that when, for instance, moral and subjective reflection give conflicting accounts of the significance of a particular project, then one of the two—say, the moral significance of the project—should take precedence in this case. The absolutist claim is rather that moral significance should take precedence over subjective significance generally, regardless of the identity of the agent and the project. The argument in support of this claim would have to show the greater importance, weight, depth, primacy, or whatever of moral reflection when it conflicts with subjective reflection. A way of doing this would be to show that when the conflicting accounts of significance are compared on the basis of independent standards, then the account given by one mode of reflection always proves to be superior. This, of course, requires the specification of the independent standards.

One of these standards is conformity to the rules of classical logic. The denial of this standard is absurd because conformity to it is necessary for making sense. It is a standard to which even the denial that it is a standard must conform. So its attempted denial is either nonsense or self-refuting. Another standard is that a mode of reflection must take into account all the relevant facts. The central aim of all modes of reflection is to provide a general understanding of the significance of all the relevant facts. If a mode of reflection ignores any of them, it fails in its central aim. It may have difficulties with accounting for some facts, but these difficulties must be temporary and few, otherwise the adequacy of the entire mode of reflection is called into question. Yet a further standard is that each mode of reflection must acknowledge the possibility that its participants may be mistaken in their descriptions, interpretations, and reflections. What appear to them as facts may not be. Each mode of reflection, therefore, must draw a distinction between appearance and reality, and, consequently, a distinction between true claims that accurately reflect reality and false claims that do not. Moreover, all modes of reflection must strive to make true claims and avoid false ones, that is, they must aim at rationality and condemn irrationality. Otherwise, their attempts to understand the significance of relevant facts will fail, because they will be directed toward the wrong objects. What are taken to be true claims, and how best to make them, may well vary with modes of reflections. But there can be no variation among adequate modes of reflection in the recognition that conformity to the standards of truth and rationality is a necessary condition of adequacy.

It must be admitted, however, that meeting these independent standards—conforming to logic, accounting for relevant facts, and seeking rationality and truth—still leaves room for conflicts between modes of reflection. These standards help to ascertain what the facts are and how to make coherent claims about them, but they do not help to resolve conflicts between modes of reflection that do meet them and yet give incompatible accounts of the significance of bona fide facts. There remain many conflicting scientific, historical, moral, religious, aesthetic, and subjective accounts of the significance of the same set of facts.

Yet another independent standard may be thought to alter the picture, however: the capacity that adequate modes of reflection must have of coping with the disruptions of everyday life. One important reason for reflecting in a particular mode is that the approaches to coping with the disruptions raise internal and external questions that can be answered, if at all, only by further reflection. Obviously, one standard for judging the adequacy of a mode of reflection is whether it succeeds in answering these questions in a way that makes it possible to cope with the disruptions. There is, of course, much more to modes of reflection than assistance with such practical matters, but their adequacy depends on coping with the disruptions that prompted them.

This will not be the end of the matter, however, because different modes of reflection propose incompatible ways of coping with the disruptions of everyday life. These incompatibilities cannot be removed by this standard because it is the attempt to conform to the standard that causes the incompatibilities. But this is no longer a reason for regarding such conflicts as intractable. It is, rather, a reason for carrying reflection further. For the availability of incompatible ways of coping with the disruptions of everyday life is an embarrassment of riches. The problem is no longer to protect the conditions required for living good lives but to choose one protection among several. Any one will do, but, of course, the best one would do best. Finding out which is the best requires further reflection. The upshot is that there are independent standards by which the adequacy of modes of reflection can be judged.

Absolutists, therefore, are right: it is justified to give precedence to accounts of significance that conform to independent standards over accounts that do not. The fact remains, however, that these independent standards are so elementary that neither side in a long-standing philosophical argument is likely to violate them. When religious believers and secular moralists dispute about the meaning of life, determinists and libertarians about the possibility of free action, egoists and moralists about the place of morality in good lives, classicists and romantics about the art of life, and materialists and historicists about human self-understanding, then it is most unlikely that the highly sophisticated and well-informed defenders of these incompatible accounts would make simple mistakes. The two sides are typically alike in their dedication to rationality and truth, they are trained equally well in expressing their accounts in logically coherent forms, and they normally agree about the facts. They nevertheless give incompatible accounts of the significance of agreed-upon facts. It is precisely because they are committed to rationality and truth that the incompatibility of their accounts bothers them. So the appeal to these independent standards is not going to resolve conflicts between sophisticated versions of different modes of reflection.

This still leaves, however, the capacity of modes of reflection to cope with the disruptions of everyday life as an independent standard that could justify the assignment of precedence to one mode of reflection. Since one reason for giving the incompatible accounts is ultimately to cope with the disruptions, it must surely count in favor of a mode of reflection if it provides a better way of coping than its rivals. The problem for absolutists is that it is not enough to show that a mode of reflection copes better with a particular disruption. According to absolutists, good reasons are general. The justification of precedence, therefore, must be not merely that one way of coping is better in a *particular* context, but that it is *generally* better in *all* contexts.

The thought behind the assumption that good reasons must be general is the following. Take, for instance, a conflict between the religious and the moral modes of reflection about how to cope with the disruption of everyday life caused by the loss of meaning. Both sides recognize that meaning depends on the agents' having reasonable projects. But they disagree about the respective importance of the factors that make their projects reasonable. Religious reflection stresses conformity to a transcendental order; moral reflection stresses autonomous commitments. As soon as this is understood, absolutists see the conflict raised from the particular to a general level. For, absolutists will say, participants in the religious mode of reflection will find religious reasons better, whereas participants in the moral mode will find moral reasons better, and those who participate in both will have to decide where their primary commitments lie. The question, therefore, can be answered only by answering first the more fundamental question of whether, when those two modes of reflection conflict, precedence should be given to one or the other. Only if that question is answered will there be a principled way of settling conflicts about how to cope with the loss of meaning. But if absolutists are right in assuming that good reasons must be general, then they cannot justify giving precedence to one mode of reflection on the basis of its superior capacity to cope with the disruptions of everyday life because different modes will recommend different ways of coping, and each will consider its own way superior. This independent standard, therefore, will not provide what absolutists need.

III

Unless absolutists can point to a hitherto unheard-of independent standard, they are in a position that is painfully familiar from the history of philosophy. As Descartes puts it: "I shall not say anything about Philosophy, but that seeing that it has been cultivated for many centuries by the best minds that have ever lived, and that nevertheless no single thing is to be found in it which is not subject of dispute, and in consequence which is not dubious."[3] Hume agrees: "Principles taken upon trust, consequences lamely deduced from them, want of coherence in the parts, and of evidence in the whole, these are every where to be met with in the systems of the most eminent philosophers, and seem to have drawn disgrace upon philosophy itself. . . . [E]ven the rabble without doors may judge from the noise and clamour, which they hear, that all goes not well within. There is nothing which is not subject of debate, and in which men of learning are not of contrary opinions. The most trivial question escapes not our controversy, and in the most momentous we are not able to give any certain decision."[4] Kant is of the same opinion: "It seems almost ridiculous, while every other science is continually advancing, that in this, which pretends to be wisdom incarnate, for whose oracle everyone inquires, we should constantly move round the same spot, without gaining a single step. . . . [I]n this domain there is actually as yet no standard weight and measure to distinguish sound knowledge from shallow talk."[5] Mill repeats the same sentiment: "From the dawn of philosophy, the question concerning the *summum bonum*, or . . . the foundation of morality, has been accounted the main problem of speculative thought. . . . And after more than two thousand years the same discussions continue, philosophers are still ranged under the same contending banners, and neither thinkers nor mankind at large seem nearer to being unanimous on the subject than when the young Socrates listened to the old Protagoras."[6]

It is a wry thought that these devastating observations about philosophy were offered by first-rate philosophers as preambles to their own efforts to put right what has been wrong before them. If it had not been for their modesty, each could have echoed Wittgenstein's claim about his own work that followed his preamble: "The *truth* of the thoughts that are here communicated seems to me unassailable and definitive. I therefore believe myself to have found, on all essential points, the final solution of the problems."[7] But the "final solution" of each of these philosophers has fared no better than the earlier ones. The history of philosophy is a graveyard of the failed attempts of "the best minds that have ever lived" to solve the problems of philosophy.

The champions of these attempts typically proceed by noting the absence of a method that would make it possible "to distinguish sound knowledge from shallow talk." Then they propose a method of their own and claim to have inaugurated a revolution in philosophy. Some of these methods are: the elenchus for Plato; revelation for Augustine; clear and distinct ideas for Descartes; Euclidean geometry for Spinoza; a tough-minded empiricism that demands, *"Does it contain any abstract reasoning concerning quantity and number?* No. *Does it contain any experimental reasoning concerning matters of fact and existence?* No. Commit it then to the flames for it can contain nothing but sophistry and illusion" for Hume;[8] the dialectic for Hegel; phenomenological analysis for Husserl; some version of the verifiability principle for positivists and logical empiricists; dialectical materialism for Marxists; falsifiability for Popper; the scientific method for Quine, and so forth.

All of these methods, of course, are derived from the context of one or another mode of reflection or way of thinking that the original proponent of the method regards as superior. The proposed solution of philosophical problems is the outcome of the application of the method to them. The result is the "solution" of the problem, reached by the application of the method, that one of the two modes of reflection or ways of thinking whose conflict causes the problem is superior to the other. The method thus puts to work the absolutist assumption with which the proponent of the method has begun. The elenchus will lead to the conclusion that eudaimonistic moral reflection is primary; revelation will show the superiority of religious reflection; Hegelian and Marxist dialectic will privilege historical reflection; the clear and distinct ideas of the agent and phenomenological analysis will point to the primacy of subjective reflection; and the verifiability principle, falsifiability, and the scientific method will imply the superiority of scientific reflection. Other methods may be derived from other modes of reflection or ways of thinking, such as logic, psychoanalysis, geometry, economics, literary criticism, and so forth. They too will strengthen the belief with which their proponents began that their modes of reflection or ways of thinking must be given precedence over conflicting ones.

The perfectly justified response of the counterrevolutionary critics is to point out the arbitrariness of the revolutionary method and the failure of the favored mode of reflection or way of thinking to accommodate the significance of the facts. They stress, for instance, that scientific reflection is neutral about the moral significance of facts; that religious reflection does not account for the historical contingency of all religious thought; that historical reflection leaves unanswered the all-important question of how to distinguish between what is true and good and what is thought to be true and good during a particular period; that aesthetic reflection is indifferent to the moral significance of works of art; that moral reflection ignores subjective projects that give meaning to life; and that subjective reflection grossly inflates the significance of the agent's point of view.

The epigoni of the revolutionaries then respond by proposing ingenious ways of accommodating the significance that critics charge them with missing. Critics, in turn, offer ingenious objections to these ingenious proposals. And so the argument goes back and forth, centering on increasingly abstruse issues, familiar only to experts, who recall, only with embarrassment and only when forced by students or the general public, the deep and serious philosophical problems whose "final solution" was the aim of the revolution that has bogged down, once again, in the swamps of pedantry.

This dismal picture will be familiar to anyone who is acquainted with the past and present of philosophy. It is an oddity of the subject that absolutists combine the acknowledgment of the failure of past absolutist attempts to solve philosophical problems with the proposal of yet another version of absolutism. The impression that forces itself on nonabsolutist observers is of ever-renewed energetic banging of philosophical heads against the unyielding wall of philosophical problems.

The problem for absolutists, however, is not just that the ultimate arbitrariness of their position invariably leads them to deny the significance of facts that do not fit into their favored mode of reflection. They also have to explain why dissenting absolutists and nonabsolutists—philosophers who are as committed to rationality and truth, as logically savvy, as familiar with the facts, and as desirous of coping with the disruptions of everyday life as they are—refuse to accept their solutions to philosophical problems. How could it happen that such people fail to embrace the solutions to the problems they are dedicated to solve when the solutions are given to them? The obvious answer, that the proposed solutions are wanting, is of course not one that their champions are going to accept, but the fact is that they do not have a convincing alternative to the obvious answer. It is perfectly understandable, therefore, that doubts about absolutism make people doubt the feasibility of the whole philosophical enterprise. This *will* save them from the arbitrariness of absolutism, but it *will not* help to solve the philosophical problems that stand in the way of coping with the disruptions of everyday life.

Some hard-headed and clear-minded philosophers respond to this state of affairs by showing quite uncharacteristic signs of humility. Colin McGinn says: "The hardness of philosophy is both subjective and irremediable," and this is because "philosophical perplexities arise in us because of definite inherent limitations on our epistemic faculties. . . . Our epistemic architecture obstructs knowledge of the real world."[9] Thomas Nagel says: "Philosophy . . . is an extremely difficult subject, and no exception to the general rule that creative efforts are rarely successful. I do not feel equal to the problems treated in this [his own] book. They seem to me to require an order of intelligence wholly different from mine. Others who have tried to address the central questions of philosophy will recognize the feeling."[10] Bertrand Russell agrees: "There are many questions—and among them those that are of the profoundest interest to our spiritual life—which, so far as we can see, must remain insoluble to the human intellect, unless its powers become of quite a different order from what they are now."[11] The question we are left with, therefore, is whether there is an alternative to the absolutist arbitrariness in coping with philosophical problems and the loss of intellectual nerve in the face of their difficulty.

IV

One answer follows from the version of relativism that was introduced but left undeveloped in the preceding chapter. It will be referred to as skeptical relativism in order to distinguish it from other versions and to pay homage to its ancient source.[12] Skeptical relativists deny that the absolutist aim of finding the true significance of the facts can be realized. They acknowledge that this leaves the philosophical problems that concern us here without solutions. The answer, however, is not to continue the hopeless search for solutions, but to treat the problems as symptoms of misdirected reflection. "Philosophy is a battle against the bewitchment of our intelligence."[13] And "the real discovery is the one that makes me capable of stopping doing philosophy when I want to. —The one that gives philosophy peace, so that it is no longer tormented by questions."[14] The proposed solution of our philosophical problems, then, is to understand that they are symptoms of reflection having gone wrong. The remedy is to avoid the misdirection of reflection. If we do that, there will be nothing left to worry about. "The philosopher's treatment of a question is like the treatment of an illness."[15]

There is something deeply right and deeply wrong with skeptical relativism. What is right is the criticism of absolutism. What is wrong is the supposition that if absolutism were abandoned, then the philosophical problems that concern us would disappear. Let us begin, then, with understanding what is right with skeptical relativism.

Consider the position of reflective agents who have a conflict because their reflections have led them to give incompatible accounts of the significance of facts. They are committed to two modes of reflection: they regard their respective accounts of significance as correct, and they think that they have good reasons both for their commitments and for their acceptance of the incompatible accounts. According to skeptical relativists, this is the typical situation of reflective agents. Their reflections have landed them in an impossible situation; they have to cope with the disruptions they face; they are driven to cope in incompatible directions by the conflict within themselves; their peace of mind is shattered; and they do not know how to go on. Skeptical relativism offers a way out of their predicament.

What reflective agents should do is recognize that the conflicting accounts of significance derived from different modes of reflection are equally convincing and that neither takes precedence over the other. They should acknowledge that this is so and stop trying to resolve the conflict by reducing one mode of reflection to another. The intellectual agitation produced by the conflict will then be replaced by the peace of mind that comes from understanding that it is in the nature of modes of reflection to conflict in this manner. This proposal raises two questions that must be answered before it can be taken seriously.

First, why should it be supposed that the conflicting accounts that give rise to philosophical problems are *equally* convincing? Is it not obvious that sometimes at least the scientific or the aesthetic or the moral significance of facts outweighs the conflicting significance that may be attributed to them by other modes of reflection? Skeptical relativists, of course, acknowledge that this is how we in fact proceed. We view concentration camps as having primarily a moral significance, Picasso's *The Tragedy* as having primarily an aesthetic significance, and the theory of relativity as having primarily a scientific significance. But, skeptical relativists say, how we proceed is one thing, whether we are justified in proceeding that way is quite another. And it is the justification for giving precedence to one mode of reflection over another that skeptical relativists are dubious about. They base their doubt on the unavailability of a standard that could be appealed to in justifying the assignment of precedence.[16]

Part of the strength of skeptical relativism is that, unlike other versions of relativism, it does not deny that logical consistency, the explanation of relevant facts, the pursuit of rationality and truth, and the capacity to cope with the disruptions of everyday life are independent standards to which all modes of reflection must either conform or forfeit the claim to attention. The doubt of skeptical relativists about there being such a thing as the true significance of the facts rests on these independent standards being too

elementary to settle the conflicts among modes of reflection that give rise
to our philosophical problems.

All the modes of reflection we have been discussing conform to these elementary standards. What sets them apart are disagreements that arise on a
higher level. These modes of reflection agree about the description of the
relevant facts and about their interpretations by science, history, religion,
aesthetics, morality, and subjectivity, but they disagree about the mode of
reflection that would lead to the best way of understanding the significance
of the facts provided by the descriptions and interpretations.

Skeptical relativists claim that these disagreements cannot be settled by
appealing to independent standards because there are no such standards beyond the elementary level. There are, to be sure, standards beyond the elementary level, but they are not independent; they presuppose the context of
one or another mode of reflection. If reflective people encounter philosophical problems because they are committed to two modes of reflection that
provide conflicting accounts of the significance of the facts, then they cannot reasonably solve the philosophical problems by appealing to the standards accepted by one of their own modes of reflection but not by the other,
for that would be arbitrary and question-begging. What they should do instead, according to skeptical relativists, is recognize that they have carried
their reflections beyond reasonable limits. If they stay within these limits,
then the problems will not arise.

This brings us to the second question that skeptical relativists must answer. Suppose that reflective people heed their advice, eschew excessive
reflection, and avoid philosophical problems. There still remains the question of what they should do about the disruptions of everyday life that forced
them to reflect in the first place. If reflection guided by modes of reflection
is not the answer, then what is? We can extract an answer from David Hume,
who said: "A Pyrrhonian cannot expect, that his philosophy will have any
constant influence on the mind; or if it had, that its influence would be
beneficial to society. On the contrary, he must acknowledge, if he will acknowledge anything, that all human life must perish, were his principles universally and steadily to prevail. All discourse, all action would immediately
cease; and men remain in total lethargy, till the necessities of nature, unsatisfied, put an end to their miserable existence. It is true; so fatal an event
is very little to be dreaded. Nature is always too strong for principle."[17]

What skeptical relativists oppose, then, is not the beliefs of everyday life
but the speculative beliefs that follow from excessive reflection. As Hume put
it: "Shou'd it here be ask'd me, whether I . . . be really one of those sceptics,
who hold that all is uncertain, and that our judgement is not in *any* thing pos-
sesst of *any* measures of truth and falsehood; I shou'd reply . . . that neither

I, nor any other person was ever sincerely and constantly of that opinion. Nature, by an absolute and uncontroulable necessity determin'd us to judge as well as to breathe and feel; nor can we any more forebear viewing certain objects in a stronger and fuller light . . . than we can hinder ourselves from thinking as long as we are aware."[18] Eschewing speculative beliefs based on excessive reflection, therefore, does not mean that we should not hold any beliefs.

Holding beliefs, however, must be done with caution. In the words of Sextus: "When we say that Sceptics do not hold beliefs, we do not take 'belief' in the sense in which . . . belief is acquiescing in something; for Sceptics assent to feelings forced upon them by appearances—for example, they would not say, when heated or chilled, 'I think I am not heated (or: chilled)'. Rather, we say that they do not hold beliefs in the sense in which . . . belief is assent to some unclear object of investigation in the sciences; for Pyrrhonists do not assent to anything unclear."[19] Skeptical relativists thus hold clear beliefs and do not hold unclear ones. In the terms of our discussion, skeptical relativists regard as clear the beliefs of everyday life. They are the beliefs that arise from human nature and the conventions of society. Unclear beliefs, by contrast, are suggested by participation in various modes of reflection. Skeptical relativists distrust beliefs about the significance of facts, not beliefs about facts.

But this still leaves the question of what we should do to cope with the disruption of everyday life. Sextus's answer is: we should "live in accordance with everyday observances, without holding opinions—for we are not able to be utterly inactive. These observances seem to be fourfold, and to consist in guidance by nature, necessitation by feelings, handing down laws and customs, and teaching of certain kinds of expertise."[20] This fourfold guide to conduct may be understood as including those that follow from having to satisfy basic needs by exercising our basic capacities; from having feelings associated with basic needs, such as fatigue, hunger, sexual desire, and so forth; from having local laws and customs regarding how needs are to be satisfied; and from having certain kinds of expertise for satisfying them.

It may thus be said that skeptical relativists regard human nature and the conventions of everyday life as appropriate guides to conduct. These guides include expertise, such as the various approaches to coping with the disruptions of everyday life. Reflection beyond this point is misdirected because it will yield incompatible conclusions and because there is no independent standard that could be appealed to in order to resolve their incompatibility. In Hume's words, "Custom, then, is the great guide of human life."[21] Our nature compels us to hold everyday beliefs. When these beliefs are inadequate to cope with the disruptions of everyday life, we turn to the customary forms of expertise that exist in our society. And for us, in this day and age, the expertise takes the form of science, history, religion, morality, aesthetics, and subjectivity. The temptation to go beyond the available expertise leads to unsolvable philosophical problems. Those who wish to have peace of mind, will resist the temptation. They will see that "What has to be accepted, the given, is—so one could say—*forms of life*."[22]

V

Let us now consider what is wrong with skeptical relativism. The first problem concerns the claim that if reflection is kept within the limits set by everyday life, if we suspend judgment about "unclear matters" (as skeptical relativists call those with which modes of reflection deal), then peace of mind will follow. The reason why this claim is false is that we are driven by disruptions to go beyond the context of everyday life and seek better ways of coping with them than what is provided by the inadequate resources of that context. Skeptical relativists acknowledge that the disruptions endanger the conditions of good lives, but they think that reliance on the fourfold guide to conduct within everyday life—needs, feelings, conventions, and expertise—will make coping possible.

Needs and feelings, however, are obviously helpless to cope with disruptions such as AIDS. Conventions are abundant, but it is most unclear how they apply. In the first place, there is the problem of deciding which conventions should be followed. Should AIDS be treated as an epidemic? as the risk that people with certain lifestyles take? as the responsibility of taxpayers, of insurance companies, or of the families, friends, or lovers of the people with AIDS? Is its prevention a task for science, morality, or religion, or should it be left to individuals? How important is research into its cure in comparison with cancer research, the alleviation of poverty, the reduction of the crime rate, or the improvement of education? Having conventions will not answer these questions. In the second place, conventions are old and AIDS is new. There has never been anything like it before, partly because it is a consequence of the on-going sexual revolution, one of whose effects is to call many of our conventions into question. The appeal to conventions, therefore, will not help in such cases.

This leaves the last resource that the fourfold guide has to offer: expertise. Expertise includes all the available approaches to coping with the disruptions of everyday life: science, religion, morality, history, aesthetics, and subjectivity, to which may be added whatever other approach may be offered as a way of coping. The reason why relying on expertise is bound to be inadequate is that experts following the same approach disagree about what procedure their own expertise suggests. Nonexperts also disagree about which of the various available forms of expertise should be accepted as a guide. Finally, there is widespread disagreement about the comparative importance of coping with the numerous disruptions of everyday life that confront a society at any given time. Current debates about AIDS reflect these disagreements, but AIDS, of course, is just one example among many. Drugs, poverty, terrorism, pollution, and crime are some others.

It is clear that since the resources of everyday life are inadequate to answer these questions about the applicability of conventions and reliance on expertise, what must be done is to go beyond the available conventions and expertise and reflect on their significance. This is what leads to philosophical problems. AIDS, drugs, poverty, terrorism, pollution, crime, and so forth certainly disrupt everyday life, but, equally certainly, they are not *philosophical* problems. Our aim, in each case, is to put an end to them. But we do not know how to do that, and in the meantime we have to cope with them as well as we can. Each of these disruptions has deep roots in the kind of life that we have made for ourselves, and the problems they present force us to reflect on our form of life. We cannot just accept our form of life as a given because, as the disruptions show, it has features that hinder, rather than aid, our aspiration to live good lives. When we are compelled to reflect in this manner, our first problem is about what mode of reflection we should follow. This is a problem because reflection may be scientific, historical, religious, moral, aesthetic, or subjective, because most reflective people regard themselves as having good reasons to reflect in several of these modes, and because their reflections suggest incompatible ways of understanding the significance of the facts constituted by the disruptions in the background. It makes all the difference to how we cope with AIDS whether our reflection on its significance occurs in a scientific, moral, or subjective mode.

If we are reflective enough to understand this, then we are in the grip of a philosophical problem. The problem is not a by-product of excessive reflection but the result of the difficulty of the disruption that prompts the reflection. The skeptical relativist claim that peace of mind will follow if we teach ourselves not to reflect in this way is dangerously mistaken, because if we do not reflect, we endanger not only our peace of mind but also the conditions necessary for good lives that are threatened by the disruptions. Skeptical relativists fail to see that we must go beyond how the facts appear to us in everyday life and ask about their significance because the apparent facts threaten us and because we disagree about how we should cope with this threat. If we stay within the context of everyday life, calamity, not peace of mind, will follow. But if we leave that context and reflect on disagreements about the applicability of conventions among both experts and nonexperts, then we inevitably run up against philosophical problems, because our modes of reflection conflict with one another. Whatever may be true of the prospect of solving philosophical problems, the recommendation of skeptical relativists to ignore them is badly mistaken.

Another difficulty is that skeptical relativists misunderstand how philosophical problems are experienced by those who are in their grip. It is only because of this misunderstanding that skeptical relativists could recommend ignoring philosophical problems and suppose that peace of mind will follow. People in the grip of philosophical problems will find them impossible to ignore. If they are to have peace of mind, they have to achieve it in some other way.

Consider facing a situation in two different ways. Say that I know that in Stalinist Russia dedicated artists had to choose between some degree of collaboration with the regime or being unable to pursue their art. I am not sure what I would do in that situation, and I am not even sure what would be the reasonable thing to do. I recognize the problem, I see that one must choose and that what one chooses has a lasting effect on one's life, but I can ignore the problem because I am not a dedicated artist and I do not live in Stalinist Russia. I look at the lives of Mandelstam, Pasternak, and Shostakovich from the outside, and I may cultivate my peace of mind because I do not allow myself to be bothered by their problem. I can still have an intellectual appreciation of their predicament, but I do not feel it, at least not in the way in which they had felt it. They had to make a choice, I do not.

If, however, I were in their situation, it would be psychologically impossible for me, as it was for them, not to feel the predicament. I would then have to make the wrenching choice and I could not have only an intellectual appreciation of it. It would necessarily engage my feelings. The ghastly options available to me would be emotionally charged. To say that they, or I, ought to ignore the problem and cultivate my peace of mind would be to recommend an impossibility. The recommendation is not impossible for those who have the good fortune to be outside of that situation, but it is impossible for those who are in it. It is this contrast between the inside and outside views that skeptical relativists fail to appreciate in the case of philosophical problems.

Just as AIDS and other social ills are not philosophical problems, so also the choice between collaboration and artistic life in a dictatorship is not one. But it gives rise to one if we start to reflect on how that choice should be made. If our reflection is moral, it will lead us to oppose, or at least not to support, the vicious regime. If the price of that choice is that we cannot pursue our art, then so be it. If, on the other hand, our reflection is aesthetic, we shall opt for living an artistic life. We shall conclude that the potential worth of what we might create is great enough to outweigh the seaminess of the moral compromises we might have to make. But if we are reflective enough, we shall be open to reflection in both the moral and the aesthetic modes. We shall understand that they both represent something of great value, and that whichever we choose, we shall forfeit something essential to good lives. If our reflection has come this far, then we shall encounter the familiar cluster of philosophical problems connected with the art of life. How should we live? we shall ask ourselves. Should the requirements of morality be our primary guides, or should it be the cultivation of our creative talent? Should we see the significance of the facts of our lives and circumstances as moral or as aesthetic? We must choose, and whatever we choose will have a lasting effect on the kind of life we shall end up having.

It is possible to take an outside view of this philosophical problem. If I think that aesthetic reflection is decadent when it is cut loose from its moral moorings, then I will have an easy way of resolving the conflict between aesthetic and moral reflection. I could then see that some other people may be gripped by their conflict because they are equally committed to both modes of reflection, but I would see that from the outside. I myself have an answer to the question of what I would do if I were experiencing their conflict, and so I can cultivate peace of mind regarding that conflict. The crucial point, however, is that I could take an outside view of many philosophical problems only if I were insufficiently reflective. If I think through the implications of my commitment, say, to the moral mode of reflection, then I could not simply conclude that aesthetic reflection should be subordinated to it. The reason for this is that I would then see that aesthetic reflection is partly motivated by questions with which moral reflection has serious problems. Some of these questions are: Why should I be moral if it does make my life better? What makes lives meaningful once duty is done? Why are moral lives so often drab, boring, and philistine? Why is the sense of beauty and liberation that great art gives to many people valued so highly by them?

These questions will bring me to the realization that while moral considerations are, of course, important to living a good life, so are aesthetic ones. If it is a good life I want, then I must value both considerations, and if they come into conflict, as they often do for creative artists in dictatorships, then the conflict does not have a simple resolution. I have to balance their conflicting claims on me. But in my reflection on what a reasonable balance would be, I cannot rely on either moral or aesthetic reflection. To do so would be an arbitrary resolution of their conflict, and it would, in any case, abandon an essential element on which the goodness of my life depends. What should I do then? How should I think about this conflict?

If I carry my reflection this far, then I will ask not merely internal questions that are answerable *within* a mode of reflection, but external questions *about* that mode of reflection. These questions will be prompted by my understanding that there are incompatible ways of understanding the significance of the facts that have a serious effect on how I myself live. This will unavoidably grip me, not merely as an intellectual problem, but as an emotional issue. The conflict is partly about the significance of facts that affect *my* world, *my* place in it, and *my* life. If I have reached this point in my reflections, I can no longer take a detached view of this philosophical problem; I cannot ignore it; and it would be psychologically impossible for me not to be intellectually and emotionally engaged with it. This psychological impossibility would remain even if I could not decide where the significance of facts is to be sought. Against this background, the skeptical relativists' recommendation to ignore the problem will seem to be about as helpful as the recommendation to people being tortured to cultivate detachment.

This criticism of skeptical relativism was couched in terms of the philosophical problem that is caused by the conflict between the moral and the aesthetic modes of reflection. It could have been equally well couched in terms of the conflicts between other modes of reflection that give rise to the problems of the meaning of life, the possibility of free action, the place of morality in good lives, or human self-understanding. All these would have served the same purpose, because, for those who understand what is at stake in these philosophical problems, ignoring them in the way skeptical relativists recommend is a psychological impossibility. The inside view of many philosophical problems is forced on sufficiently reflective people. Those who have the outside view give conclusive evidence of having wittingly or unwittingly arrested their reflections. The recommendation of skeptical relativists can be followed only by unreflective people, who do not need it; and it is useless for those who have lost their peace of mind as a result of their reflections.

These criticisms are intended to show that skeptical relativism is mistaken about how to cope with these philosophical problems. But the criticisms do not show, and were not meant to show, that skeptical relativism is mistaken about the origin of many philosophical problems. Skeptical relativism is right in some respects, wrong in others. It is right in its diagnosis that many philosophical problems are the result of misdirected reflection that leads to an intellectual impasse and shatters one's peace of mind. It is wrong in proposing as a remedy the cessation of reflection. We cannot cease to reflect because it is psychologically impossible, and it should not be done because we cannot cope with the disruptions of everyday life without reflection.

VI

To conclude, the philosophical problems that concern us here arise because modes of reflection conflict with one another. These conflicts are the unavoidable products of the disruptions of everyday life, of the internal and external questions raised by the various approaches to coping with them, and of the reflective efforts to answer these questions. On the basis of what has been said so far, skeptical relativists appear to be right in finding that the philosophical problems to which these questions lead are unsolvable. This conclusion may be resisted in two ways. One is to show that the philosophical problems are not unsolvable by solving them. This is what absolutists have been trying to do with no success. The other is to show that the philosophical problems only appear to be unsolvable because they are wrongly framed and that if they are framed rightly, then they can be solved. This second approach is the subject of the rest of the book.

4

The Pluralistic Approach

There are philosophers who assure us that all human utterance
is in one mode. They . . . hear only one authentic voice. And
there might be something to be said for this view if we were
considering some primordial condition of the race when death
was close, when leisure was scarce, and when every utterance . . .
may be supposed to have had a practical bearing. But it is now
long since mankind invented for itself other modes of
speaking. . . . Nevertheless, the view dies hard that Babel was
the occasion of a curse being laid upon mankind from which it
is the business of philosophers to deliver us, and a disposition
remains to impose a single character upon significant human
speech.

MICHAEL OAKESHOTT, "The Voice of Poetry
in the Conversation of Mankind"

I

This chapter proposes an alternative to the line of thought
that leads to unsolvable philosophical problems. The source of these problems is that modes of reflection give incompatible accounts of the
significance of the facts. The resulting problems are unsolvable *if* their solution is taken to involve finding a general reason for attributing overriding
significance to the account given by one of the conflicting modes of reflection. No such general reason can be found because all candidates arbitrarily
and unavoidably denigrate the significance attributed to the facts by one or
another of the conflicting modes of reflection. The alternative proposed in
this chapter proceeds by accepting that the source of the philosophical problems that form our present concern is the conflict among modes of reflection, while denying that a rational solution requires finding a general reason
that establishes the superiority of a mode of reflection. According to this ap-

proach, our philosophical problems have rational solutions, but they are not general solutions because there is no such thing as the one true account of the significance of the facts.

It must be emphasized that this chapter presents only the outlines of a proposed approach. Its aim is merely to introduce a way of thinking. A convincing case for it depends on filling in the details and giving the promised rational solutions. That, however, will be done only in the five chapters that follow, in which the approach will be applied to each of the five philosophical problems that concerns us here.

The argument has so far led to the conclusion that if people carry their reflections far enough, they unavoidably find themselves in a predicament from which there seems to be no reasonable way out. Their predicament arises from the combination of four interconnected elements. The first is some disruption of everyday life that threatens the conditions of good lives. It may be the sense of futility caused by the endless routine drudgery that one's life involves; or the feeling of powerlessness in the face of the overwhelming forces of one's physical and social environment; or the obstacles to living as one wishes created by the prevailing moral and political arrangements; or the inability to make one's life more meaningful, bring it more under one's control, and have it embody a more harmonious relation between the requirements of morality and personal satisfactions; or the failure to understand the conditions in which one lives and to which one is vulnerable. These disruptions are the ultimate sources of the philosophical problems of the meaning of life, the possibility of free action, the place of morality in good lives, the art of life, and the nature of human self-understanding. But the disruptions do not give rise to these philosophical problems directly. The customary approaches to coping with the disruptions and the various modes of reflection mediate between the disruptions and the problems. The second element that contributes to the predicament of reflective agents consists of the external and internal questions concerning the comparative merits of the attempts through science, history, religion, aesthetics, morality, and subjectivity to cope with these disruptions. Coping depends on answering the external and internal questions, and that, of course, provides a strong reason to seek answers to them. The third is the result of understanding that the approaches that prompt the questions and the disruptions that create the need to answer them give rise to modes of reflection that yield conflicting accounts of the significance of the facts on which coping with the disruptions depends. This conflict requires making a reasonable choice among the alternative accounts. The fourth element is the recognition that the reasonable choice is neither to eschew reflection, as skeptical relativism suggests, nor to assert the superiority of one of the conflicting modes of reflection, as absolutism claims. For the first makes it impossible to cope with the disruptions and the second arbitrarily ignores much of the significance of the facts upon which coping depends. It is thus reasonable to try to resolve the conflicts by avoiding both skeptical relativism and absolutism. But if the disruptions call for reflection and if no mode of reflection can be reasonably privileged, then it seems that both the failure to reflect and the effort to arrive at a reflective choice are unreasonable. This is the predicament to which the argument has led. Now we need to find a way out.

The discussion of skeptical relativism and absolutism in the preceding chapter has prepared the ground for an alternative approach. We have seen that something close to the skeptical relativist account of the origin of the philosophical problems that concern us is right, but the skeptical relativist way of trying to cope with them is wrong. We have also seen that although absolutists are right in seeking to solve philosophical problems by trying to reflect further and better, they are wrong in assuming that the aim of continued reflection is to find a general reason that establishes the superiority of one mode of reflection and of its account of significance. The alternative approach that will now be presented agrees that continued reflection is necessary for solving our philosophical problems, but it disagrees that this reflection must aim at finding a general reason. Reasoned choice among conflicting modes of reflection is possible without relying on a general reason for regarding one mode of reflection superior to the others.

II

The alternative approach is that of pluralism. Anyone defending pluralism must answer three basic questions: What are the items that are said to be plural? What are the reasons for regarding them as plural? and What improvement in understanding follows from regarding them as plural?

The items among which plurality holds are modes of reflection. They are scientific, historical, religious, aesthetic, moral, and subjective ways of understanding the significance of facts. This list of modes of reflection is by no means closed. The longer the list, the stronger the claim for the plurality of the items that appear on it. But pluralism regarding modes of reflection is not the only, or the usual, form of pluralism. Other forms concern the ultimate constituents of reality, cognitive stances, values, or cultures. Pluralism thus may be metaphysical, epistemological, moral, anthropological, and so forth.[1] There is as little reason to limit forms of pluralism as there is to limit the particular items a form of pluralism recognizes.

All forms of pluralism take the fact of diversity as their point of departure, and all take diversity to be real, rather than apparent. This is the most fundamental respect in which pluralism and absolutism differ. Absolutists believe that diversity is merely a surface phenomenon and that deeper understanding will reveal an underlying unity among diverse facts. To the ancient question of whether the world is one or many, absolutists give the first answer, whereas pluralists give the second.

Absolutists typically seek a unity below diversity by imposing a hierarchy on the apparently diverse facts. This may be a hierarchy that orders facts from simple to complex, as in logical atomism; from being closer to, rather than farther from, the whole truth, as in Hegelian idealism; from having more to less good in them, as in Platonism; and so forth. The apparently diverse facts can then be assigned a position in the hierarchy; they can be ranked, compared, evaluated—a unitary way of ordering them can be established. Pluralists reject the idea that a hierarchy can be found that would command the assent of all or most reasonable people who seek to understand the significance of the relevant facts. The reason pluralists give against this absolutist ambition is that there is plurality not only of different ways of understanding the significance of relevant facts but also of the hierarchical orderings of these ways of understanding. The history of metaphysics, epistemology, morality, and cultures is a history of competing attempts at the imposition of rival hierarchies, and the failure of all such attempts provides ample support for pluralism. It also imposes an obligation on absolutists to explain how it is that reasonable and informed people seeking understanding have not been able to agree on the comparative merits of the incompatible hierarchies they have championed. Absolutists have not been able to discharge this obligation, and that lends further support for pluralism.

There is, however, also agreement among the various forms of pluralism that their shared rejection of absolutism stops short of relativism. Relativists reject absolutism, but they conclude from its difficulties that it is futile to search for a kind of truth and rationality that transcends the diverse hierarchical orderings of the relevant items and permits their objective comparison and evaluation. Relativists view all the various ways in which diverse facts may be ordered as ultimately arbitrary because there is no standard external to these hierarchies which could be appealed to by way of justification. Relativists need not reject truth and rationality altogether. But they must at least relativize them to the various hierarchies, and treat them as merely internal standards that have application only within particular hierarchies but not outside them. Pluralists disagree with relativists on this point.

According to pluralists, truth and rationality are external standards that can be used to compare and evaluate various hierarchies. In this respect, pluralists agree with absolutists. But they disagree with the absolutist assumption that these external standards will provide a general reason, which, if only it were found, would settle once and for all the respective merits of the various hierarchies. Pluralists think that their respective merits can be reasonably ascertained, but not once and for all. It has to be done over and over again, as the context of the comparisons and evaluations changes. And this, incidentally, explains why the same questions and the same arguments recur in the history of philosophy.

Our present concern, however, is not with pluralism in general but with the version of it that has to do with modes of reflection. This version ("pluralism" from now on) is that the scientific, historical, religious, moral, aesthetic, and subjective modes of reflection are all candidates for genuine, important, and independent attempts to account for the significance of facts. Their accounts can be true and rational; they can be criticized for failing to be such; and their criticisms or justifications can appeal to standards external to them. This is why pluralism is incompatible with relativism. The reason why it is incompatible with absolutism is that pluralism denies, whereas absolutism asserts, that the criticisms and justifications could lead to the conclusion that one of these modes of reflection is superior to the others. We have seen that the reason for the absolutist assertion is the belief that there is one true account of the significance of the facts. Insofar as the accounts provided by particular modes of reflection are true, they are so because they form some part of the true account provided by whatever is the superior mode of reflection. The absolutist cannot regard these accounts of significance as compatible because each aims to be general and thus either includes alternative accounts as more or less imperfect approximations of its own or rejects them as mistaken. We have now to understand what reason pluralists have for rejecting the absolutist view that there is one true account of the significance of the facts. This leads to the second basic question that defenders of pluralism must answer.

III

The question is: What are the reasons for regarding modes of reflection as plural? The past failure of absolutist attempts to establish the superiority of one mode of reflection is not a strong enough reason for accepting the plurality of modes of reflection. For the failure may betoken stupidity, ignorance, stubbornness, pride, or prejudice, and it may have no connection with the nature of modes of reflection. The failure may be the result of obstacles to reflection rather than of modes of reflection themselves. A strong enough reason would have to show why the failure is an unavoidable consequence of absolutism, why the superiority of a mode of reflection would not be shown even if human limitations were overcome.

The argument, however, has already provided such a reason. Modes of reflection are plural because they are irreducibly different, so that no mode of reflection can share the significance that another mode of reflection attributes to the facts. This is not a correctable defect of modes of reflection but a consequence of their very nature. A mode of reflection is what it is because it forms a general outlook that aims to account for the significance of the facts in its own way. The consequence of reducing one mode of reflection to another is to replace one general outlook and its account of significance by another. This, of course, can be done, but not without the crucial loss of the essential feature of the reduced mode of reflection.

The same set of facts can be understood in terms of the scientific, historical, religious, aesthetic, moral, or subjective modes of reflection. Understanding them in a particular mode will include understanding what significance would be attributed to them if they were viewed in the terms of other modes. It is a consequence of absolutist assumptions, however, that that understanding must carry with it the rejection of alternative attributions of significance. To revert to an earlier example, take the absolutist claim that the significance of Picasso's *The Tragedy* is aesthetic. Absolutists may, of course, allow that it also has scientific, historical, religious, moral, and subjective significance. The aesthetic mode of reflection can take cognizance of these other kinds of significance, but it must regard them, at best, as merely aids to its own account or, more likely, as missing the point. How the painting fits into the nomological network, what historical antecedents have led up to it, whether it points beyond itself to a transcendental realm, how it affects good lives, and what personal meaning it has for different individuals are all either partial or irrelevant considerations from the aesthetic point of view. And its aesthetic significance will be similarly partial or irrelevant from each of the other modes of reflection. For each is, by its very nature, committed to providing an account of the true significance of the facts.

The same point holds of other examples, such as the theory of relativity, the French Revolution, original sin, concentration camps, or the place of security in the life of an individual. We may begin to see their significance in terms of the scientific, historical, religious, aesthetic, moral, or subjective modes of reflection. We may, then, reflect further and understand their significance in the contexts of other modes of reflection. As we do, however, so the significance that has been attributed to them earlier recedes into the background and the significance that characterizes the then current mode of reflection comes to occupy the foreground. Given the absolutist assumption, this is an unavoidable feature of modes of reflection because the essential aim of each is to understand the true significance of the facts, to which each supposes its own way of proceeding to hold the key.

It follows from absolutism that when a mode of reflection accommodates the significance that has been attributed to facts in other modes of reflection, what is happening is not that the significance of facts is now understood in the same way in the different modes of reflection, but rather that it is understood why the other modes attribute to facts the significance they do. To understand that, however, is not to share those attributions of significance, but to appreciate why participants in other modes have it. If, led by absolutism, I reflect on concentration camps in the moral mode, I can readily acknowledge that they have aesthetic significance in novels about them; historical significance as the product of long trends of intolerance, dehumanizing use of technology, and ideological fervor; religious significance as God's punishment or the result of original sin; scientific significance as the unavoidable effects of natural causes; or subjective significance as the source of one's recurrent nightmares. But if I reflect in the moral mode, then absolutism obliges me to hold that what really matters is the significance of the evil that concentration camps embody, and these other ways of understanding their significance are more or less insensitive diversions from the salient point.

This may appear persuasive until it is realized that reflection in other modes leads to equally persuasive but incompatible accounts of significance. Scientific, historical, or religious reflection may each regard the focus on evil that follows from moral reflection as a symptom of a superficial sentimentalism that prevents asking deeper and more searching questions about the causes of the undoubted evil that concentration camps represent. And each of these modes of reflection will regard the others as misguided because they look for a deeper understanding in the wrong place. Each mode may well have something important to say about the significance of concentration camps—and this is to be prized—but the absolutist urge prompts the champions of each mode to attempt to subordinate the alternative accounts of significance to its own. Because the cost of this attempted subordination is the falsification of the alternatives, the attempt is to be deplored.

The main reason for regarding modes of reflection as plural is that they are irreducibly different ways of understanding the significance of facts. The basic defect of absolutism is that it attempts to reduce different modes of reflection to one that is supposed to be superior. But the reduction cannot succeed because it unavoidably results in denying the significance that the supposedly inferior modes of reflection attribute to the facts. It is because these attempts persist that so much of the history of philosophy is a history of recurrent arguments. For the same reason, absolutists cannot explain the lack of agreement on these matters among reasonable people. What stands in the way is the false absolutist assumption that there is a mode of reflection that is superior to the others and that the task of philosophers is to find it.

IV

If it is accepted that pluralism is preferable to absolutism, there still remains the question of skeptical relativism: Why should reflection be pushed to the point where it will produce the kind of conflict that pluralists inevitably experience? Why pursue various modes of reflection when the outcome is incompatible accounts of the significance of facts? Why not just accept the facts that human nature and the prevailing conventions force on us, refuse to worry about their significance, and prudently keep out of deep waters? This leads to the third question that defenders of pluralism must answer: To what improvement in understanding does pluralism lead? How does it help to regard modes of reflection as many rather than as one? Or, in short, what is the good of pluralism? To these skeptical questions there are two answers. One is to point to the practical benefit pluralism yields. This is to view the good of pluralism as instrumental. The other is to point to the gain in understanding that pluralism makes possible. This may be said to be the intrinsic good of pluralism.

The practical benefit of pluralism is its contribution to coping with the disruptions of everyday life. Such force as the skeptical relativist question about the cultivation of reflection has derives from missing the links between reflection and the disruptions. The disruptions and the difficulties in the way of coping with them force reflection on reasonable agents. Reflection is not a luxury that minds unoccupied with practical matters may enjoy, but a practical necessity. Everyday life does not have the resources to cope with many of its disruptions, so we rely on science, history, morality, religion, aesthetics, and subjectivity to help us cope with them. But reliance on them is insufficient because practitioners within these approaches disagree with one another and because different approaches suggest different ways of coping. Reason requires making a decision about which practitioners of which approach should be followed, and that depends on asking and answering the deeper question of whether the significance of the facts relevant to coping with the disruptions should be understood from the point of view of the general outlook of the scientific, historical, moral, religious, aesthetic, or subjective mode of reflection. And this, of course, is precisely the question that reflection aims to answer.

If pluralists give a better answer than absolutists, if their answer has the rational credentials that skeptical relativists deny any answer can have, then skeptical relativists are mistaken in supposing that reflection yields no practical benefit and ruins one's peace of mind. Such peace of mind as the human condition permits can be enjoyed only if there are reflective agents who make reasonable decisions about the respective merits of practitioners and approaches that make conflicting recommendations about how to cope with the disruptions of everyday life.

The good of pluralism, however, is not only the instrumental one of yielding practical benefits, but also the intrinsic one of providing a deeper kind of understanding than either absolutism or relativism. Whatever virtues may be ascribed to relativism, the possession of depth is not one of them. Relativists recognize that there are various hierarchical orderings of the facts, but, denying that it is possible to make reasonable choices among them, they arbitrarily accept one of the orderings. Absolutists, however, promise depth. They promise to reveal the unity that underlies diverse facts. They aim to explain why it is that the facts appear as they do by exhibiting the causes whose effects they are, and they rely on reason in trying to redeem their promise. The metaphysical systems of Plato, Aquinas, Spinoza, and Hegel; the religions of the Judeo-Christian tradition, Buddhism, and Islam; the physics of Einstein; the evolutionary theory of Darwin; the psychoanalytic view of Freud; the dialectical materialism of Marx; the poetic visions of Lucretius, Dante, and Goethe all exemplify the absolutist search for depth. If the world were as they understand it, it would account for the significance of the facts in a much more basic and illuminating way than what was possible before them. The search for this kind of depth is the basic motivation of absolutism. It is also the feature that many reflective people find so attractive that they persist in searching for it, even though what they find is at best a partial truth about a smallish segment of reality, and usually a prodigious intellectual construction to which reality fails to conform.

Pluralists are also moved by the motivation to find depth. They think, however, that the absolutist search for it is misdirected. What underlies the facts on the surface is not unity but deeper diversity. At no point, according to pluralists, does unity replace diversity. Diversity permeates everything and is without end. Depth consists in understanding that and in giving up all hope for an intellectual resting place from which everything could be explained and which is secure from reasonable challenges. It is to take seriously the implications of Nietzsche's dictum that God is dead.[2] Absolutists, by contrast, continue to hope for this mythical resting place, even though the finest minds have failed innumerable times to find it.

It is crucial to understand that, for pluralists, the thoroughgoing diversity that constitutes depth is not a diversity of facts but a diversity of understandings of the significance of facts. Pluralists are realists about facts. The facts are what they are quite independently of what anyone thinks or believes about them. Pluralists also hold that the best guides to facts are such approaches as science, history, aesthetics, religion, morality, and subjectivity, each of which is concerned with facts of a certain type: science with natural phenomena; history with formative past influences; aesthetics with works of art; religion with prayer, salvation, miracles, sin, and revelation; morality with virtues and vices, obligations, ideals, punishment, right and wrong actions, and good and evil aims; and subjectivity with one's experiences, projects, hopes, fears, and the sense of one's life. These facts constitute the subject matter of these approaches, and if what they take to be facts are not facts, as they may not be, then the approach is partly or totally mistaken. And whether the facts in any of these areas are what they are taken to be is an objective question to which there are true or false answers that rationality can help to find.

Facts, however, are one thing, understanding their significance is quite another. Crucial to pluralism is an irreducible diversity in understandings of the significance of facts—that is, an irreducible diversity of modes of reflection. What pluralists are saying is that it is a constitutive feature of human understanding that it has these modes. According to pluralists, it is a truth about *us*, not about the facts, that we can attribute to them these different kinds of significance. And, unlike absolutists, pluralists think that this truth about us reveals a diversity that is intrinsically good, for the diversity of modes of reflection makes possible a fuller, more complete understanding of the facts. It enriches us by enlarging our view of them and by opening up for us possibilities of appreciation, enjoyment, judgment, and conduct that we would otherwise lack. The realization of these possibilities, the living of a life so as to actualize them, is an intrinsic good that reflection confers and the mark of those who possess the depth that pluralism makes possible.

This is not an easy point to make convincingly. It will seem platitudinous to reflective people who already have depth; it will ring hollow to relativists and philistines who question its possibility or value; and it will be found frustratingly imprecise by those who recognize its value, hope to acquire it, but have not yet succeeded. Adding general description to what has already been said would merely strengthen these unreceptive responses. The best that can be done is to show in concrete terms what depth is like and how its absence impoverishes.

Take as an example a fact whose significance can be understood in terms of diverse modes of reflection: the discovery and widespread availability of anesthesia. The significance of this fact can be understood scientifically, in terms of the physiology of the nervous system and its pharmacological manipulation; historically, in terms of the radical change that the control of pain has introduced into people's expectations and attitudes; morally, in terms of the betterment of human lives brought about by the decrease of suffering; religiously, in terms of yet another sign of divine grace that lightens the hardships we have brought upon ourselves through original sin; aesthetically, in terms of how the amelioration of the harrowing effects of pain enhances the grace, ease, and enjoyment of life; and subjectively, in terms of the relief one experiences for being that much less vulnerable to the contingency of life. There is, of course, nothing special about anesthesia as an example. Space exploration, contraception, electronic music, computers, bullfights, and so on and on, are also facts whose significance can be understood in terms of diverse modes of reflection.

The point that anesthesia, or some other example, helps to make concrete is that it is grossly impoverishing to insist that *the* significance of any of these facts is scientific, historical, moral, or whatever. There is no such thing as *the* significance of any fact. Facts have many different kinds of significance, and diverse modes of reflection help us to understand what they are. It forecloses possibilities, corrupts one's judgment, and reduces one's options to insist, as absolutists must, that when all is said and done, the understanding of one mode of reflection is superior to all the others. Of course anesthesia can be understood scientifically, and of course the historical, religious, moral, aesthetic, and subjective understandings of it involve natural processes that can also be understood scientifically. But to suppose that a scientific understanding makes the historical, moral, religious, aesthetic, and subjective understandings dispensable is wittingly or unwittingly to falsify the significance of anesthesia, or of whatever else. And the falsification is the same, although perhaps not as tempting, if the dominant mode of reflection is supposed to be one of the others, rather than the scientific. Anesthesia, space exploration, contraception, electronic music, computers, bullfights, and so forth are facts whose significance is complex, manifold, and irreducibly different. It is a sign of civilized minds to resist falsifying facts by assimilating their various kinds of significance to one that is arbitrarily held to be superior.[3]

The intrinsic good of pluralism, then, is the good of having a civilized, as opposed to a philistine, mind; the good of being open, as opposed to closed, minded; and the good of appreciating the variety of the possibilities of life, as opposed to being ruled by a simplifying vision. It is a good that affects not the acquisition of facts, but what is made of the acquired facts. It leaves the world as it is, but it changes how one understands, appreciates, enjoys, and evaluates the world. It improves life not by making the world better, but by making people better—although, of course, if people are better, the world is too.

V

The appreciation of pluralism and the recognition of its advantages over relativism and absolutism must not lead us to forget the central difficulty posed by the philosophical problems that concern us. It is fine and good to cherish having diverse modes to reflect on the significance of anesthesia, space exploration, electronic music, computers, and bullfights, for these diverse modes lead to complementary understandings. That is why seeing the many different kinds of significance that may be attributed to these facts enriches one's understanding. Not all facts, however, lend themselves to this kind of understanding. There are facts to which different modes of reflection attribute incompatible significance. This is what produces the philosophical problems of the meaning of life, the possibility of free action, the place of morality in good lives, the art of life, and the nature of human self-understanding.

The outcome of pluralism, then, is not just civilized minds but also minds in conflict. If modes of reflection are ultimately prompted by the disruptions of everyday life, and if they lead to incompatible ways of coping with the disruptions, then pluralists seem, once again, to be in the awkward position of having to choose between options that they have good reasons to reject. They could resolve the conflict by arbitrarily assigning superiority to one of the conflicting modes of reflection, but that would make their efforts to cope with the disruptions violate their commitment to rationality and truth. Or they could continue to search for some general reason that would establish once and for all the superiority of one mode of reflection over the others, but that would make it impossible for them to cope with the disruptions because the search for such a general reason is futile. What, then, should pluralists do?

They should, contrary to relativists, hold fast to their commitment to rationality and truth as the best means of coping with the disruptions of everyday life, but they should reject the absolutist assumption that the commitment requires searching for a general reason that would justify the subordination of all modes of reflection to one superior mode. They should recognize that many philosophical problems have the same general form: a conflict between the incompatible accounts of the significance of facts that follow from different modes of reflection. But they should not assume that their solutions must also have a general form. That assumption is held not only by absolutists but also by relativists. They all believe that *the* solution depends on finding *the* general reason establishing the superiority of one mode of reflection. Relativists give up on rationality and truth because they think that the general reason cannot be found; absolutists think that rationality and truth guarantee that a general reason can be found, even if they have not found it.

Pluralism is free of this stultifying assumption. It abandons the doomed search for a general solution that will hold once and for all. Instead it works out the implications of the idea that the requirements of rationality and truth would be satisfied if particular solutions for particular occurrences of many philosophical problems were found. These solutions will not hold once and for all, and they will not dissolve philosophical problems. But they will make it possible to cope with the particular disruption of everyday life that threatens the conditions in which particular people in a particular context can live human lives.

If it is understood that although the five philosophical problems that interest us have a general form, reflective agents nevertheless encounter them as particular problems that occur in particular contexts, then it becomes apparent that two quite different things may be meant by solving them, depending on whether one has in mind their general or particular form. One solution is to dissolve them, and the other is to resolve them. If a problem is dissolved, it disappears. If a theorem is proved, a murderer found, a code broken, a poem understood, then what was problematic before is no longer so. If a problem is resolved, it is defused, but it does not disappear. Settling the conflicts between freedom and equality, perfection of life and perfection of work, personal sympathy and official responsibility, or benevolence and impartiality is to find a way of balancing their competing claims. The balance will hold for a while, but the context will change, the conflict will recur, and it will have to be settled again. If a problem is dissolved, it ceases to exist; if it is resolved, it ceases to press. The first solution is general and reached once and for all; the second is particular and temporary. The first is final because the problem in the background is an obstacle that, once removed, stays removed. The second lacks finality because the problem in the background is a conflict between two prized alternatives, each with defenders unwilling to abandon it. There may be a compromise, in order to have as much of both as possible, but the compromise will be unstable because the conflicting claims will crop up again and again in a wide variety of contexts, and because the settlement reached in one context need have no bearing on that reached in another.

The pluralistic approach to our five philosophical problems is to treat them as problems that need to be resolved rather than dissolved. In this respect pluralism is a break with the history of philosophy because absolutists and relativists have both supposed that solving philosophical problems requires dissolving them. Absolutists have thought that this can be done, relativists have denied it, but they have both agreed that the solution of philosophical problems ought to lead to their dissolution. Pluralists disagree, and their disagreement rests on their understanding of the nature of the five philosophical problems that concern us here. They cannot be dissolved because they are caused by conflicts between modes of reflection. Reflective agents could not reasonably aim to dissolve these conflicts by abandoning one of the conflicting modes because it would lead to ignoring a crucial part of their understanding of the significance of facts and make it impossible to cope with the disruptions of everyday life. But this still leaves the possibility that these philosophical problems can be resolved, and be resolved in conformity with the requirements of rationality and truth.

The key to the realization of this possibility is to give up the search for a general answer to the question of which mode of reflection is superior to the others, and to ask instead the particular question of which mode of reflection is more likely to be helpful in coping with a particular disruption in a particular context. The answer will be particular because it depends on the particularities of the disruptions and of the contexts in which reflective agents try to decide how they ought to think about the significance of the relevant facts. There is no reason, apart from human fallibility, why the answer they give could not be logically consistent, account for the relevant facts, help to cope the particular disruption, and be rational and true.

The argument in this chapter has not, of course, led to the resolution of any philosophical problem. It has led to an approach showing what their resolution would be like. Whether this approach is acceptable depends in part on whether it can be successfully applied to the resolution of particular philosophical problems. The next part of the book shows that this can be done.

PART TWO

Applications

PREAMBLE

The theory developed in the preceding part will now be applied to five perennial philosophical problems: the meaning of life, the possibility of free action, the place of morality in good lives, the art of life, and the nature of human self-understanding. The discussion will have the same structure in all five cases. Each starts with a disruption of everyday life that presents an obstacle to good lives. Since the resources of everyday life are insufficient to cope with the disruption, it is necessary to turn to some approach outside of everyday life: science, history, religion, aesthetics, morality, or subjectivity. Conflicting recommendations about how to cope with the disruption and internal disagreements among experts regarding the right recommendation force reflection on those who want to cope with the disruption. Their reflections occur in scientific, historical, religious, aesthetic, moral, and subjective modes. These modes of reflection, however, also conflict because they lead to incompatible ways of understanding the significance of the relevant facts. Their conflicts are the source of the problems that will be discussed. The absolutist assumption is that these problems can be dissolved by finding some general reason for assigning precedence to one of the conflicting modes of reflection.

The next step is to argue that no general reason has been found, and so the absolutist assumption leads to the painfully familiar impasses in the history of philosophy. The apparent intractability and recurrence of these perennial philosophical problems can, however, be overcome by abandoning the absolutist approach in favor of the pluralistic one. This requires abandoning the assumption that the way out is to find general reasons that would permit the dissolution of the problems. The pluralistic approach looks instead for particular reasons that will help to resolve particular occurrences of the problems. Although such resolutions will not dissolve the problems once and for all, they make it possible to cope with them. The pluralistic approach recognizes that it is a consequence of the plurality of modes of reflection that they will conflict with one another. These conflicts are unavoidable but nevertheless rationally resolvable, provided rational resolution is understood to be particular, not general.

Two observations need to be made about arguments proposed in the next five chapters. First, each resolution is an application of the theory that was presented in Part One. If a resolution is successful, it is evidence that strengthens the case for the theory. And the theory itself is intended to stand as a general explanation of why the particular resolutions are successful, if indeed they are. Nevertheless, the theory and its particular applications are logically independent. The theory may be correct even if these particular applications of it are failures. And the resolutions may succeed even if the theory fails on other grounds.

The second observation is that the merits of the particular resolutions will emerge in comparison with the impasse to which the absolutist assumption has led. The argument requires, therefore, consideration of the traditional arguments about each of the problems to be discussed. These traditional arguments are extremely complex, and they have ramified over the centuries as a result of numerous criticisms and defenses. Books have been written attacking or championing the various traditional arguments about these problems. The purpose of the present discussion, however, is not to provide a detailed reconstruction of these hoary arguments but to form an overview, to show how they are mired in an impasse, and to present the pluralistic approach to resolving them.

5

The Meaning of Life

The conviction common to Aristotelians and a good many
Christian scholastics and atheistical materialists alike, that
there exists . . . a discoverable goal, or pattern of goals, the
same for all mankind . . . is mistaken; and so, too, is the notion
that is bound up with it, of a single true doctrine carrying salvation to all men everywhere, contained in natural law, or the
revelation of a sacred book, or the insight of a man of genius,
or the natural wisdom of ordinary men, or the calculations
made by an elite of utilitarian scientists set up to govern
mankind.

ISAIAH BERLIN, "John Stuart Mill and the Ends of Life"

I

This chapter proposes a way of resolving the philosophical
problem of whether life has a meaning. This may seem like a grandiose ambition, but it will perhaps appear less so if it is understood that the aim is not
to end up with a conclusion that completes the sentence "The meaning of life
is . . ." The aim is rather to show what conditions must be met so that individuals could reasonably judge their lives to be meaningful. The main reason
for adopting this more modest aim is that there is no such thing as *the* meaning of life. The pluralistic approach rejects the possibility that there is a general solution that would dissolve this philosophical problem. The argument
will show only what individuals need to do to resolve the problem for themselves. And the assumption is that different individuals will have to do different things in order to live meaningful lives. This philosophical problem, like
many others, has a general form, but it does not have a general solution.

That there is a general solution, that the problem can be dissolved, is an
assumption shared by two modes of reflection that provide unsatisfactory

approaches to the problem. One of these modes is religious, and the other is moral. Both agree that the problem initially arises in the context of everyday life. They also agree that the resources of everyday life are inadequate to cope with the problem and that coping with it requires leaving that context and reflecting on the significance of the relevant facts. But they disagree about how that reflection ought to proceed, about how the significance of the relevant facts ought to be thought about. Religious reflection proceeds by trying to find the meaning of life in a transcendental order. Moral reflection seeks the meaning of life either in the natural world or in individuals who try to make their lives meaningful. After showing how both modes of reflection fail, the argument will conclude by formulating the pluralistic approach to resolving the problem.

II

In chapter 5 of his *Autobiography*, John Stuart Mill makes wonderfully concrete what it is like for one's life to have meaning and then to lack it. He writes: "I had what might truly be called an object in life: to be a reformer of the world. My conception of my own happiness was entirely identified with this object. The personal sympathies I wished for were those of my fellow labourers in this enterprise. . . . [A]s a serious and permanent personal satisfaction . . . my whole reliance was placed on this; and I was accustomed to felicitate myself on the certainty of a happy life which I enjoyed, through placing my happiness in something durable and distant, in which some progress might always be making, while it could never be exhausted by complete attainment. This did very well for several years, during which the general improvement going on in the world and the idea of myself as engaged with others in struggling to promote it, seemed enough to fill up an interesting and animated existence."

Mill lived in this manner until "the time came when I was awakened from this as from a dream. . . . [I]t occurred to me to put the question directly to myself: 'Suppose that all your objects in life were realized; that all the changes in institutions and opinions which you are looking forward to, could be completely effected at this very instant: would this be a great joy and happiness to you?' And an irrepressible self-consciousness answered: 'No!' At this my heart sank within me: the whole foundation on which my life was constructed fell down. . . . The end has ceased to charm, and how could there ever again be any interest in the means? I seemed to have nothing left to live for."

Reflecting on what has gone wrong, Mill offers the following diagnosis: "All those to whom I looked up, were of the opinion that the pleasure of sympathy with human beings, and the feelings which made the good of others . . . the objects of existence, were the greatest and surest sources of happiness. Of the truth of this I was convinced, but to know that a feeling would make me happy if I had it, did not give me the feeling. My education, I thought, had failed to create these feelings in sufficient strength to resist the dissolving influence of analysis, while the whole course of my intellectual cultivation had made . . . analysis the inveterate habit of my mind. I was thus left stranded . . . without any desire for the ends which I had been so carefully fitted out to work for: no delight in virtue, or the general good, but also as little in anything else."[1]

Mill's explanation of what had deprived his life of meaning is convincing, but we can go beyond it. He became indifferent to his projects and ceased to care about the goals he used to pursue because he became disengaged from them. The circumstances of his disengagement and the nature of his project are peculiar to Mill, and so is the extraordinary education that was partly responsible for both his achievements and his life's lost meaning. But we can abstract from these peculiarities and recognize Mill's case as typical of many lives whose meaning has been lost. The precipitating experience is waking up, as if from a dream, and realizing that what mattered before no longer does. The loss of religious faith, the death of someone deeply loved, the recognition that our decisive choices were based on self-deception, the realization that we have devoted our lives to pursuing a hollow goal, the discovery that our passionate commitment is to an irremediably tainted cause are such experiences. The result is disillusion, and life becomes a tedious burden.

These experiences may bring us to regard our activities as worthless. We see ourselves as engaged in the endless drudgery of some soul-destroying job. We do what we do, not to attain some positive good, but to avoid poverty or starvation. Yet, some intrinsically worthless activities may have a point if they lead to goals we value. If, however, chores lacking in either intrinsic or instrumental value dominate in our lives, like tightening bolts day in, day out, as in Chaplin's *Modern Times*, then we can rightly judge them meaningless because they are pointless. In other cases the activities that dominate our lives have a point, and yet our lives are still meaningless because their goals are destructive, such as finding enough drugs to support an addiction. Lives of this sort are misdirected. Other lives are meaningless because their goals are trivial, like keeping one's childhood toys in working order. There are also lives with goals that are impossible even to approximate, for example, communicating with the dead. These lives are futile.

We reach a deeper understanding of what it would be like for lives to have meaning if we see that it is not enough to avoid these defects. Mill reasonably judged his life meaningless, yet it had worth, for it was dedicated to a good cause; it aimed at the important goal of bettering the condition of humanity, thus it was not pointless, misdirected, destructive, or trivial; and it was not futile either, for the amelioration of misery and the increase of general happiness are goals capable of approximation, if not of realization. Mill recognized that his project in life had these meaning-conferring attributes, yet they were insufficient to give it meaning.

One element that Mill's life lacked was his wish to stay engaged in his project. Before his crisis he identified himself with his project and actively pursued it; afterwards he did not. The connecting link he had with his goal—the worthwhile, purposeful, and feasible project of improving the condition of humanity—was broken. Mill's case shows that it is a mistake to suppose that meaning is inherent in some lives, so that if we live them we cannot fail to find them meaningful. Meaningful lives must have the features just described, but we must also identify with them, we must want to engage in them. Our motivation is as essential as the intrinsic features of the lives.

The fact is, however, that the combination of the intrinsic features and our motivation is still not sufficient for meaning. We may come to think that reflection excludes the possibility of meaning because it brings home to us the absurdity of even the most reasonable projects. Thomas Nagel gives an account of the philosophical sense of absurdity that "must arise from the perception of something universal—some respect in which pretension and reality inevitably clash for all of us."[2] What is this clash? "Two inevitable standpoints collide in us, and that is what makes life absurd." One is that we "cannot live lives without energy and attention, nor without making choices which show that we take some things more seriously than others. . . . Think of how an ordinary individual sweats over his appearance, his health, his sex life, his emotional honesty, his social utility, his self-knowledge, the quality of his ties with family, colleagues, and friends, how well he does his job, whether he understands the world and what is going on in it." The other viewpoint is that "humans have the capacity to stand back and survey themselves, and the lives to which they are committed, with that detached amazement which comes from watching an ant struggle up a heap of sand. Without developing the illusion that they are able to escape from their specific and idiosyncratic position, they can view it *sub specie aeternitatis*. . . . Yet when we take this view . . . it does not disengage us from life, and there lies our absurdity: not in the fact that such an external view can be taken of us, but in the fact that we ourselves take it, without ceasing to be the persons whose ultimate concerns are so coolly regarded."[3]

This is a perceptive analysis of the philosophical sense of absurdity, but it does not help to understand the kind of meaninglessness that overtook Mill. It is true that we have a capacity to view ourselves from an impersonal cosmic perspective, but the fact is that the few of us who do are by no means uniformly assailed by a sense of meaninglessness. Plato, Spinoza, and Kant among philosophers, Sophocles and Wordsworth among poets, Einstein among scientists come to mind as combining a cosmic view with an intense concern with human welfare. The truths that in the long run we shall all be dead and that from Alpha Centauri we seem like ants lead many reflective people to a heightened appreciation of the importance of human concerns. Nor do people find their lives meaningless, as Mill did, because of a philosophical sense of absurdity. Mill's trouble was not that from a cosmic perspective it appeared absurd to care about his project. What bothered him was that he lost the capacity to "sweat over his appearance, his health, his sex life, . . . whether he understands the world and what is going on in it." His life became desultory because he stopped caring, not because his caring appeared to be absurd from a nonhuman point of view.

The experience we need to understand is the disruption that occurs in everyday life between us and our projects. The projects used to matter, but they no longer do. This may happen because our projects are worthless, pointless, misdirected, trivial, destructive, or futile. Or it may happen because, although our projects have none of these defects, they may still lack meaning as a result of our changed attitude to them. Our attitudes may sometimes be sapped by a sense of absurdity, but they are more often sapped by a disengagement of our will and emotions that has nothing to do with absurdity. It must also be allowed that people may find their lives meaningless because they *are* meaningless. But not all lives are. The question is: What is it that engages our will and emotions, infuses our lives with meaning, given that our projects are not defective and we do not suffer from a sense of absurdity? Two modes of reflection provide incompatible answers: the religious and the moral, and we shall examine them in turn.

III

The religious approach to the question is pithily expressed by Wittgenstein: "The sense of the world must lie outside the world. In the world everything is as it is, and everything happens as it does happen: *in* it no value exists. . . . If there is any value . . . it must lie outside the whole sphere of what happens and is the case."[4] The world is the natural world, and it is a world of facts, not of values. If anything in the natural world has meaning or value, it must come from the outside it. And it is on the outside that religious reflection concentrates. As Wittgenstein puts it, "Ethics is transcendental,"[5] and he means that "Ethics is the enquiry into what is valuable, or, into what is really important, or . . . into the meaning of life, or into what makes life worth living, or into the right way of living."[6]

We know then the direction in which to look for the religious answer, but before we can look an obstacle needs to be overcome. Religious reflection varies greatly in scope, ranging from the very general to the quite specific. Specific religious answers are given by Christianity, Buddhism, Islam, and so forth. The general religious answer is based on the belief that there is a transcendental order that is the ultimate source of meaning. Specific religious answers, then, are interpretations of this supposed transcendental order in terms of revelation, religious experience, miracles, sacred books, the deliverances of prophets, sages, mystics, and various gnostics. In trying to understand the religious answer, it is best to begin with the general one, leaving aside the respective merits of different specific interpretations of it.

Part of the general answer, then, is that there is a transcendental order and that the natural world in which we live reflects that order. Through science we may discover some aspects of this order, but there are large and deep questions to which there can be no scientific answers. Why is there a natural world? How did it come into being? Why does it have the order it has? Why is it that of the countless alternative possibilities in the natural world, it is self-conscious human beings that have been realized? Scientific theories about relativity, the big bang, and evolution do not even begin to answer these questions because the questions can take for granted the scientific answers and go beyond them. Science answers questions internal to the natural world. Religious reflection, if it is reasonable, accepts these answers, asks questions external to the natural world, and endeavors to answer them. One of these questions is about the significance the transcendental order has for the meaning of our lives.

Let us suppose for a moment that there is a transcendental order and that the natural world that science aims to understand reflects it. Why, if that were so, would it have anything to do with the meaning of life? A Stoic parable will help here. Take a dog tied to a cart drawn by a horse. The dog's position is unenviable, but it can still be made better or worse depending on what the dog does. It can understand its position and act accordingly: move when the cart moves, rest when the cart does. Or, it can try to resist, in which case it will be dragged, and the going will be much rougher than it needs to be. And so it is for us. We can try to understand and live according to the transcendental order, or we can ignorantly or unreasonably pit ourselves against it. As William Faulkner put it: "There are ways and still ways of accepting what you have no chance of refusing."[7] The meaning of human lives is given by our place in the transcendental order, and our lives will go well or badly, depending on how well or badly we understand and conform to it.

The Stoics did not think that human beings have a special place in the transcendental order, or that if we live reasonably, then we shall somehow free ourselves from the necessity it imposes on us. They thought that the only freedom we can have is to understand the necessity to which we are subject. Platonists, Jews, Christians, and a host of philosophers and theologians go beyond this and take the more optimistic view that the transcendental order is not just necessary but also good. If our lives are governed by understanding it, then we shall not only avoid unnecessary suffering but enjoy positive benefits. This is called salvation, and the hope that its possibility creates is the dominant tradition in religious reflection. Whatever has meaning in the natural world has it as a result of being in harmony with the good transcendental order. Meaning is not made but found, and it is found outside the natural world. The key to meaningful lives thus is to cultivate our understanding of the good transcendental order and to bring our projects in harmony with what we have thus understood.

One problem with the religious answer becomes apparent if we reflect on the mythical fate of Sisyphus, as Albert Camus did in *The Myth of Sisyphus*.[8] Sisyphus revealed divine secrets to humanity, and for this he was condemned by the gods to roll a heavy rock uphill to the crest of a mountain only to watch it roll down, then to roll it up again, and so on for all eternity. Sisyphus's life is the epitome of meaninglessness. Camus's suggestion is that our time-bound lives are like Sisyphus's, albeit on a less heroic scale. Religious reflection needs to show that this is not true.

Richard Taylor offers an interesting suggestion that bears on this: "Let us suppose that the gods, while condemning Sisyphus . . . at the same time, as an afterthought, waxed perversely merciful by implanting in him . . . a compulsive impulse to roll stones. . . . I call this perverse, because from our point of view there is clearly no reason why anyone should have a persistent and insatiable desire to do something as pointless as that. Nevertheless, suppose that is Sisyphus' condition. He has but one obsession, which is to roll stones. . . . Now it can be seen why this little afterthought of the gods . . . was . . . merciful. For they have by this device managed to give Sisyphus precisely what he wants—by making him want precisely what they inflict on him. . . . Sisyphus' . . . life is now filled with mission and meaning, and he seems to himself to have been given an entry to heaven."[9]

Taylor's suggestion provokes a doubt. Sisyphus's belief that his life has meaning is false. He believes that his meaningless life has meaning only because the gods have manipulated him. We may wonder, however, whether meaning can be based on false beliefs. But let us set this doubt aside for the moment and observe that, whatever we may think of Taylor's suggestion, it is not the religious one. Taylor suggests that the meaning of life comes from living the way we want to live, whereas the religious answer is that meaning comes from living according to the transcendental order. A further twist to the myth of Sisyphus, however, will show how it might give rise to the religious answer.

Suppose that Sisyphus's fate remains as before, but when he reaches the crest, the rocks are incorporated into a gigantic monument glorifying the gods. Sisyphus's life then is no longer pointless or futile. He is part of a larger scheme, and his activities, difficult as they are, have a purpose. It may be further supposed that Sisyphus understands this purpose because the gods have explained it to him. This, of course, is the religious answer to the question about the meaning of our lives as we face the endless struggles our various projects involve. The transcendental order is God's self-designed monument, and the ultimate purpose of all reasonable projects is to enact the small role assigned to us in this monumental scheme. We know that there is such a scheme, and we know that it is good, even if its details remain obscure to our limited intellects, because it has been revealed to us by a sacred book, by prophets, or by our own interpretations of our experiences.

The religious answer is unpersuasive. In the first place, it is impossible to adduce any evidence in its favor because all evidence available to human beings comes from the natural world. There can thus be no evidence of what may lie beyond the reach of evidence. Sacred texts and prophets make various claims about what there is beyond the natural world, but there can be no reason to believe their claims because the authors of the texts and the prophets are human beings who, like us, have access only to the natural world. The authors and prophets, of course, typically claim to have access to the transcendental realm, but that claim is also bound to lack evidential support. There undoubtedly are events and experiences that have, at least at present, no natural explanation. But to call the events miracles or the experiences religious is once again to go beyond what the evidence permits. To acknowledge that there are events and experiences in the natural world that we cannot explain lends no support whatsoever for explaining them in terms of a transcendental order. If there is such an order, we cannot know anything about it: not *that* it exists, and even less *what* form it takes. The questions raised by religious reflection about what exists external to the natural world have no rationally defensible answers. This does not make the questions uninteresting or illegitimate, but it does make all answers to them arbitrary. Arbitrary answers can be accepted on faith, but that does not make them less arbitrary. If the meaning of life depends on understanding and on being motivated to live according to a transcendental order, then we do not know what meaning life has because we cannot understand the transcendental order and consequently cannot be motivated by it.

Assume, however, that these doubts about religious reflection are misplaced. Assume that the natural world points toward a transcendental order. Assume further that we can extrapolate from features of the natural world and form some views about the transcendental order because the natural world reflects it. Knowing some things about the transcendental order, however, is still not enough for meaning, as the last twist to the myth of Sisyphus makes obvious. Why would it make Sisyphus's life meaningful if he knew that the rocks he is rolling help to construct a monument for the glory of the gods? He knows that he is part of a plan, that his endless drudgery has a purpose, but neither the plan nor the purpose is his own. He is, in effect, enslaved by the gods. Having a part in monument building gives no more meaning to Sisyphus's life than having had a part in pyramid building gave to the slaves of the Egyptians. Neither Sisyphus nor the real slaves had a choice in the matter; they both had to do what they had to do—just like the dog tied to the cart. They may resign themselves to it; they may accept the inevitable; but why would that make their lives meaningful? Meaningful lives require more than understanding the uselessness of opposing the immense force that coerces us to do its bidding.

What would have to be added to the transcendental order to make our lives meaningful is for it to be not merely necessary but also good. If we understood this about it, it would motivate us to live according to it. We would then see its necessity as the key to living a good life, and this, of course, is just what the dominant tradition in Western religious thought claims. But is this a reasonable claim? Why should we think that the transcendental order is good? Perhaps it is indifferent; perhaps it is not good but bad; or perhaps it is a mixture of good, bad, and indifferent. What reason is there for accepting one of these possibilities rather than the others?

In answering this question let us assume, for the sake of argument, that it is reasonable to derive inferences about the transcendental order from features of the natural world. What features of the natural world, then, imply that the transcendental order is good? These features, it might be said, are that the natural world sustains life and the human form of life, that many human beings live happy and beneficial lives, that there are many acts of honor, decency, and self-sacrifice, and that people often strive to be kind and just. In general, we can attribute our moral successes to the transcendental order.

This approach, however, is fundamentally flawed. For every form of life that the natural world sustains, numerous others have perished in the struggle for survival. Lives that are unhappy and destructive are at least as common as those that are happy and beneficial, and usually our lives go sometimes one way, sometimes the other. Selfishness, cruelty, greed, aggression, envy, and malice also motivate people and often lead them to cause serious unjustified harm to others. If we extrapolate from how things are in the natural world to what the transcendental order must be like, then we cannot just concentrate on the good and ignore what is bad and indifferent. If the natural world reflects a transcendental order, much must be bad and indifferent in that order.

If the transcendental order has to be good in order to endow our lives with meaning, then we have no reason to believe that our lives have meaning. For our understanding of the transcendental order will then motivate us not to live according to it but to avoid its malignity or indifference. If Sisyphus had remained reasonable in the midst of what the gods forced him to endure, he would not have concluded that the monument the gods were building to glorify themselves was good or that his enforced contribution to it gave meaning to his drudgery.

We have therefore no reason to accept the religious answer to the question of whether our lives have meaning because we have no reason to believe that there is a transcendental order. Moreover, even if there is such an order, we have no reason to believe anything about it; and if we hold beliefs about it on the basis of what the natural world implies, reason tells us that it is a mixture of the good, bad, and indifferent.

IV

Let us, then, turn from the religious to the moral mode of reflection on the meaning of life. The distinction between them has been broached by Plato in *Euthyphro*.[10] The subject there is piety or holiness, but it has become customary to pose the question Socrates puts to Euthyphro in more general terms about the source of the good. Assuming that there is a God, what is the relation between God and the good? Does God make the good good or does God's will reflect the good that exists independently of it? The religious answer is the first, the moral answer is the second. Because morality is about the good, regardless of whether there is a God whose will could or would reflect the good, the concern of morality is not with God but with what God's will might reflect.

According to the moral mode of reflection, Wittgenstein was wrong to think that "Ethics is transcendental."[11] It is revealing, however, to bear in mind Wittgenstein's reason for thinking as he did. Commenting on Moritz Schlick's view about "two conceptions of the essence of the Good," Wittgenstein says that "according to the superficial interpretation, the Good is good because God wills it; according to the deeper interpretation, God wills the Good because it is good." Wittgenstein, then, goes on: "I think that the first conception is the deeper one: Good is what God orders. For this cuts off the path to any and every explanation of 'why' it is good, while the second conception is precisely the superficial, the rationalistic one, which proceeds as if what is good could still be given some foundation."[12] The moral mode of reflection on the meaning of life assumes, for reasons given in the preceding section, the failure of what Wittgenstein thinks of as the deeper conception. Wittgenstein is wrong to regard moral reflection as "the superficial, the rationalistic one," precisely because it recognizes the obligation (which Wittgenstein spurns) to give reasons for claims about what the good is, if its pursuit is to endow life with meaning. It is a further feature of moral reflection that it looks for these reasons within the natural world, rather than outside of it.

Before we can address the question of where in the natural world these reasons could be found, clarity requires distinguishing between a wide and a narrow sense of morality. In the narrow sense, the concern of morality is with what is right. In this sense, morality is about the formulation of impersonal, impartial, disinterested rules that ought to govern human interactions. In the wide sense, the concern of morality is not merely with what is right, but also with what is good. In this sense, morality is not only about rules, duties, actions, and obligations, but also about ideals, virtues, conceptions of a good life, personal aspirations, intimate relationships, private projects, supererogation, and so forth. The moral approach to the meaning of life is moral in the wide sense: what gives meaning to life is the pursuit of good projects. Doing what is right is an important part of that, but it is only a part. Right actions are impersonal conditions of a moral life, whereas the meaningfulness of moral lives derives from the personal sphere in which there are great individual variations.

We can begin to understand moral reflection by returning to the earlier suggestion of Richard Taylor about where, in the wide sense of morality, the source of meaning may be found. Taylor thought that Sisyphus's life would have meaning if he wanted to pursue the project to which the gods have doomed him. According to Taylor, the crux is the wanting, not the nature of the projects or how we came to have them. Meaning thus comes from us, not from our projects. We confer meaning on them. On this view, meaning is subjective.

The distinction between the subjective and objective can be drawn in a number of different ways, and there is much confusion about the whole question. It is important, therefore, to make it clear that what is meant by the meaning of life being subjective is that its meaning depends wholly on how the agents regard their lives. According to this view, a life has meaning if the agent thinks so, and it lacks meaning if the agent sincerely denies it. The subjective view, then, is that the agents' conviction that their lives have meaning is the necessary and sufficient condition for their lives' having meaning. The objective view, by contrast, grants that the agents' attribution of meaning to their lives is necessary for their lives' having meaning, but it denies that it is sufficient for it. According to the objective view, lives may lack meaning even if their agents sincerely think that their lives have meaning. The objective view claims that agents may be sincere and mistaken about their lives' having meaning.

There are three reasons for rejecting the subjective view and accepting the objective one. The first emerges if we recall the doubt we ignored earlier. We may want to pursue a project only because we have been manipulated, just as Sisyphus was by the gods in the last twist to the myth. It seems clear, however, that there is a difference between wanting to pursue a project because of indoctrination or artificial stimulation of the cortex and wanting to pursue it as a result of having reflected and discovered that it makes our lives meaningful. If meaning were subjective, if it were created *merely* by our wants and beliefs, it would make no difference to meaning whether our wanting to pursue a project is genuine or manipulated. And it would be inexplicable how the discovery of manipulation could lead us to regard as meaningless a project that we regarded as meaningful before the discovery. Wanting to pursue a project is certainly connected with the meaning of life, but there is more to meaningful lives than just that.

The second reason grows out of the first. Suppose that we genuinely want to pursue a project, so that we have not been manipulated. Suppose that Sisyphus just found himself wanting to roll rocks. That wanting to do something is not sufficient to make it meaningful is shown by the fact that the bare having of a want is not enough to make us try to satisfy it. The satisfaction of a want has to matter to us. And its mattering depends on its fitting into the overall causal nexus that connects that want to our other wants and to hopes, plans, ambitions, goals, memories, and so forth. If all of a sudden we discovered in ourselves an urge to roll rocks, we would not automatically act on it. We would ask ourselves why we want to do that and how it would affect our lives and projects if we did it. We would want to give ourselves some explanation, especially since the want in question is assumed not to be trivial, like scratching one's nose, but a meaning-conferring one, like deciding to make rock rolling one's project in life.

It might be thought, however, that excluding manipulation and having an explanation of why the satisfaction of a want matters to us are requirements that the subjective view can meet. But this is not so. To ascertain whether we have been manipulated, or to explain why something matters to us, inevitably involves reference to objective conditions that exist independently of what we think. Manipulation is interference from the outside by people, the media, the gods, or whatever. To exclude it requires having reasons to believe that we have not been unduly influenced in these ways. And the explanation of why something matters to us must have to do with the influence of our upbringing, education, family, society, and so forth, the strength of which is similarly independent of what we think.

The third reason against the subjective view emerges from the recognition that we want to pursue a project because we believe that to do so would make our lives better than the available alternatives. But whether this is true depends on whether its pursuit would actually make our lives better. After all, we may pursue a project because we mistakenly believe that it would make our lives better, we may discover that we are mistaken, and we may change our minds about its meaningfulness. If the mere belief that a project is better than the alternatives were sufficient to make the project meaningful, this change of mind could not occur.

It may be said in defense of the subjective view that the sincere belief that our lives have meaning is necessary and sufficient for our lives' having meaning that what these three objections show is that the truth of our beliefs may affect how good our projects are, but it will not affect our sense that our lives are meaningful, if we believe them to be so. This defense is partly right and partly wrong. It is right that we may find our projects meaningful even if our wants are, unbeknownst to us, manipulated and if our beliefs in the importance and goodness of our projects are, unbeknownst to us, false. But it is wrong to conclude from this that the subjective view that meaning depends *merely* on our beliefs is correct. The very recognition that meaning requires both that we should fail to know that our wants are being manipulated and that we should fail to realize that our beliefs are false implies the relevance of objective considerations. For the knowledge that our wants are manipulated and beliefs false would destroy our belief in the meaningfulness of our projects. That we may be ignorant of the objective conditions of our projects' having meaning does not show that those conditions are irrelevant to their meaning. It shows that we may be mistaken in believing that our projects have meaning. It strengthens this point that if we realize that we are mistaken, that our wants are manipulated, or that our beliefs in the importance or goodness of our projects are false, then we would be the first to think that the projects we regarded as meaningful were in fact meaningless. This is just what would happen to Sisyphus if he knew the facts.

We are justified in concluding, therefore, that, in addition to the relevant wants and beliefs, there are objective conditions that must be met by meaningful lives. One of these conditions is that the wants must be genuine; and the other is that the beliefs must be true. Consequently, meaning depends on both subjective and objective conditions. To think otherwise, as Taylor does, is not to suppose that meaning depends on what God wills, as religious reflection claims, but that it depends on what the agent wills. As religious reflection relativizes meaning to God's will, so subjective moral reflection relativizes it to the agent's will. Both leave it unexplained how the subjective state of willing, whether it be God's or human agents', could be sufficient to establish what it is that makes lives meaningful.

The strongest case for the moral mode of reflection on the meaning of life will therefore recognize that meaning depends on both the subjective and the objective conditions. The subjective condition requires us to be in the appropriate psychological states of wanting and believing. The objective condition requires that our projects actually make our lives better. Meaning then depends on both of these two conditions: on our psychological states being successfully directed toward the appropriate objects. As David Wiggins puts it: "Psychological states and their objects [are] equal and reciprocal partners. . . . It can be true both that we desire x because we think x good, and that x is good because we desire x. . . . The quality by which the thing qualifies as good and the desire *for* the thing are equals and 'made for one another.'"[13]

It need not be supposed that this presupposes commitment to a transcendental order. It is not surprising that in the course of evolution there has emerged something like a correlation between what we want and what is good for us. We would be extinct if it were otherwise. Yet the correlation is less than perfect. Objective conditions both shape and constrain our wants, but, within the limits they impose on our projects, there is much scope for experiments in living. Evolutionary success has not freed us from necessity, but it has opened numerous possibilities that we may pursue within the limits of necessity.

We may conclude, then, that according to the moral mode of reflection our lives have meaning if the following conditions are met: first, they are not worthless, pointless, misdirected, trivial, or futile; second, we have not succumbed to the view that all human projects are absurd; third, we have identified with projects that we genuinely want to pursue; and fourth, our belief that successful engagement in our projects will make our lives good or better is true.

The problems of the moral mode of reflection begin to emerge if we recognize that the fourth condition of meaningful lives is ambiguous. It may mean that successful engagement in our projects will make our lives *morally* better or that it will make them better in *nonmoral* ways. This ambiguity derives from the ambiguity of the "good" in good lives. Our lives may be good because they conform to the requirements of morality, or they may be good because we find them satisfying. Satisfaction in this context should not be identified either with pleasure or with the feeling that results from having met one's own physiological or psychological needs. To be sure, these experiences are examples of satisfaction, but satisfaction may also be derived from doing our duty at considerable cost to ourselves, from imposing hard, self-denying discipline on ourselves, from beholding the success of other people that does not reflect on us at all, or from seeing that justice is done even though it does not benefit us. These two constituents of good lives—morality and satisfaction—may coincide, or they may not. Morally good lives may not be satisfying, and satisfying lives may not be morally good. It is a moral ideal dating back at least to Socrates that our satisfactions should derive from living in conformity to the requirements of morality. If the ideal holds, the ambiguity of the "good" will disappear. The projects we pursue then will be morally good, and our lives will be at once good and meaningful because we will find our engagement in our morally good projects satisfying. This is the ideal that motivates the moral answer to the meaning of life. The ideal, however, is flawed, and the moral answer fails.

Two different lines of argument lead to this conclusion. The first is that morally good projects need not be satisfying. What happened to Mill makes this obvious. Morally good projects may be tedious or painful; they may involve doing our duty at the cost of self-sacrifice, self-denial, and the frustration of our desires. The modicum of satisfaction we may take in doing what we feel we ought to do is often greatly outweighed by the dissatisfactions that are the by-products of having to act contrary to our nonmoral projects.

The second line of argument that leads to the failure of the moral answer is that even if it were true that morally good projects are satisfying, it would not follow that *only* morally good projects are satisfying. There may be satisfying immoral and nonmoral projects, and successful engagement in them may give meaning to our lives. That immoral lives may be meaningful is shown by the countless dedicated Nazi and Communist mass murderers, by those many sincerely committed terrorists who aim to destabilize a society through committing outrageous crimes against innocent civilians, and by people whose rage, resentment, greed, ambition, selfishness, and sense of superiority or inferiority give meaning to their lives and lead them to inflict grievous unjustified harm on others. Such people may be successfully engaged in their projects, derive great satisfaction from them, and find their lives as scourges of their literal or metaphorical gods very meaningful.

The moral answer, however, is vitiated not only by the meaningful lives of moral monsters but also by lives dedicated to the pursuit of nonmoral projects. These may be athletic, aesthetic, horticultural, erotic, or scholarly, or they may involve collecting, learning languages, traveling, cultivating connoisseurship, inventing ingenious gadgets, and so forth. Many people find meaning in projects that are morally indifferent. Such people may by and large conform to morality, but the meaning of their lives derives from their engagement in nonmoral projects, not from conformity to the requirements of morality. If immoral and nonmoral projects may give meaning to lives, it follows that the moral answer is mistaken in regarding successful engagement in morally good projects as a necessary condition of meaningful lives.

In sum, the moral answer that meaning derives from living good lives founders because of the ambiguity of "good." If the good is taken to be moral good, then the claim is false, because morally good lives may not be meaningful and meaningful lives may not be morally good. If, on the other hand, the good is interpreted as nonmoral good, then the answer ceases to be moral, since it allows that meaningful lives may be immoral or nonmoral. The moral answer, therefore, turns out to be either false or not moral. Its defenders, of course, normally intend it to be interpreted in the moral sense, so the likely charge they have to contend with is that their answer is false.

V

There are, then, strong and independent reasons that show that neither the religious nor the moral mode of reflection provides a satisfactory approach to the meaning of life. But there is yet another and deeper reason why both fail: they seek a general answer. Their basic assumption is that meaning is derived from something that applies equally to all lives. Religious reflection looks for that something in a transcendental order; moral reflection seeks it in morality. Both recognize individual differences, but they treat them as mere variations on the same basic theme. Individual differences matter only because they compel us to do different things to conform to the same general meaning-conferring requirement. Given our characters and circumstances, we may have to serve the will of God in different ways, you as an artist, I as a soldier, or we may have to apply the categorical imperative in different situations, or pursue the common good by means of different actions. But they both assume that, for all of us, meaning is derived from the same source, be it the will of God or some moral principle. This assumption makes it impossible for both modes of reflection to recognize the possibility that individuals may derive the meaning of their lives from different sources. It also prevents them from acknowledging that individual differences have a fundamental influence, not only on what we must do to pursue a meaning-conferring project, but also on which of many meaning-conferring projects we should aim to pursue. It is the assumption that all meaning-conferring projects must ultimately be variations of one or perhaps a few general patterns that leads to the mistaken view that the phrase "The meaning of life is . . ." can be completed by some general formula that will make it hold true for all lives.

The problem is that if we give up the assumption that there is a general answer to the question of what gives meaning to life, then we seem to be led back to the subjective view that we had good reasons to reject earlier. But these reasons continue to hold even if no general answer provides the additional necessary objective condition that must be added to the subjective condition. The wants whose satisfaction we seek may be manipulated, self-destructive, trivial, inconsistent, or otherwise detrimental and thus fail to make our lives meaningful. And the beliefs we hold about the kind of life that would be meaningful may be false. Conformity to the subjective condition is necessary but insufficient for meaningful lives, and conformity to the objective condition by searching for a general answer exacts the unacceptable cost of denying that different lives may be made meaningful by conformity to different meaning-conferring requirements.

Answering the question "Does life have a meaning?" has in this way become a perennial philosophical problem. The problem originates in a disruption of everyday life. Because we are unsuccessful, bored, poor, tired, sick, grief-stricken, victims of injustice, or readers of subversive books, we start reflecting on the point of the routine activities we endlessly perform. Once we embark on this reflection, it is very hard to stop. Reflection puts an end to the unreflective innocence with which we have unquestioningly lived. As we question, we feel the need for answers, and we turn to religion or morality. But the religious answer fails because no reason can be given for thinking that there is a good transcendental order that would confer meaning on lives lived in conformity to it. And the moral answer fails because meaningful lives may be immoral or nonmoral and moral lives may not be meaningful. Defenders of the religious answer insist that the problems of morality can be met only by appealing to a transcendental order that would guarantee the identity of good and meaningful lives. Defenders of the moral answer insist that there must be moral reasons for regarding the transcendental order as good and that these reasons are either unavailable or, if available, cannot themselves be transcendental.

The religious and moral approaches to this perennial philosophical problem agree in seeking a general answer, but they disagree whether it is to be found in the transcendental or in the natural world. They see the significance of the relevant facts differently, and they charge each other with missing their true significance. If the transcendental order is not seen as having primary significance, then, according to the religious mode of reflection, the moral answer to the meaning of life is groundless. If good lives for human beings are not seen as having primary significance, then, according to the moral mode of reflection, the religious answer to the meaning of life is groundless. But seeing the significance of facts in one way excludes seeing them in the other. Thus each side accuses the other of failing to see the point. And each attempts to reduce the other to its own terms. Religious reflection sees morality as a part of religion; moral reflection sees religious morality as one kind of moral theory. Both reductive attempts fail because they leave out an essential aspect of the mode of reflection they are trying to reduce. Defenders of both approaches keep pointing this out about each other's reductive attempt. And so the argument goes perennially back and forth between those who give conflicting answers to Socrates' question to Euthyphro.

VI

The way out of this impasse is to give up the search for a general answer. And that finally brings us to the pluralistic approach, which is free of the defects of the religious and moral modes of reflection. The description of the pluralistic approach is now a simple matter because it involves no more than assembling the conclusions that have been reached in the preceding argument. These conclusions may be formulated as conditions of meaningful lives. According to the pluralistic approach, then, lives have meaning if

1. they are not dominated by worthless, pointless, misdirected, trivial, or futile activities;
2. they are not vitiated by the belief that all human projects are absurd;
3. they involve the pursuit of projects with which the agents have genuinely identified (they thus exclude all forms of manipulation);
4. their agents' genuine identification with their projects is based on their true belief that successful engagement in them will make their lives better by providing the satisfactions they seek (they thus exclude all projects in which the agents' subjective identification is not correlated with objective conditions);
5. their objective conditions are located in the natural world, not outside of it (they thus exclude the religious answer);
6. their agents' subjective identifications are based on the pursuit of projects that yield either morally good, immoral, or nonmoral satisfactions (they thus exclude the moral answer);
7. their agents' subjective identifications with their projects reflect individual differences (they thus exclude all general answers).

These conditions are individually necessary and jointly sufficient to make lives meaningful. The main purpose of the preceding argument has been to attempt to explain and justify them.

The argument has been meant also to make evident that the proposed approach is pluralistic, not in the trivial sense that there are many conditions that meaningful lives must meet, but in the important sense that meaningful lives may take a wide plurality of forms. The plurality of meaningful lives reflects, in addition to individual differences in our characters and circumstances, differences in the types of projects that we pursue. These projects may be religious or moral, but they may also be scientific, aesthetic, athletic, scholarly, horticultural, military, commercial, political, poetic, and so on. The rejection of the religious and moral answers, therefore, should not be mistaken for a denial that religious and moral projects may be meaningful. In rejecting these answers, the pluralistic approach rejects only the general claim that meaningful projects must be religious or moral. The pluralistic approach insists that any project may contribute to making a life meaningful, provided it meets the conditions listed above. Meeting these conditions excludes many possibilities, but, for present purposes, perhaps the most important among them is the possibility of a general answer to the question of what project or what type of project would make all lives meaningful. The basic difference between the pluralistic approach, on the one hand, and the religious and moral modes of reflection, on the other, is that the first denies and the second assert that there is a general answer.

It remains to point out that this difference constitutes a radical break between the pluralistic approach and traditional moral and religious reflection on the meaning of life. One central claim of the pluralistic approach is that individuals must make their lives meaningful by genuinely identifying themselves with their projects and that doing so must reflect the individual differences among their wants, beliefs, capacities, interests, and preferences. It is because of these differences that there can be no acceptable general answer to the question of whether life has a meaning. A general answer must apply to all human lives, but if meaningful lives must reflect individual differences, then general answers, by their very nature, are doomed.

Part of the reason why the pluralistic approach constitutes a radical break with traditional moral and religious reflection on the meaning of life is that it does not aim to provide a general answer. Providing such an answer is what all the major religions, metaphysical systems, and moral theories seek to do. For Jews, it is the Covenant; for Christians, the life of Christ; for Buddhists, karma; for Moslems, the law as laid down in the Koran; for Platonists, the Form of the Good; for Stoics, natural necessity; for Kantians, duty as prescribed by the categorical imperative; for Hegelians, the dialectic; for utilitarians, the maximization of general happiness; and so on. If the pluralistic approach is right, then all these general answers are fundamentally misguided because they are essentially committed to denying individual differences in what can make different lives meaningful. The pluralistic approach is an attempt to proceed differently.

Another central claim of the pluralistic approach is that meaningful lives may not be morally good and that morally good lives may not be meaningful. The fundamental reason for this is that meaningful lives often depend on engagement in nonmoral projects. Such projects may be crucial to making lives meaningful, but engagement in them may violate or be indifferent to the requirements of morality. This claim is also contrary to the traditional religious and moral modes of reflection about meaningful lives because these assume that only morally good projects could make lives meaningful.

The assumption that underlies this religious-moral tradition is that the scheme of things is such that ultimately only morally good lives will be satisfying and immoral or nonmoral lives cannot be. The pluralistic approach rejects this assumption as groundless. Immoral or nonmoral lives could have sufficient satisfactions to make them meaningful. This is hard to accept because it outrages our moral sensibility, which is deeply influenced by this tradition. Accepting it, however, has the virtue of doing justice to the plain fact that many evil and morally unconcerned people live meaningful lives. It also explains what this tradition has great difficulty with explaining, namely, why so many people live lives in which immoral and nonmoral satisfactions dominate over moral ones. The explanation is that such satisfactions may make their lives meaningful. It is thus a consequence of the pluralistic approach that the questions of what makes lives meaningful and what makes them morally good are distinct and should not be conflated.

The upshot of the argument in this chapter is that at least one philosophical problem can be resolved by the pluralistic approach. Its resolution consists in the specification of the conditions that meaningful lives must meet. It should be clear, however, that this does not dissolve the problem because the disruptions of everyday life will continue to force it on reflective agents, who will continue to have to resist the blandishment of the mistaken religious and moral attempts to cope with the problem with the help of some general answer. Nor does its resolution make individual effort dispensable, because coping with the problem requires both specifying the conditions that would make lives meaningful and actually living in conformity to these conditions. And that is something that individuals must do for themselves.

6

The Possibility of Free Action

It is through the various degrees of self-consciousness in action, through more and more clear and explicit knowledge of what I am doing, that in the first place I become comparatively free, free in the sense that my achievements . . . directly correspond to my intentions. . . . A man becomes more and more a free and responsible agent the more he at all times knows what he is doing, in every sense of this phrase, and the more he acts with a definite and clearly formed intention. . . . It is not by itself a threat to the reality of human freedom that some close observers are able to predict . . . that which a man is going to do before he actually does it. The threat arises when his own evidently sincere declarations of intention turn out to be comparatively worthless as a basis for predictions of his actions.

STUART HAMPSHIRE, *Thought and Action*

I

The possibility of free action is problematic because the scientific and the subjective modes of reflection give incompatible accounts of it, yet both accounts are based on reasons whose strength no reasonable person can deny. There is, on the one hand, the universal subjective experience that some of our actions are based on reasoned decisions. We perform the actions because we have decided to do so. We have reasons for our decisions, and we could have decided and acted differently. There is also, on the other hand, science, whose immense authority derives from its great success in understanding the natural world. Reflection on science tells us that everything that happens fits into a nomological network, that if certain specifiable causes occur, then certain specifiable effects will follow. But if what scientific reflection tells us is true, then how could our actions be free, since it is the laws of nature in conjunction with antecedent events, rather than our reasoned decisions as subjective reflection suggests, that determine what actions we perform. It seems, therefore, that reflection on our universally shared subjective experience and reflection on the implications of science yield incompatible conclusions about the possibility of free actions.

If scientific reflection is correct, then we cannot act freely and our subjective experience is mistaken. If subjective reflection is correct, then we can act freely and the scientific understanding of the natural world comes to end with human actions. Neither of these possibilities is believable, for the testimony of our direct subjective experience of what goes on in our own minds is more certain than the conclusions reached by any other means, especially since that experience is universally shared. And the scientific understanding of the natural world is bound to include us and our actions, since we are part of the natural world. It is incredible that the nomological network includes everything from galaxies to quarks, from evolution to DNA, from global tectonics to the chemical composition of distant stars, from neurophysiology to artificial intelligence, but when it comes to human actions, then a gap appears.

Given the conflict and the implausibility of resolving it one way or another, it is natural to ask why we should worry about it. Perhaps it is just another idle conundrum that we can shrug off along with such others as whether God can create a rock he cannot lift, whether chicken or eggs came first, or whether "This statement is false" is true or false. There are two powerful reasons, however, why we should not evade the problem of whether free actions are possible. Both concern serious matters about how we conduct ourselves in the context of everyday life.

The first has to do with how far, if at all, we are in control of our lives and actions. We all believe that we can learn from the past and influence our future, form and break habits, indulge or discipline ourselves, express or keep private some of our emotions, weaken or strengthen the habits that form our characters, and that through these and similar activities we can shape how we live and act. Exercising such control over ourselves is often difficult because it takes effort and deprives us of pleasures and satisfactions. But if we cannot act freely, then the belief that we can do all this is false, for our actions are not up to us. In that case, however, why make any effort? Why forego pleasure and satisfaction? Why not just let nature take its course? Why struggle rather than accept what is in any case unavoidable? How we answer these questions will shape our attitudes to our lives and actions. If we have no control, then the appropriate attitude is resignation, despair, cynicism, nihilism, irony, or some combination of them. And we shall have one attitude or another regardless of whether or not we are free to form it. For the attitudes reflect our beliefs independently of whether the beliefs are true or false, whether they are the results of what we regard as good reasons or of other antecedent causes.

The second serious matter that makes the evasion of the problem inadvisable is the assignment of responsibility. It is a basic assumption of morality, politics, and the law that people should be held responsible only for their free actions. If they are forced to do whatever they do, either by external or internal influences that they are powerless to resist, then it would be wrong to reward or punish, to praise or blame them, for in that case they are not the originators of their actions but merely one of the many links in the causal chain that has led up to them. We may nevertheless hold them responsible, but that would simply be a way of manipulating them to do what they would not do without manipulation. If free actions are impossible, then the assignment of responsibility must be rethought, and this rethinking would transform our moral, political, and legal judgments.

It appears, therefore, that the possibility of free action is indeed problematic and that the problem should not be evaded. But it is not yet clear why the problem is philosophical or, if it is, how the pluralistic approach could resolve it. The discussion of these issues will begin by considering the reasons for and against the various traditional approaches whose conflict makes the problem philosophical. The next step is to describe the pluralistic approach and show why it is an improvement over the traditional approaches to coping with the problem.

II

In order to make the problem concrete, let us focus on the case of a man who finds it offensive if strangers or superficial acquaintances call him by his first name. He objects to the familiarity, the patronizing, the pretense of intimacy, and to the failure to observe the difference between what is proper in personal and impersonal encounters. As time goes on, he is more and more easily offended in this way. If circumstances make it prudent to bear it silently, he seethes, and it takes him quite some time to calm down. It so happens that he has to go into a hospital for an operation. He knows that everyone from physicians to cleaners will address him in the offending manner. He also knows that having an operation is not the right time to fight battles, especially not with those on whom he relies for comfort and recovery. So he tells himself not to be a fool, to swallow his pride and put up with it. He reminds himself that these people mean no harm; they are merely following a custom and will probably treat him decently, given their understanding of what that involves. He succeeds so well that by the time he leaves the hospital he does not even notice that he is bid good-bye as Adolf.

If we reflect on this case in the subjective mode, we shall think of it as a paradigm of free action. Adolf takes account of his feelings and actions; he has a good reason to refrain from acting on his feelings; led by this reason, he decides to break the connection between his feelings and actions; and his subsequent actions implement his decision. In all of this, Adolf does the sort of things that countless people do all the time in everyday life. And that sort of thing is just what we mean by free actions. It would be absurd to deny that we often perform such actions. Moreover, it would diminish but not destroy the freedom of Adolf's actions if the reason that he thinks leads him to act in the way he does turns out not to be the real reason. Perhaps he is offended when people call him by his first name because he hates sharing it with a monster. The reason he believes himself to have, therefore, is not the real reason. He does not really care about the distinction between the private and the public; he fears that he will be tarred by Hitler's evil deeds. Even if that were so, however, he would still be acting freely because he decides to break the past pattern of his feelings and actions, and he successfully acts on that decision. What makes actions free is that their agents make a decision on the basis of their beliefs and that they act on their decisions. If their beliefs are false, they are less free, but they are still not without freedom.

Subjective reflection thus leads us to see the significance of the relevant facts in a certain way. We need not deny that Adolf's feelings and actions have causes, but we will not think that that is what is significant in this case. We will think that what really matters is that although many causes push Adolf in various directions, it is nevertheless ultimately he who decides on the direction in which he moves, and he does move that way. The customary label for this way of reflecting on the significance of the facts is libertarian. Libertarianism is the account of the possibility of free actions that follows from the subjective mode of reflection.[1]

If we reflect on Adolf's case in the scientific mode, libertarianism appears to be superficial because it fails to take into account the full significance of the facts. It may be granted that Adolf believes that he is making a reasoned decision about which of the causes influencing him he should allow to lead him to act one way or another, but his belief rests on a mistake. The reasoned decision he makes also depends on causes that are acting on him. It may seem to Adolf that he is making a decision, but what is actually happening is that he ends up doing what the strongest cause acting on him compels him to do. The truth is that Adolf's fear of being tarred by Hitler's monstrosity is weaker than his desire not to alienate the staff of the hospital. It is, however, not his decision that makes his fear weaker than his desire, but antecedent causes that are acting on him. His decision registers, but does not alter, the causes that are influencing him. When he gives to himself, or to others, the reasons for his decision, he is merely expressing in a misleading way the motivational force of the strongest causal influence to which he is subject. If Adolf thinks that he is acting freely on the basis of a reasoned decision he has made, he is mistaken.

According to the scientific mode of reflection, the correct account of what is happening to Adolf is that he is the point at which a particular conjunction of causes occurs. He may be more or less aware of the play of these causes, but, contrary to his belief, he is the theater, not the star or the director. The traditional name for this kind of reflection on the significance of the facts is determinism. Determinism is the account of the possibility of free actions that follows from the scientific mode of reflection.[2]

Determinists and libertarians thus agree about the relevant facts but disagree about their significance. Libertarians assert, and determinists deny, that the fact that Adolf believes that he is making a reasoned decision has a special significance. Libertarians think that the type of belief that Adolf has is centrally important to understanding his actions. Determinists think that the importance of that type of belief is the same as what may be attributed to the other causes of Adolf's actions. Libertarians claim that beliefs of that type are among the decisive causes upon which subsequent actions depend. Determinists claim that beliefs of that type are also the effects of causes that influence people independently of their decisions, so that it is a misunderstanding to attribute special significance to the beliefs. The conflict between libertarians and determinists thus turns on the significance of the beliefs people often have about making reasoned decisions regarding how to act. Libertarians think that free actions are possible because actions can be based on reasoned decisions. Determinists think that free actions are impossible because what seem like reasoned decisions never are.

Libertarians and determinists have a deep disagreement, but they agree about the incompatibility of their positions. If one is right, the other is wrong. They hold, therefore, two different versions of incompatibilism. Incompatibilism may be rejected, however, on the ground that the two positions are not really incompatible. This is the position of compatibilists. Their key idea is that free actions and causes that lead to them are compossible, provided a distinction is drawn between external and internal causes. Actions are unfree if causes external to their agents compel their performance. But if actions are the effects of certain types of causes internal to their agents, then they may justly be regarded as free. Reasoned decisions are precisely the type of internal causes that is compatible with free actions. People act as they do not because outside forces make them, but because they make themselves act as they do.

According to compatibilists, Adolf has acted freely even though his actions had causes. The true significance of the facts, according to compatibilists, is that the most important causes were internal rather than external. So compatibilists agree with libertarians about the possibility of free actions and the significance of reasoned decisions. But they also agree with determinists about free actions and reasoned decisions having a place in the nomological network. There is a causal chain that leads to free actions, but it is a special causal chain because the reasoned decisions of the agents are internal causes that form an indispensable link in it.[3]

Compatibilism is rejected by both determinists and libertarians on the ground that its defenders fail to explain why internal causes should be thought to have a special significance. It is true that actions that compatibilists call free have internal causes, but internal causes have external causes. If the external causes are present, then the agents' reasoned decisions are their effects. The agents may appear to themselves to be weighing alternatives that they believe themselves to have, but what is actually happening is that they end up doing what the conjunction of laws of nature and antecedent events compels them to do. They decide as they do, not because reasons incline them one way or another, but because causes leave them with no alternative possibilities. Determinists and libertarians agree that free actions are possible only if reasoned decisions have a special significance in causing them, but they disagree about whether the attribution of special significance is justified. Compatibilism fails to address that issue, so they both reject it.

Compatibilists, of course, attempt to defend their position. Perhaps their strongest argument is based on the intrinsic desirability of reconciling the scientific and subjective modes of reflection and on the implausibility of both determinism and libertarianism. Determinists cannot consistently deny that there are free actions because they believe that they themselves must attribute a special significance to their reasoned decision to accept determinism and reject libertarianism and compatibilism, as well as about countless other matters in the context of everyday life. Determinists are committed to truth and rationality, but pursuing them would be pointless if their position were true, because their decisions would be the effects of causes acting on them, not of reasons that they have themselves reached. Libertarians, in turn, have the daunting task of explaining what precisely is the special significance of reasoned decisions. Determinists and libertarians endeavor, of course, no less than compatibilists, to defend their respective positions and to criticize those of their rivals.

These debates have a familiar form. When defenders of the three approaches argue constructively, they offer ever more fine-grained and analytically sophisticated accounts of their own views. Libertarians do this with what is involved in making reasoned decisions; determinists with borrowing from science the most recent theories about the workings of the brain; and compatibilists by refining the distinction between external and internal causation. But the champions of these approaches also argue critically against one another. And then their arguments take the form of charging their opponents with leaving out of their accounts the true significance of the facts. Libertarians stress the centrality of human agency, which, according to them, determinists and compatibilists miss. Determinists stress that human beings are part of the natural world and subject to its laws, and they claim that their opponents fail to acknowledge the full implication of that. Compatibilists stress the role of internal causation in human agency and accuse the other two approaches of overlooking either that the causation is internal or that it is causation. Then the defenders respond by revising their positions in minute ways to show how their accounts can accommodate the significance of the facts that their critics charge them with missing. The critics deny that they have succeeded. And so the debate goes perennially on.

This sketch of the problem and of the three approaches to solving it will probably be tediously familiar to anyone who has thought about the matter. The observation will also be familiar that the problem is extremely complex because it is connected with a host of other problems in addition to the previously noted ones of self-control and responsibility, such as causality, the relation between the mental and the physical, the nature of scientific laws, the logic of conditionals, the scope of the scientific world view, the reliability of immediate experience, and so forth. All these problems are interconnected because the conclusions reached about one simultaneously presuppose and imply beliefs about the others. The result is the proliferation of technical literature of great difficulty in which arguments concerning minute issues exfoliate and the prospect of dealing with the basic problem recedes ever further. The big questions raise a multitude of smaller questions, and the answers to smaller questions depend on the answers to many other small questions. The problem of the possibility of free action has thus become a multidimensional maze.[4]

III

Let us now go a little deeper and try to understand what is behind the dispute among these three approaches. The problem they share is the significance of the belief people universally hold that they often make reasoned decisions about what action to perform. It is important to understanding the problem that it is about significance rather than truth. The problem is not whether it is true that human agents actually hold the belief in reasoned decisions. They obviously do, and it would be absurd to deny it. Nor is the problem merely whether the universally held belief in reasoned decisions is true. Defenders of the three approaches certainly disagree about that. What really matters, however, is not their disagreement but its implications. One of these implications is that the outcome of the conflict between the scientific and subjective modes of reflection hinges on it. If the belief in reasoned decision is false, then the scientific mode of reflection triumphs because human actions fit into the nomological network. If the belief is true, then the subjective mode of reflection prevails, either because human actions form an area of freedom that is an exception in an otherwise deterministic universe, or because, although there is a nomological network that includes human actions, there is sufficient difference between internal and external causation to leave room for free actions. The defenders of all three approaches thus take the significance of the belief in reasoned decisions to be that its truth has an important consequence for the credibility of the scientific and subjective modes of reflection, both of which deeply inform our understanding of the world and ourselves.

Well, then, is the belief in reasoned decisions true or false? Part of the reason why the problem of the possibility of free action is philosophical, if it is taken to be about reasoned decisions, is that no fact could help to resolve it. Suppose that the most favorable case for the scientific mode of reflection actually obtains. Through neurophysiology, cognitive psychology, computer modeling, or whatever, scientists succeed in discovering laws that govern both the internal workings of the brain and its interaction with the environment. Defenders of the scientific mode of reflection would then claim that they have provided a causal account of the chain of events that results in human actions, and consequently the belief in reasoned decisions is shown to be false. Defenders of the subjective mode of reflection would respond by accepting the causal account and denying that it shows that the belief in reasoned decisions is false. According to them, the trouble with the scientific mode of reflection on this problem is not that it rests on insufficient evidence but that it is logically flawed. The scientific mode of reflection could not show that the belief in reasoned decisions is false because it presupposes the subjective mode of reflection, of which the belief in reasoned decisions is an essential part.

Part of the reason given for thinking that the scientific mode of reflection presupposes the subjective mode is that the subjective mode is the inevitable starting point of all human inquiries. We must begin with our own beliefs.

They are the initial data of all inquiries, including the scientific one. More-over, the subjective mode of reflection provides not merely the inevitable ini-tial beliefs but also the means for testing the credibility of the beliefs subse-quent inquiries yield. For all beliefs, including scientific ones, must ultimately be tested by the sort of subjective experience that the subjective mode of reflection concentrates on. There comes a point at which theoriz-ing must stop and instruments be read, observations made, and drops, stars, intervals, or clicks be counted to test the theories. At that crucial point, as well as at the starting point where the initial beliefs are held, the scientific mode of reflection presupposes the subjective one. It is, therefore, logically inconsistent for defenders of scientific reflection to claim that the beliefs ac-credited by the subjective mode are false. Since the belief in reasoned deci-sions is among these beliefs, its truth cannot be consistently denied on the basis of any evidence that may be provided by defenders of scientific reflec-tion. Or so it is argued on behalf of subjective reflection.

Defenders of scientific reflection, of course, remain unconvinced. They concede that subjective reflection provides both the initial beliefs and the tests of scientific theories, but they think that these beliefs can be legiti-mately criticized from the point of view of scientific reflection. Many beliefs accredited by subjective reflection have been shown to be false. The earth may look flat, but it is not; the pain felt in an amputated limb is not there; the sea looks blue on a clear day even though it is colorless; and so forth. Scien-tific reflection, therefore, may result in beliefs that are not only inconsistent with but much better warranted than subjective beliefs. The belief in rea-soned decisions is one of these discredited subjective beliefs. So the argu-ment goes for scientific reflection.

The subjective response is then to argue that there is a core of beliefs that cannot be falsified in this way because they are so fundamental as to make scientific reflection impossible without assuming their truth. The scientific rejoinder is to deny that any belief is immune to falsification if scientific ev-idence tells against it. The subjective response is to deny that such falsifica-tion is possible; the scientific rejoinder is to insist on it. And so the debate goes back and forth. The dispute about the belief in reasoned decisions is, of course, but one instance of the general conflict between the scientific and the subjective modes of reflection.[5]

What emerges from this interpretation of the dispute about reasoned de-cisions is that it is not about facts but about the significance of the facts. De-fenders of both modes of reflection can readily accommodate all the facts the other adduces in support of its own view, and then proceed to give incom-patible accounts of their significance. The incompatibility cannot be elimi-nated by showing that one of the two modes of reflection is mistaken because it leaves some facts unaccounted for, since both modes of reflection account for all the facts. Nor can the incompatibility be eliminated by reconciling the two modes of reflection because one asserts and the other denies that the belief in reasoned decisions is true. They are thus contradictory views: if one is right, the other must be wrong. The dispute between them turns on the question of which mode of reflection is more basic to understanding the world. If one could be shown to be more basic, then the other could be argued to presuppose the first. If they come into conflict, then the more basic mode of reflection should prevail over the less basic one. The root of the problem is that it cannot be shown that one is more basic than the other because each has a very plausible explanation of why it is more basic; their explanations are incompatible, and it does not seem to be possible to decide between them.

The explanation of why the subjective mode of reflection is more basic is that all attempts to understand the world must begin with and be tested by the agents' subjective beliefs. To be sure, these beliefs need to be refined, elaborated, and enlarged, and entirely new beliefs may be formed. Science does an excellent job of going beyond its subjective starting point. But no matter how successful science is, it presupposes the subjective mode of reflection because it builds on it and it is tested by it. If the two modes of reflection come into conflict, the subjective mode must prevail because it is prior.

The explanation of why the scientific mode of reflection is basic is precisely that it abstracts from the subjective beliefs of individual agents and endeavors to understand the world as it is, rather than as it appears to human observers. It is but a contingent fact that scientific inquiry is conducted by human agents who perforce begin with their subjective beliefs. The very point of science is to go beyond subjective beliefs and to correct them, if necessary, from a point of view that is as objective as possible. The test of scientific beliefs is not how closely they conform to subjective beliefs but how well they fit into the nomological network that science aims to formulate. The subjective mode of reflection forms merely a small part of the scientific mode of reflection. If the two modes of reflection come into conflict, the scientific mode must prevail because it is more objective.

If the question of which mode of reflection is more basic is answered by appealing to priority, then the subjective mode of reflection is more basic; if it is answered by appealing to objectivity, then the scientific mode of reflection is more basic. But whether we appeal to one or the other itself depends on the mode of reflection from whose point of view we ask and answer the question. If defenders of the two modes of reflection are willing to engage each other in sufficient depth, they will reach a point at which it becomes obvious to each that the other is begging the question. And each will be right.

The dispute about the belief in reasoned decisions is a particular instance of this general state of affairs. From the subjective mode of reflection, the priority of the belief in reasoned decisions appears to be a decisive reason for regarding the belief as true. From the scientific mode of reflection, the objectivity of the causal explanation of human actions appears to be a decisive reason for regarding the belief in reasoned decisions as false. So the dispute goes endlessly on without the possibility of resolution, as each side devises better, stronger, analytically more sophisticated arguments that beg the question.

The problem of the possibility of free actions, therefore, is a symptom of the deeper problem that results from the conflict between the scientific and the subjective modes of reflection. Each is general, in the sense that each aspires to accommodate all the relevant facts that may come to its attention, one by trying to fit them into the nomological network, the other by trying to view them as dependent on and accredited by subjective beliefs. There is no reason to suppose that either mode might fail. That is why the conflict between them is not about facts but about the significance of the facts. The two modes understand the significance of the facts in incompatible ways, and each faults the other for missing the true significance of agreed-upon facts.

The implication of the preceding account is that the problem is philosophical, *if* it is interpreted as a conflict between the subjective and scientific modes of reflection about the significance of the belief in reasoned decisions. It is because this interpretation underlies determinism, libertarianism, and compatibilism that their dispute has reached what seems like a dead end. In an influential book, Thomas Nagel writes: "My present opinion is that nothing that might be a solution [of the problem of free will] has yet been described. This is not a case where there are several possible candidate solutions and we don't know which is correct. It is a case where nothing believable has . . . been proposed by anyone in the extensive public discussion of the subject."[6] Richard Taylor, describing the problem in an encyclopedia article, says: "The question, then, of whether determinism is true or of whether men have free will is no longer regarded as a simple or even a philosophically sophisticated question by many writers. Concealed in it is a vast array of more fundamental questions, the answers to which are largely unknown."[7] Gary Watson concludes a survey article: "Although the terms of the debate have been considerably sharpened, it is fair to say that the basic issue . . . still lives. . . . It is hard to say where this argument will go, or even where it should go. . . . Either free agency is ineffable, free agency . . . is illusory, or compatibilism is true. Take your pick (if you can)."[8] Nevertheless, coping with the problem remains urgent because forming the appropriate attitude to our lives and actions and the assignment of responsibility depend on how we deal with it. There is, therefore, a good reason for trying to resolve the problem by a different approach. This approach is the pluralistic one.

IV

The basic idea of the pluralistic approach is the combination of a critical and a constructive claim. The critical claim is the conclusion of the argument just completed: it is futile to try to resolve the abstract and theoretical dispute between the subjective and the scientific modes of reflection. The constructive claim, to be discussed now, is that the problem of the possibility of free action should be regarded as the practical question of what agents can do in their specific circumstances to increase their self-control.

The point of increasing self-control is to leave us less at the mercy of forces that we cannot control. These forces are the laws of nature and the conditions in which they operate. The laws of nature obviously cannot be the subject of self-control, but the same is not true of the conditions in which they operate. These conditions may be external or internal to their agents, and it is some of the internal conditions that are open to the possibility of self-control. These internal conditions are the psychological states of the agents: desires, capacities, evaluations, and reflections. In taking the problem of the possibility of free action to be the problem of increasing self-control, the intent is to focus on the question of whether we can increase our control over our desires, capacities, evaluations, and reflections.[9]

Self-control begins with a desire. We want something in the belief that it would be better to have it than not. "Desire" is to be understood in the widest possible sense. Its object may be to have or do something, or to avoid or refrain from doing it; it may be our own pleasure or someone else's; it may be revenge, justice, a good insect repellent, death, recognition, a quick lunch, anonymity, wealth, or some combination of these and similar goals. The desire may be strong or weak, serious or trivial; it may involve a long-term project, planning, and much application, or it may be a fleeting impulse soon forgotten, whether satisfied or not. Its satisfaction may be a matter of life and death or a dispensable frivolity.

The desire may or may not be accompanied by awareness of it. Correspondingly, the belief that its satisfaction would be good need not be conscious or articulate. The belief may be held only in the weak sense that our actions imply it. Furthermore, although the belief is that it would be good to satisfy the desire, the good could be the lesser of two evils, or, for that matter, the lesser of two goods. A desire need not be for the best; not even for what is believed to be the best. Also, the belief that the satisfaction of the desire would be good may be mistaken. Such mistakes can occur because what we take to be good or bad may not be. Understood in this way, then, wishes, whims, wants, needs, impulses, aspirations, efforts, inclinations—anything from the vaguest velleities to ruling passions—may count as desires.

The satisfaction of desires partly depends on the capacities of the agents. Desires may be arranged on a continuum from largely inborn physiological ones to those that are largely acquired as a result of various environmental influences. Members of species that have survived the rigors of evolution are likely to have the capacity to satisfy their physiological desires, but the possession of the capacity to satisfy psychologically variable and socially conditioned desires is much more chancy. Yet without the capacity to satisfy them, desires are doomed to frustration. They may be doomed, however, even with it because the opportunity to exercise the capacity is also necessary, and it may be lacking. Self-control, therefore, requires having a desire, the capacity to satisfy it, and the opportunity to do so. Although these conditions are necessary, they are not sufficient for self-control. We often have virtually irresistible desires that we cannot help having. If it were in our power to get rid of them, we would, but it is not in our power. If we act to satisfy them, the action may still not be in our control, even though the conditions of having a desire and the capacity and the opportunity to satisfy it are met. Obvious cases in point are desires driven by addiction, perversion, rage, shame, or guilt.

These cases point to an additional condition necessary for self-control. It is a fact about our psychology as normal and mature adults that we have a large number of desires of which only a fraction are satisfied. Yet we do not, on that account, live in a state of permanent frustration. If we are frustrated, it is not merely because of unsatisfied desires but because of the importance of our unsatisfied desires. It is a psychological truism that we seek to satisfy some of our desires and avoid or suppress the satisfaction of others. We thus routinely evaluate our desires, and our subsequent actions often reflect these evaluations. The evaluations need not involve deliberate or articulate decisions. They may be nothing more than quick, intuitive, routine approvals or disapprovals, relying on education, past experiences, and the unquestioning acceptance of conventions. But the evaluations may also be reflective, involving soul-searching and the questioning of priorities. What matters for the moment, however, is that in one way or another we routinely evaluate very many of our desires.

The additional condition necessary for self-control, then, is that the desires we seek to satisfy should have been favorably evaluated by us. Actions prompted by our unevaluated or adversely evaluated desires are, of course, possible, but they are not in our control. These actions are performed either because our desires are so strong as to override adverse evaluations or because, for a variety of reasons, we are ignorant of the desires that prompt them or indifferent to the reasons against acting on them. Such actions may be caused by strong passions, addictive cravings, fanatical commitment to some cause, stupidity, self-deception, prejudice, propaganda, or various forms of mental illness. By contrast, if we are aware of having a desire, if we have the capacity and the opportunity to satisfy it, and if we have favorably evaluated it, then, it may be thought, the resulting action intended to satisfy the desire is in our control.

According to this way of thinking, we are in control of our actions insofar as we identify with the desires that prompt them.[10] If the occasion or the need arose, requiring us to be reflective and articulate about our favorable evaluation, then we would say that the satisfaction of these desires fits in with the kind of life we want to live. We may not be consciously engaged in reflecting on our lives, but we would say, upon reflection, that we do or would approve of that particular episode in our history. The aim of this identification or, as the case may be, rejection, proceeding by way of our evaluations of our desires, therefore, is not merely to satisfy a desire but to decide whether it should be satisfied. The decision is based both on the importance of the hoped-for satisfaction and on whether the desire fits in with how we want to live.

These four conditions are necessary for self-control, but they are not sufficient for it because the evaluations of our desires may go wrong. The most obvious way in which this can happen is that we are not reflective enough. We think that the satisfaction of a particular desire fits in with our lives, but it does not because it is inconsistent with other desires whose satisfaction we value as much or more; or we attribute greater importance to a desire than it has in our lives because we are carried away by the prospect of immediate pleasure; or we do not realize that the satisfaction we seek has prudential or moral consequences that we would find unacceptable upon further reflection, and so forth. A less obvious way in which evaluations can go wrong is that, although we judge well whether or not the satisfaction of a desire would fit in with our lives, our conception of how our lives should be is faulty, as we ourselves would acknowledge if we were more reflective. Our conceptions may be impoverished because they are too narrow and exclude possibilities that would make our lives better in our own eyes; or our conceptions may be lacking in depth because they involve mistakes about the true nature of the possibilities we have accepted or rejected; or we have formed our conceptions on the basis of inadequate self-knowledge, and if we knew our own desires better, we would substantially alter our conceptions, and so forth.

Reflection can thus go wrong in many ways, and, given human fallibility and the ingenuity with which we deceive ourselves, it is impossible to give a complete or even a sufficiently full list of its pitfalls. But what has already been said is surely sufficient to support the claim that the more reliable our reflection is, the less likely it is that the evaluations of our desire will go wrong. Consequently, in addition to the four necessary conditions already noted, self-control requires also the fifth condition that our evaluation must pass the test of reflection. In sum, self-control requires a desire, the capacity and the opportunity to satisfy it, the evaluation of the desire, and the evaluation to have passed the test of reflection. Evaluation and reflection both appeal to our judgment of whether the satisfaction of the desire in question fits in with the kind of life we want to live.[11]

To avoid misunderstanding, it should be stressed that understanding self-control in this way does not mean that its exercise is either error-free or morally good. It means only that self-controlled actions are more likely to fit in with how we want our lives to be than uncontrolled actions. Morally bad actions can be just as much, or as little, under our control as good actions. Self-control mediates between our conception of how to live and the actions that constitute living that way. If the conceptions are morally bad, then the more self-control we have, the worse our actions will be. It may often be that what makes self-controlled actions morally bad are mistakes we make in the evaluation of and reflection on our desires. But it may also be that the evaluations and reflections accurately reflect how we want to live, but we want to live in morally bad ways. If we realize this, we may want to change our ways; or we may not. Self-control is one thing, morality is another.

The pluralistic approach to the problem of the possibility of free action casts the problem not merely in terms of the possibility of self-control but in terms of the possibility of *increasing* self-control. There are two reasons for concentrating on increasing self-control rather than on simply having or not having it. The first is to make clear that the possession of self-control is rarely a question that allows for a yes-or-no answer. It is an activity in which all normal human beings engage more or less. It is very hard to imagine human beings who at least to some extent do not evaluate and reflect on their desires, who do not sometimes inquire how the satisfaction of desires affects their lives. Such evaluation and reflection is part of ordinary prudence without which human lives stand in jeopardy. We differ, of course, in the frequency with which we ask this question, as well as in the reliability of the answers we give. Those with subnormal intelligence or who are brutalized by disasters, extreme poverty, enslavement, or live on the subsistence level may lack self-control altogether. Normal people in normal circumstances, however, have it at least to some degree. This is one consideration relevant to self-control that the pluralistic approach stresses. Another consideration is that different people possess different degrees of self-control, and the same person varies in the degree of its possession in the course of a lifetime. But whatever the degree of self-control we have, increasing it is important because, according to the pluralistic approach, the more self-control we have, the more likely it is that we can live the life that accords with our evaluations and reflections.

The second reason for concentrating on increasing self-control is to resist the tendency to treat its possibility as a general problem that stands in need of the sort of abstract and theoretical solution that libertarians, determinists, and compatibilists strive in vain to provide. The problem of increasing self-control is concrete, specific, and psychological. It is the problem of what specific agents can do in their specific circumstances, given their specific characters, history, and experiences, to achieve greater control over the satisfaction of their desires. Taking the problem in this way does not assume question-beggingly that we all have self-control and the question is merely how to increase it. It may be that there are people whose characters and circumstances make self-control impossible. But such cases require an explanation that will point at some adversity—brain damage, shipwreck, enslavement, derangement—that makes it impossible to do what is normally and routinely done. So the pluralistic approach to the problem allows that people may have great, average, little, or no self-control. In each case, however, the claim is that they would be better off if they had more of it, and that in the vast majority of cases they have the capacity and the opportunity to increase the degree of self-control they have by improving their evaluations and reflections. Doing so depends not on the miraculous suspension of the laws of nature but on the normally feasible effort to alter some of the internal conditions in which the laws of nature operate. These conditions and alterations, however, are psychological, they differ from person to person, and that is why the problem of increasing self-control is concrete, specific, and psychological, rather than abstract, theoretical, and general. Of course, a particular resolution of the problem has wider implications, but that does not change the fact that the resolution itself is not abstract, theoretical, and general, and not the kind that libertarians, determinists, and compatibilists vainly seek.

The pluralistic approach to the problem of increasing self-control claims, then, that because increasing self-control is a matter of degree and varies with agents, times, and psychological states, there is no general answer to the question of what we can do to increase it. What we can do, if anything, varies with our characters and circumstances. The kind of general answer that determinists, libertarians, and compatibilists seek is not obtainable because our characters and circumstances vary. We have to deal with the problem differ-

ently, and part of the reason why the problem has been found to be so difficult is that determinists, libertarians, and compatibilists have been looking
for a general solution. The problem of increasing self-control is like the
problem of making one's marriage better, one's children less ill-behaved, or
oneself more attentive to others. If we succeed, we will have resolved the
problem for ourselves, but we will not have dissolved it; others will have to
repeat what we have done in order to succeed. They will also have to resolve
the problem for themselves, since their characters and circumstances will
be sufficiently different to preclude imitation. The pluralistic approach
stresses that the problem is concrete, specific, and psychological; increasing
self-control requires doing many small things that vary with persons and
circumstances.

V

Let us now return to Adolf to illustrate what is involved in one case of increasing self-control. It will be remembered that he has made a reasoned decision to control the offense he feels and the actions he performs when other
than intimates call him by his first name, and he succeeds. He tells himself
not to express his feeling, and he does not. But he does more than just make
himself not do something that he is usually inclined to do. He succeeds so
well that he reduces the strength of the offense that he earlier felt. He has
not changed his mind about the offensiveness of strangers calling him by his
first name. He still has the same objections as before, and he would also have
the feelings, if he let himself. But he does not. He now does not allow his
feeling of the offensiveness of the custom to get to him. He emphasizes to
himself the importance of prudence in his situation, the impersonality of the
custom, the good intentions of those who offend him, and his own tendency
to stand too much on his pride. These considerations weaken the offense he
feels, and by keeping them assiduously in mind he learns to reduce the feeling to such an extent that controlling it and his subsequent actions no longer
takes effort. The feeling of offense, however, is still there, and if he wanted
to, he could easily call forth its full force by dismissing from his mind the
considerations whose presence has helped him to control it. Thus Adolf has
increased his self-control by changing some of his psychological states.
These changed states were among the internal conditions of his actions, and
by changing them, he changed from one way of acting to another.

It does not undo, although it does diminish, Adolf's achievement of increased self-control if it turns out that he is deceiving himself. Suppose that
he does not really care about maintaining the distinction between intimate

and impersonal encounters, what motivates him is that he wants avoid the association with Hitler. The reasons he gives for being offended are rationalizations, not genuine reasons. Even if that were so, however, he would still
have increased his self-control because he has learned to control the offense
he felt, whatever its source is, and that was something he did not do before.
He might, of course, increase his self-control even more by achieving greater
self-knowledge, which would enable him to realize what is really bothering
him. That he could, and perhaps should, have even more self-control, however, is not a reason for denying that he has increased what he had before.

The possibility of self-deception is nevertheless instructive because it reinforces the earlier point: by changing our psychological states we increase
our self-control. One of the many things wrong with self-deception is that it
involves us in misleading ourselves. This results in giving ourselves the
wrong reasons for doing whatever it is that we do. And this in turn opens up
the possibility, which may remain unrealized, that if we knew the real reasons, we would change our conduct. Thus, once again, we find that by moving from self-deception to self-knowledge, we increase self-control by
changing the internal conditions of our actions.

It should also be noted that what Adolf has succeeded in doing, regardless
of whether he was deceiving himself, is not a rare feat but a common and
low-level achievement that many of us at many times in our lives can justifiably claim to be our own as well. We routinely control our temper, suppress
various desires, discipline how we think, teach ourselves to be more or less
critical, learn to be polite to people we dislike, keep our mouths shut, dismiss
unworthy suspicions, put up with obnoxious children. Increasing self-
control is a frequent and familiar occurrence. So the answer to the question
of whether we can increase our control over some of the psychological states
that affect our actions is that we certainly can.

The discussion of this case is but a reminder of familiar psychological truisms. They contain nothing new, it would be absurd to deny them, and that,
of course, is their point. There is no question that we often succeed in increasing our self-control. What is in question is whether these truisms help
to deal with the problem of the possibility of free actions. The reason for
thinking that they do, that increased self-control shows that there are free
actions, is that it shows that Adolf, like many of us, reflects on his habitual
patterns of action. Concluding that he should alter one of them, he realizes
that doing so requires changing his motivation, which in turn requires revising his thoughts, feelings, desires, and attitudes; he sets about doing so
and succeeds, and he breaks the pattern by coming to act in a different way.
Nobody forces Adolf to do any of this. He is sane, normal, and not under
undue stress. There is no emergency, and he is not manipulated by an evil

demon, a superscientist, or the media. He decides on the basis of good reasons to act differently from the way he had been acting, and he does. He is now less at the mercy of conditions he cannot control. He has reasoned, acted accordingly, and successfully controlled himself. We can do likewise, even though what doing so requires varies with our characters and circumstances. And when we do so, it is right and proper for others to hold us responsible for our actions and to praise or blame us. The implication of the assembled truisms is that we all can, to some extent, control our lives and actions, and that we can be justifiably held responsible for our self-controlled actions. The failure of nerve that the impasse involved in the problem of the possibility of free action has produced can be avoided, therefore, by adopting the pluralistic approach in preference to libertarianism, determinism, or compatibilism.

VI

The pluralistic approach to dealing with the problem will not remove the doubts of those who are accustomed to thinking along the tracks laid by determinists, libertarians, and compatibilists. They will acknowledge that the assembled truisms are true, but they will deny that they have the implication that has been attributed to them. They will say that although some of us can sometimes in some respects increase our self-control, that we can or cannot do so is not something that we can control. Increasing self-control, they will argue, depends, in particular, on intelligence, reflectiveness, and fortunate circumstances and, more generally, on genetic inheritance and environmental conditioning, and these are not within our control.

That this is so must, of course, be acknowledged. Its being so, however, does not tell against the pluralistic approach. Thinking that it does comes from overlooking two crucial aspects of the approach. One is that self-control is a matter of degree. If self-control had to be total, then showing that it depended on some conditions that we could not control would show that we could never have it. But that is a misunderstanding of self-control. We can have more or less self-control, and the amount we have depends, in part, on the balance between the external and internal conditions of our actions. The further back one goes in any life, the more the balance tilts toward the external conditions. There is never a time in our lives when some of the conditions that affect our actions are not beyond our control. From that, however, it does not follow that we do not have some self-control. And the degree of self-control that we do have is often sufficient to enable us to deliberate about, evaluate, and alter the patterns of our actions. If self-control is not mistaken for total control, then one source of the persisting doubts about self-control is removed.

The other overlooked aspect of the pluralistic approach is that it is not about having self-control but about increasing it. The question is whether we can diminish the extent to which we are at the mercy of conditions that we cannot control. The question is not how much self-control we happen to have, but whether we can have more than we had before. That our actions are affected by pre- and postnatal conditions is obvious, but it leaves unaffected the truisms illustrated by the case of Adolf. What matters is that we can increase our self-control. To dwell on the extent to which our genes and environment influence the degree of self-control we have is to dwell on the wrong thing. For what we care about is that we can increase whatever degree of self-control our genes and environment conditioned us to have, and thus we can better direct our lives and actions. The recognition that this is so should remove the second source of doubt about the pluralistic approach.

The point may be expressed thus: Our actions are free to the extent to which we increase our control over them. Those who have more control over their actions are freer than those who have less. Being freer matters because it enables us to have greater control over our lives and actions, and because it leaves us less at the mercy of conditions we cannot control. It is, of course, true that the extent to which we can increase our self-control depends on genetic and environmental conditions that we cannot control. But that does not change the fact that it is better to have more rather than less self-control. It is just a fact of life that we differ in respect to how intelligent, beautiful, imaginative, musical, or contemplative we are. That we differ also in how self-controlled we are is another fact. Denying it is silly; wishing it otherwise is futile. Facts are facts.

It may now be asked: Is the pluralistic approach determinist, libertarian, or compatibilist? The answer is that it is none of these, although it resembles each in important ways and closely enough to be confused with it. Take determinism first. The pluralistic approach is deterministic insofar as it agrees that everything that happens has causes and is subject to the laws of nature. Human actions are no exceptions. From this, however, it does not follow that human actions cannot be free. They can be free because we can often increase our control over our actions. If determinists deny that, then the pluralistic approach is not determinist. Consider libertarianism next. The pluralistic approach is libertarian insofar as it agrees that human actions can be free, if freedom is understood as increasing self-control. But that does not mean that free actions do not have causes and are not subject to the laws of nature. If libertarians deny that, then the pluralistic approach is not libertarian. Last comes compatibilism. The pluralistic approach is compatibilist insofar as it agrees that free actions have causes and are subject to the laws of nature. But this is so, not because determinists and libertarians are mistaken in supposing that their beliefs about human actions are incompatible, but because both are mistaken in what they deny. If compatibilists believe that determinists and libertarians hold compatible beliefs about human actions, then the pluralistic approach is not compatibilist. The pluralistic approach thus agrees with what defenders of each of the other three approaches assert and disagrees with them about what they deny.

The deepest difference, however, between the pluralistic approach and the other three is that it proposes a new way of dealing with the problem of the possibility of free action. It refuses to see the problem either as a conflict between the subjective and scientific modes of reflection because that conflict has only a question-begging resolution; or as a question that requires an abstract, theoretical, and general answer that applies to everyone equally because the answer is specific, concrete, psychological, and thus varies with agents; or as a problem of either having or lacking freedom because freedom is a matter of degree and depends on the extent to which we increase our self-control. It is because determinists, libertarians, and compatibilists see the problem in their mistaken ways that it has appeared to be intractable.

7

The Place of Morality in Good Lives

> It is often felt, even if obscurely, that there is an element of deception in the official line about morality. And while some have been persuaded by talk about the authority of the moral law, others have turned away with a sense of distrust.
>
> PHILIPPA FOOT, "Morality as a System of Hypothetical Imperatives"

I

What is the place of morality in good lives? Its place is problematic because the subjective and the moral modes of reflection give conflicting accounts of it, and each has apparently good reasons for the account it gives. Stating the problem requires an initial clarification of how good lives should be understood. It is generally agreed that good lives should be both personally satisfying and morally commendable. Personal satisfaction depends on meeting subjective interests. Moral commendation depends on meeting moral responsibilities. Good lives should be understood to require both because a personally satisfying life may be deeply immoral and a morally commendable life may be filled with frustration. Lives in which immorality or frustration preponderate cannot reasonably be described as good. They are in need of improvement, which consists in making them less immoral or less frustrating. The "good" in good lives should be understood, therefore, to include both moral and nonmoral components. The primary concern of the moral component is with good lives for human beings, and that is what imposes moral responsibilities on agents. The primary concern of the nonmoral component is with a good life for the agent, and that is what requires the satisfaction of the agent's subjective interests.

It is a plain fact of everyday life, however, that actions motivated by subjective interests often violate moral responsibilities and actions that discharge moral responsibilities are often detrimental to subjective interests. Since most people place a high value both on satisfying their subjective interests and meeting at least some of their moral responsibilities, it is important to resolve conflicts between them. The subjective and the moral modes of reflection, however, suggest apparently reasonable but incompatible resolutions, and that is what makes the place of morality in good lives a philosophical problem.

By way of illustration, consider the life of a man whose ruling passion is gardening. He has enough land, skill, and knowledge to pursue his interest, and he does. He wants to see his plants grow and respond to the changing seasons; he wants to understand their habits, try out ideas, plant and replant them to achieve pleasing aesthetic effects; he takes delight in them; he gets excited about rarities and new techniques; he fights inclement weather, rabbits, deer, and bugs; he exchanges ideas with other gardeners whom he visits and who visit him. Gardening provides ample scope for the exercise of his intelligence, imagination, emotions, body, and sociability.

He has a job, a family, and, of course, he lives in a community and in a country. He is moderately thoughtful, educated, decent, and he knows perfectly well that he has moral responsibilities as a parent, husband, neighbor, employee, and citizen. He finds that many of these responsibilities interfere with his gardening. They consume much of his time, oblige him to spend his moderate income in ways other than he prefers, divide his attention, dissipate his energy, and just generally intrude and disrupt his engagement with the gardening that he deeply cares about. The gardener is thus conflicted in his life because his psychological, physical, and financial resources are insufficient to satisfy the demands of both his moral responsibilities and his subjective interests. He is, therefore, frustrated because he frequently has to make choices that are forced on him. Whatever he chooses, he is bound to act contrary to something he values. The more he discharges his moral responsibilities, the less he can satisfy his subjective interests; the more he satisfies his subjective interests, the less he can meet his moral responsibilities. What, then, should the gardener do?

The gardener's case illustrates a type of conflict that is ubiquitous in everyday life. There seem to be only three approaches to resolving it: either subjective interests should override moral responsibilities, as the subjective mode of reflection suggests; or moral responsibilities should override subjective interests, as the moral mode reflection claims; or they should be balanced.[1] The first two approaches have less and more reasonable versions. The less reasonable ones are untenable. The more reasonable ones lead to the third approach, the pluralistic one, according to which the resolution of the conflict requires abandoning the fruitless search for a general answer in favor of concentrating on specific people in specific contexts who try to balance the conflicting demands of their subjective interests and moral responsibilities. There *are* good reasons that can guide people in such situations, but both the reasons and their weights vary with people and contexts. This counts against the claim that good reasons must be general, but it does not support a distrust of reason. But whether the pluralistic approach is reasonable depends on its explanation of *how* the conflicting claims of moral responsibilities and subjective interests should be balanced.

In the course of the argument, frequent appeal will be made to what is reasonable. This is not the place to propose a theory of rationality. It will perhaps suffice to say that throughout this book being reasonable is taken to require that one's beliefs should conform to logic, take account of relevant facts, be open to criticism, and that one's actions should be based on one's reasonable beliefs.

II

The first approach, then, is that when moral responsibilities and subjective interests conflict, the latter should override the former. This is the egoistic view. It says that people should find out what they want out of life, what is really important to them, and live accordingly. If their moral responsibilities stand in the way, then they should subordinate them to whatever they have come to regard as their important subjective interests.[2] This view rules nothing out. It justifies any crime just so long as it helps people live as they really want. It fails to take into account that even if people are not vicious, they may still be stupid, indoctrinated, inconsistent, perverse, self-destructive, or just mistaken in forming their views of what is in their subjective interests. It also misses the fact that moral responsibilities are often not obstacles to but conditions of people's satisfaction of their subjective interests.

Egoism can be reformulated to avoid these objections. It will then require that people's conception of their subjective interests should be reasonable and that they should do whatever would satisfy them, but only so long as they do not interfere with other people doing the same with their subjective interests. They should also meet their moral responsibilities because by meeting them they can satisfy their subjective interests.[3] Reasonable egoists, however, think that moral responsibilities should be met not because they are moral—because, that is, they help others to live good lives—but because they are means to a good life for the agent. Reasonable egoists recognize that they can satisfy many of their subjective interests only if they live in a stable and secure society in which people cooperate with one another and this enables them to pursue their subjective interests. Insofar as their moral responsibilities serve this purpose, reasonable egoists will meet them. What makes that reasonable, however, is not that they care about the goodness of human lives but that they care about the goodness of their own.

This is a more reasonable view than the preceding version of egoism, but it still has two unacceptable implications. One is that according to it egoists would have a good reason to inflict serious harm on others if their subjective interests required it and if they were sure that the harm would not jeopardize the stability, security, and cooperation within their society. The other is that holding it would not help people like the gardener to decide how they should live when their acknowledged moral responsibilities conflict with their reasonable subjective interests. As we have seen, the gardener's moral responsibilities as a husband, parent, employee, neighbor, and citizen interfere with his gardening. So what should he do according to the reasonable version of egoism? The obvious answer is that he should do as much of both as possible by balancing their conflicting claims. But this obvious answer is no answer at all, unless it tells him *how* to balance their conflicting claims, *how* to assign the proper weight to each, *how* to gauge their respective importance to the goodness of his own life. These, however, were the questions with which he started out. So the less reasonable version of egoism should not be accepted and its more reasonable version needs to overcome the problems just noted.

III

The second approach is that moral responsibilities should override subjective interests if they come into conflict. This view will be dubbed "moralism." According to it, meeting moral responsibilities is more important than satisfying subjective interests. In its consequentialist version, agents should recognize that the common good matters more than their subjective good. In its deontological version, agents should recognize that moral responsibilities are universal; they apply to everyone equally, regardless of subjective interests. Both versions hold that reason requires that moral responsibilities should be overriding.[4] But is this view reasonable?

There is a formalist argument for an affirmative answer. Morality just is whatever has overriding status. There are various ways of explaining why this is so. One is that moral responsibilities are nothing but the most important action-guiding considerations. Moral responsibilities, therefore, are bound to be overriding because they necessarily express what is most important.[5] Another explanation is that the requirements of reason are universal and moral responsibilities embody them as they apply to human actions. Since subjective interests hold only individually, not universally, reason requires that universal moral responsibilities should override individual subjective interests.[6] A further explanation is that morality is the all-things-considered point of view. After all relevant considerations have been duly weighed, there follows a conclusion about what should be done, and acting on it becomes the agent's moral responsibility. If agents find that their subjective interests conflict with their moral responsibilities, then either they have not considered all things, or satisfying their subjective interests is unreasonable because it ignores countervailing considerations.[7]

There are several reasons why the formalist argument fails. The first concerns the "should" in the formalist interpretation of the claim that moral responsibilities should override subjective interests if they conflict. If the "should" is interpreted as expressing a moral responsibility, then it is question-begging. It says that moral responsibilities require that moral responsibilities should be overriding. The same argument could be used to show that subjective interests should be overriding. All that needs to be done is to interpret the "should" as expressing a subjective interest. Any view can be made overriding by this expedient. If, however, the "should" is not interpreted question-beggingly, then how is it to be interpreted? Say that it is the "should" of reasonableness. The claim is, then, that being reasonable requires that moral responsibilities should override subjective interests. But making the claim is not enough. It needs to be *shown* why being reasonable requires this. It has to be shown why the gardener is unreasonable if he prefers deadheading his rhododendrons to taking his daughter to the movies when he cannot do both. There may be an argument that shows this. If there is, however, it will not be formal. It will have to show what it is about that gardener's specific moral responsibilities that makes them more important than his specific subjective interests.[8]

The second reason why the formalist argument fails has to do with the very nature of formal arguments: they leave their content unspecified. Assume that moral responsibilities are the most important ones, or those that are universal and action guiding, or those that are arrived at after all things are considered. There is nothing in these formal characteristics to prevent anyone from regarding crazy, vicious, trivial, perverse, or idiosyncratic responsibilities as moral and claiming overriding status for them, just so long as they are consistently held and followed in action. There must be limits to what moral responsibilities can reasonably be regarded as important, universally action guiding, or the result of the consideration of all things. Otherwise, the gardener could resolve his conflict by simply declaring that he finds the satisfaction of his subjective interests most important, universally action guiding, or the consequences of his consideration of all things. And if he acted accordingly, he could not be morally faulted. To avoid such absurdities, limits must be imposed on what could count as being overriding. As soon as that is done, however, the argument ceases to be formal, and it must specify some content that overriding moral responsibilities must have.[9]

The third reason for the failure of the formalist argument becomes apparent if it is recognized that claims about importance, universality, and all things being considered are hopelessly vague unless much more is said about them. Moral responsibilities are not just important, they are important for something. What is it? Why does justice count but not a sense of humor? Moral responsibilities are not just universal, they are responsibilities that hold in certain contexts. What are these contexts? Why exclude doing long division or playing chess? Moral responsibilities do not follow from all things being considered but from all relevant things being considered. What things are relevant? Is it relevant if they are unpleasant, boring, hard to figure out, or call for a great deal of tact? If such considerations are relevant, what makes them so? If they are not, why not? There are, of course, answers to these questions. Moral responsibilities are important for living a good life; universality holds in contexts where human actions cause good and evil; and what considerations are relevant depends on whether they affect the goodness of human lives. But these are just empty phrases unless it is specified what lives are good and what things are good or evil. Without specifying them, the gardener could just say that his subjective interests are important and universal in his context and that the relevant considerations bear on what enhances or detracts from their satisfaction. If, however, the necessary specifications are provided, then the argument ceases to be formal.[10]

The formalist argument for moralism therefore fails. But it is not hard to reformulate it in order to avoid these objections. If it is understood that what motivates defenders of formalism is not attachment to formal arguments as such but the conviction that moral arguments must be universal, then the reformulation can readily introduce substantive considerations, provided they can be shown to apply equally to all human agents and actions. If all good lives depend on having certain goods, then there is a good reason for there being overriding moral responsibilities to protect these goods. This good reason is that it would be unreasonable if these moral responsibilities did not override subjective interests because the moral responsibilities are to the protection of goods on which the satisfaction of subjective interests depends. Let us call this reformulated version of the formalist argument a "minimally substantive" one, and refer to the goods that all good lives require as "primary goods." The question, then, is whether moralism can be defended by a minimally substantive argument.[11]

There are two reasons for thinking that the answer is no. One is that the minimally substantive argument is too strong, and the other is that it is too weak. The trouble with the argument on account of its strength is that if it were correct, then reasonable people, insofar as they were being reasonable, could not find themselves in a conflict between the requirements of their subjective interests and moral responsibilities. In particular, the gardener's conflict could not be accepted as genuine. His predicament would have to be seen as a symptom of his being unreasonable because, if the minimally substantive argument were correct, meeting his moral responsibilities would actually be among his subjective interests. He would be unreasonable if he did not do what was necessary to satisfy his reasonable subjective interests. He should see that meeting his moral responsibilities is a necessary condition of his gardening. This, however, is plainly not so. The man could have his fill of gardening even if he was morally deficient as a parent, husband, employee, neighbor, or citizen. In fact, being morally deficient in these ways may just be what would make it possible for him to garden to his satisfaction. Something is wrong, therefore, with the minimally substantive argument.

What is wrong is that the moral responsibilities that cause the gardener's conflict are not the moral responsibilities that are concerned with protecting the primary goods that all good lives require. The gardener would not violate anyone's primary goods if he were less attentive to his wife and children than he should be, if he were unobliging as a neighbor, if he were merely a time-serving employee, and if he cheated on his income tax. If he contemplated murder, mayhem, and extortion for the sake of his gardening, that would be a different matter; that would violate primary goods and undermine the stability, security, and cooperation on which his own primary goods depend. If he were reasonable, he would not be in a conflict about committing these crimes. The vices he is flirting with, however, are relatively minor lapses that leave primary goods unaffected. No doubt they are vices, and no doubt the gardener would be morally wrong to act on them, but the reason why he should not is not captured by the minimally substantive argument based on it being unreasonable to violate conditions on which the satisfaction of his subjective interests depends. The gardener has a genuine conflict. Perhaps he should resolve it in favor of his moral responsibilities, but it has yet to be shown why.

Suppose, however, that the gardener is convinced by the minimally substantive argument, accepts that he is unreasonable in thinking that there is a conflict, and acts as moralism requires. It might be said then that he recognizes that his moral responsibilities should override his subjective interests. But this would be a misdescription of what actually happens. If the gardener meets his responsibilities as a parent, husband, neighbor, employee, and citizen because he thinks that doing so is necessary for gardening, then, as Kant put it, he is acting in accordance with morality, but he is not motivated by it. That he is acting in a morally acceptable way is an accident that occurs because his subjective interests happen to coincide with his moral responsibilities; it is just that they have not come into conflict, and there is no need to assert the overridingness of his subjective interests. So even if the minimally substantive argument escapes the objection that it is too strong, it would still succumb to the objection that it is not an alternative to, but a version of, egoism, whose problems have been noted earlier.

The other reason for thinking that moralism cannot be defended by the minimally substantive argument is that the argument is too weak. It does show something, but not enough to support the claim that moral responsibilities should override subjective interests. What it shows is that any acceptable view of morality must recognize the necessity of primary goods for living a good life. It also shows that primary goods set limits to what can be reasonably included in moral responsibilities: moral responsibilities express what is most important to living a good life, or what requirements are universal, or what the all-things-considered point of view is. But it does not show that it follows from the necessity of primary goods that moral responsibilities should override subjective interests. The reason for this is that good lives require more than the primary goods, and the minimally substantive view is silent on the subject of what these additional requirements are. They may be moral responsibilities over and above those that concern primary goods, or they may be subjective interests that enable people to live enriching and rewarding lives, or they may be some mixture of both moral and subjective requirements, where the contents of the mixture vary with the characters and circumstances of the agents.

That good lives require more than having the primary goods and respecting the primary goods of others becomes obvious once it is seen that lives that conform to these requirements may still be immoral, frustrating, pointless, boring, futile, and filled with pain, drudgery, shame, anger, guilt, humiliation, and fear—and the agents may themselves take this view of their lives. Let us call the "more" that good lives require beyond primary goods "secondary goods." Some examples of secondary goods are an interesting job, a rich emotional life, a lively imagination, appreciation of beauty, solidarity with a worthy community, loving personal relationships, justice, moderation, courage, intelligence, a satisfying sexual life, self-respect, fulfilling projects, a sense of humor, physical fitness, financial security, a pleasing appearance, public recognition of one's achievements, and so forth. Some secondary goods are moral because they primarily affect the lives of others; some are subjective because they primarily affect the life of the agent; and some are both moral and subjective. Good lives require both primary and secondary goods, and the secondary goods must include both moral and subjective goods.[12]

Defenders of moralism may be tempted to restrict good lives to those that have a sufficient amount of primary and secondary moral goods, and thus exclude secondary subjective goods. But they should resist this temptation because of the plain fact that lives that have and respect all the moral goods may nevertheless be frustrating, boring, drab, unhappy, empty, unfulfilled, and so forth.[13] This is just what Mill discovered about his life (as we have seen in Chapter 5). People who conscientiously meet their moral responsibilities may nevertheless be ciphers, incapable of the reciprocity that marriage, friendship, parenthood, and love affairs depend on. If they lack, or fail to satisfy, subjective interests, they have little to contribute that would make meaningful relationships with them possible for others. Such people are honored by Kant's notorious eulogy: "If nature had implanted little sympathy in this or that man's heart; if (being in other respects an honest fellow) he were cold and indifferent to the sufferings of others . . . if such a man . . . were not exactly . . . a philanthropist, would he not still find in himself a source from which he might draw a worth far higher that any that a good natured temperament can have? Assuredly he would. It is precisely in this that the worth of character begins to show—a moral worth beyond comparison the highest namely, that he does good, not from inclination, but from duty."[14] Now imagine this paragon as a father, husband, friend, or, God forbid, a lover. Such dutiful lives are perhaps morally good, but there is more to good lives than moral goodness. It is, therefore, an unavoidable question for moralism how the moral and subjective goods that good lives require are related. This question is particularly pressing because, as the gardener's case illustrates, the moral and subjective goods that good lives require routinely conflict. It is a weak response to such conflicts to say, as the minimally substantive argument for moralism does, that all good lives require primary goods and that subjective goods presuppose them. Even if moral responsibilities should override subjective interests when primary goods conflict with secondary subjective goods, it has not been shown that the same should be done when secondary moral and subjective goods conflict.

The conclusion that emerges from this consideration of moralism is that good lives require primary goods, secondary moral goods, and secondary subjective goods, but, since secondary moral and subjective goods conflict, good lives require balancing their conflicting claims. This is why the more reasonable version of moralism leads to the third approach to resolving the conflict between moral responsibilities and subjective interests. The consideration of egoism has led to the same conclusion, because the more reasonable version of egoism recognizes that good lives have not only a subjective but also a moral component, that these components conflict, and that good lives require balancing them. The time has come, therefore, to consider the third approach, which is pluralistic.

IV

The third approach holds that the conflict between moral responsibilities and subjective interests can be reasonably resolved by balancing their conflicting claims rather than having one override the other. Moral responsibilities involve the protection of the conditions of the good lives of people living together in a society. Subjective interests represent people's endeavors to make good lives for themselves. There is a good reason, therefore, to try to satisfy the claims of both to the fullest extent possible. If they conflict with each other, then it is impossible to satisfy both claims fully. The second best then is to satisfy them as much as possible, and that is the reason for balancing them. The question, of course, is how that should be done. The answer will be given in two steps. The first is to reach a better understanding of the conflict between moral responsibilities and subjective interests than has so far been provided. The second is to employ that understanding to show that there is no general way to achieve optimal balance because the optimum varies with agents and circumstances. This answer goes against much past and present thought about good lives, which seeks to formulate universally applicable principles.[15]

Let us then try to understand better the conflict between moral responsibilities and subjective interests. Each presupposes a mode of reflection that represents a different general approach to the evaluation of life and conduct. Subjective reflection is concerned with life and conduct as they affect the agent. Moral reflection is concerned with the same as they affect human beings in general. Each evaluates what comes under its purview as good, bad, or indifferent, depending on how the goodness of the life of the agent or of human beings is affected. Both are general because they recognize that anything may have an effect on what they are concerned with.

It is a consequence of their generality that each mode of reflection must be capable of accommodating the concerns of the other in its own terms. And certainly both set out to do this. Moral reflection makes room for subjective interests by recognizing that their satisfaction affects the lives of human beings and that the moral concern for good human lives includes concern for the life of the agent, who is one human being among others. Subjective reflection, too, makes room for moral responsibilities, because

the goodness of the lives of at least some other human beings is bound to affect the subjective interests of the agent. The moral mode of reflection thus
recognizes the satisfaction of subjective interests as a special case within itself, and the subjective mode of reflection does likewise with moral responsibilities. Both can recognize and evaluate all the facts that the other does,
and there is no reason why there could not be many cases in which they evaluate the facts in the same way. These are cases in which a good life for the
agent coincides with good lives for human beings. That such cases occur,
however, is a matter of luck, not what either mode of reflection aims at. It is
well and good if moral responsibilities coincide with subjective interests, but
this is a lagniappe, not something that can or should be counted on. There
are, of course, also many other cases in which subjective interests do not coincide with moral responsibilities. Such cases are evaluated in one way in the
subjective mode of reflection and in another in the moral modes of reflection. These are the cases that concern us here.

What needs to be noticed about them is that the incompatible evaluations
result from disagreements not about what the facts are but from disagreements about the significance of agreed upon facts. It will be granted by both
sides that if the gardener meets his moral responsibilities, then they will seriously interfere with the satisfaction of his subjective interests. But the significance of this will be seen differently from the points of view of the moral
and the subjective modes of reflection. One mode will attribute greatest significance to the gardener's discharge of his moral responsibilities, the other
to his meeting his subjective interests.

It needs to be noticed further that when either mode of reflection is accommodated as a special case in the other, then the accommodation is always
and necessarily imperfect because what is found to be significant by one is
bound to be different from what is found to be significant by the other. This
must be so because their standards of significance are different. The standard
of the subjective mode of reflection is a good life for the agent; the standard
of the moral mode is good lives for human beings. The consequence of both
attempts at accommodation is that one standard of significance must be ex-
changed for the other. This, of course, no reasonable defenders of either
mode of reflection would be willing to accept, since it would be tantamount
to abandoning their mode of reflection. That is why moral and subjective reflections are bound to conflict. And they will do so even in cases where their
evaluations happen to coincide because the reasons for conforming to their
respective requirements will be necessarily different.

The promised better understanding of the conflict between moral and
subjective reflection is, therefore, that it is a conflict not about the facts
themselves but about their significance. Moral and subjective reflections

necessarily attribute different significance to agreed-upon facts because their different standards of significance are just what make them the different modes of reflection that they are. The conflict between them is thus unavoidable so long as they exist. Egoists and moralists each attempt to resolve the conflict by bringing the other's standard of significance in line with their own. Egoists recognize moral responsibilities that are necessary for the satisfaction of subjective interests, and they regard the claims of moral responsibilities that conflict with subjective interests as unreasonable. Moralists recognize subjective interests that conform to moral responsibilities, and they regard the claims of subjective interests that conflict with moral responsibilities as unreasonable. Both attempt to resolve the conflict by calling unreasonable precisely those parts of the others' approach that create the conflict. According to egoists, the key to good lives is that people should reasonably decide how they want to live and then live that way; moral responsibilities are reasonable only insofar as they help them to do so. According to moralists, the key to good lives is that people should meet their moral responsibilities; the satisfaction of their subjective interests is reasonable only insofar as it helps them to do so. They agree that good lives require both the satisfaction of subjective interests and meeting moral responsibilities, that the claims of subjectivity and morality often conflict, and that resolving this conflict depends on placing limits on either one or the other. They disagree only about which should limit which. But the arguments each offers in defense of its view and in criticism of the other rest on ignoring what the other regards as having the greatest significance. Thus each sees the other as offering sophistical arguments that miss the point.

Dispassionate observers of these hoary arguments are unlikely to avoid a sense of weariness. They will perhaps sympathize with Socrates' attempt to thrash Thrasymachus and with Kant's inspirational words about the starry heavens above and the moral law within, but they will also welcome the efforts of Machiavelli, Hobbes, and Nietzsche to cut through the pious moral cant of the ages. Such observers may understandably wonder whether human reason has not just reached rock bottom in this perennial conflict. Perhaps the conflict between the moral and the subjective modes of reflection reveals that good human lives have incompatible requirements.[16]

V

The immodest proposal that will now be considered is that there *is* something that can be done. The key is to reject the assumption implicit in the argument for both egoism and moralism that since the conflict between the moral and the subjective modes of reflection has a general form, its resolution must also have a general form. The antecedent of this assumption is true, but the consequent is false. The sense that reason has here reached an end results from the accurate perception that this conflict can have no general resolution because the two sides accept incompatible standards of significance. There can be no reasonable doubt that both subjective interests and moral responsibilities are necessary constituents of good lives, that they often conflict with each other, and that resolving their conflicts depends on one overriding the other. But from this it does not follow that the one that overrides the other must always be the same, nor that the decision of which should override which must always involve an all-or-none choice rather than a more-or-less one.

The proposal is that there is a reasonable resolution of this general conflict, but it varies from case to case. There are individual variations, not merely in the answers to the question of which of the conflicting claims should override the other in a particular case, but also in the answer to the question of how far the conflicting claims can both be satisfied in particular cases. The proposal is thus to opt for the third and pluralistic approach introduced earlier, namely, that the way to resolve the conflict between the moral and the subjective modes of reflection is to balance them against each other. The balance, however, is taken to vary from case to case both in respect to which should override which and in respect to the extent to which one should override the other.

This proposal faces an obvious difficulty that must be dealt with before proceeding to further explanation: particular resolutions of the conflict are no more likely to be acceptable to the side whose requirements are subordinated to the other side's than the general resolution has proved to be. If moral responsibilities prevail on a particular occasion, then subjective interests are thereby thwarted; and if subjective interests prevail on that occasion, then moral responsibilities are thereby violated. Defenders of the overridden claims cannot but find this objectionable.

The way out of this difficulty is to recognize that the conflict occurs because defenders of the two modes of reflection share an assumption that is essential to their approach, yet it is mistaken. The assumption is that there is a general answer to the question of what a good life is. Only because they both hold that assumption do defenders of moral and subjective reflection disagree about which approach is more likely to lead to good lives. The key idea of the pluralistic approach is to reject the assumption that there is a general answer to the question of what a good life is. Good lives are the lives of individuals, and what makes their lives good depends on their characters and circumstances, which vary individually, historically, and culturally. It is true that no matter how variable good lives are, they require the same primary goods, and they require also secondary moral and subjective goods. But what particular secondary goods they require depends on the variable characters and circumstances of the agents. That is why good lives are individually variable and why there can be no acceptable general answer to whether the claims of moral responsibilities or of subjective interests are more important to the goodness of the life of a particular person in a particular case.

Reasonable people will agree that the claim that subjective interests should override moral responsibilities, or the other way around, is not absolute and that it allows for legitimate exceptions. They will recognize that the cost of meeting some moral responsibilities or subjective interests may be too great because the gain in one is small and the loss in the other is huge. It would be insane to insist that I should keep my promise to try out a new restaurant with you if I could do so only by putting my life at serious risk, and it would be equally crazy to let people die agonizing deaths if I could save them by missing the concert that I am on the way to attending. One can be very serious about moral responsibilities or subjective interests and still recognize that the claims of either may be overridden. The question is when reason requires that the claims be honored and when that exceptions be made. There is always a reasonable answer to that question, even if it is hard to find, but the answer depends on the importance of honoring the claim or making an exception in the context of a particular case that is an episode in the life of a particular person. And the standard of importance is the effect that honoring the claim, or making an exception to it, has on the goodness of the life of that particular person.

It may be objected to the present proposal that it does not resolve the conflict between moral responsibilities and subjective interests because the conflict will reemerge as soon as it is asked what makes lives good. Egoists will say that it is the satisfaction of reasonable subjective interests; moralists will say that it is the honoring of moral responsibilities. And they will go at each other again in the familiar, time-honored manner. But now that we have a better understanding of the conflict, we see that a resolution is available.

Lives are made good by the agents' possession of various goods. Some of these goods are primary. All good lives are alike in having satisfied certain basic physiological, psychological, and social requirements. Good lives are also alike in having both moral and subjective secondary goods. But good lives differ because different characters and circumstances lead agents to require different secondary moral and subjective goods. Individuals enter into different relationships, hold different positions, have different interests and projects, and these differences are conditioned by psychological, historical, and cultural differences that prevail in their different contexts. Good lives, therefore, are unavoidably good lives *for* individuals, and they vary with individual identities, characters, and circumstances.

For each good life it is possible to formulate a conception that enumerates the goods that make it good and explains their respective importance. Such conceptions can be formulated by the agents themselves or by other people on their behalf, or they may remain unformulated and inferable only from what their agents do or fail to do in various situations. Suppose that such conceptions of a good life are formulated, that particular agents live so as to realize them, and that the agents judge their lives to be good. They are satisfied with them, they want their lives to continue by and large in the same way, they contemplate no major changes, they harbor no serious grievances or regrets, and people respect, value, and appreciate the agents. The agents, therefore, have good reasons to think that their lives are good.

However good these reasons are, they will not be conclusive. The agents may think that their reasons are good, but they may be mistaken. The reasons may only appear to be good to them because of self-deception, indoctrination, stupidity, or a self-imposed narrowness motivated by fear or laziness. The judgments of others who agree with the agent may be flawed by similar considerations. It is also possible that people's reasons may count as truly good in a particular way of life, yet this way of life is not conducive, or not conducive enough, to good lives. If the agents' reasons are doubted on the ground that they are flawed in some such way, then the doubts deserve to be resolved.

If these doubts and the attempts to remove them are reasonable, however, they must be specific, not general. To illustrate this, let us return to the gardener once again. To say to him, You should care more about your moral responsibilities than about your subjective interests, will quite naturally make him ask why. To give him as an answer that his moral responsibilities are more important than his subjective interests will seem to him to be an irritating and empty generality unless he is shown why and how it applies to his life. And we will know, even if the gardener does not, that this answer is not only uselessly general but also that it begs the question in favor of moralism and against egoism. If, however, the answer is more specific—for example: You love your daughter, but you should pay more attention to her because she questions your love and is growing up to be full of self-doubt—then the gardener, if he is reasonable, will recognize that he has been given a reason to spend less time on weeding and more with his daughter.

What he will recognize, however, is that he has been given *a* reason, not a conclusive reason. It is only *a* reason because the gardener's attention is demanded also by his job, wife, son, neighbor, income tax, and garden. His attention has limits, his energy is not inexhaustible, and he has to have something in his life for himself, something that delights and relaxes him and gives him relief and some distance from his troubles. Living a good life requires the gardener to weigh all these reasons, balance them, and change the assigned weights as circumstances change. It is that balance that the gardener needs to think about and sustain, and in that context his daughter's needs are one consideration among many.

Egoism, whether it be that of Machiavelli, Hobbes, or Nietzsche, and moralism, whether it be based on divine commands, natural law, the common good, the categorical imperative, the Golden Rule, or the like, will ring hollow to the gardener because none of them gives him guidance about what the optimal balance is in his situation. In their different ways, all these approaches to good lives aim to give a universal principle, an answer that applies to everyone equally in a particular situation. But there is no one else in the gardener's situation, and that is not an accident. No one else combines his love of gardening, his job, his wife and children, his neighbors, and the history of his relation to each of them. Of course a universal principle will say nothing to him. Nor, if we bear in mind the specific situations in which conflicts between moral responsibilities and subjective interests occur, will it say anything to us.

There is, therefore, little that can be said about good lives in general terms. It can be said that good lives are made good by the same primary goods and by some combination of various moral and subjective secondary goods, that they include meeting both moral responsibilities and subjective interests, and that their requirements will often conflict with each other. But there is no general answer to the questions of what specific secondary moral and subjective goods must good lives have, what the comparative importance of those specific secondary goods is, and how the conflict between moral responsibilities and subjective interests should be resolved. There are reasonable answers to these questions, but they are specific, not general. The questions are asked by specific people in specific contexts, and the answers must involve reflection on their conceptions of a good life, on their characters and circumstances, and on what balance of moral responsibilities and subjective interests is reasonable, given their conceptions of a good life, their characters, and their circumstances.

The answer such reflection may yield is that the agent's conception of a good life is unreasonable, or that the agent's character and circumstances are wretched and must be greatly improved in specific ways before there is any point in talking about the place of moral responsibilities and subjective interests in the agent's life. Or reflection may suggest the more cheery answer that if the agent gardened a little less and paid a little more attention to his family, or if his family importuned him a little less and left him a little more space, then life would be better.

This is not to deny that both egoists and moralists got something essentially right about good lives. But they also got something essentially wrong. What egoists got right is that ultimately the justification for meeting moral responsibilities must appeal to the agents' conception of a good life. What they got wrong is the supposition that reason requires that reasonable subjective interests should always override moral responsibilities if they conflict. The supposition is mistaken because if the agents' conceptions of a good life are reasonable, they will recognize their moral responsibilities to respect the primary goods of others, even if doing so in particular cases requires overriding their specific subjective interests. The reason for this is *not* that meeting their moral responsibilities is a means to satisfying their subjective interests. The reason is that part of what makes a conception of a good life reasonable is that the agents' subjective interests are inseparably connected with their moral responsibilities to respect the primary goods of others. Such a respect is a condition of having a society in which the agents and others can live good lives. Egoists can reject this reason only if they are unreasonable. Those who wish to protect their society because it makes good lives possible would be justified in doing what is necessary to remove the threat that egoists present.

It should be noticed that this general argument against egoism is about the overriding moral responsibility to respect the primary goods of others. The same general argument does not apply to the secondary goods of others. There can be no general arguments about how conflicts between the secondary moral and subjective goods of the agents and of others should be resolved because reasonable resolutions depend on the agents' reasonable conceptions of a good life, and there are very many such conceptions.

What moralists got right is that reason requires that some moral responsibilities should override some subjective interests, if they come into conflict. This is a universal claim, but it is of a severely limited scope because it applies only to respecting the primary goods of others. What moralists get wrong are two suppositions: if a claim is moral, then it must be universal; and the assignment of overriding importance to the moral responsibility to respect the primary goods of others, which reason requires, does not have to appeal to the agents' reasonable conception of a good life. Moral claims are typically made on agents in the context of everyday life, and in that context, in civilized societies, the conflicts are normally between secondary moral and subjective goods. These conflicts have no universal resolutions, although they have reasonable ones. Such resolutions appeal to the agents' conceptions of a good life, and it is because there are very many reasonable conceptions that no universal resolutions are possible.

The approach defended here thus agrees with moralism about there being overriding moral responsibilities on the level of primary goods. It also agrees with egoism about the overriding importance of the agents' subjective interests on the level of secondary goods. But it disagrees with both as well, because moralism mistakenly aims to extend overriding moral responsibilities to the level of secondary goods, and because egoism mistakenly aims to extend the agents' overriding subjective interests to the level of primary goods.

The pluralistic approach defended here does not fully resolve this conflict, but it indicates the kind of considerations that are relevant to its resolution. In order to have a full resolution, it would be necessary to write a not-so-short story about the gardener's marriage, his relationship with his children, the nature of his job, the political climate in his country, and so forth, including details about his and his family members' lives, characters, and circumstances. The argument does not require such a story because the case is merely an illustration intended to show that the resolution of the conflict depends on adding details, not on appealing to universal considerations. The more detailed the context, the more particularized the resolution. The case was meant to illustrate that the key to good lives is in their particularities, and the generalities sought by egoists and moralists are so many ways of missing the point.

VI

The argument is now complete, but it would be a mistake to end the chapter here because it is unlikely to convince egoists and moralists, whose minds are ruled by the craving for generality. They will remain unconvinced because they want an answer that expresses the requirements of reason, which they take to express what any agent in that kind of situation ought to do. They want an answer that applies universally, regardless of the identity, characters, and circumstances of the particular agents. They want a universal specification of all or most of the goods required for good human lives, not just of primary goods. They remain unconvinced by the pluralistic approach because it allows that an answer about what secondary moral and subjective goods are required for the goodness of the life of a particular agent can be reasonable even if it is not universal, and because it holds that reason allows agents to resolve the conflict between moral responsibilities and subjective interests in different ways precisely because of the individual differences among them.

The pluralistic approach, on the one hand, and reasonable egoists and moralists, on the other, disagree, then, about how to interpret the requirements of reason beyond those of primary goods. They agree in being committed to its requirements, but they disagree about what the requirements are. It is this disagreement that underlies the dissatisfaction of egoists and moralists with the pluralistic approach.

Disagreements about standards by which disagreements can be settled are particularly intractable. Nevertheless, this chapter makes a weighty case for the pluralistic side in this disagreement. The case has a critical and a constructive component. The critical one is to point to the failure of all historical attempts to provide a principle that would be a universal resolution of this conflict, one that all reflective people would either have to accept or be unreasonable in rejecting. The history of philosophy is a graveyard in which the many formulations and reformulations of proposed principles await—rarely in vain—resurrection. It must count against the view that the requirements of reason must be universal that, notwithstanding strenuous attempts throughout the centuries, the requirements in this case have not been met. It ought to occur to those who keep searching for a way of meeting them that perhaps they are searching for the wrong thing. That they are doing so is the critical component of the case for the pluralistic approach.

The constructive component consists in showing how individual agents can resolve specific instances of the conflict in specific cases. They need to appeal to the standard set by their own conception of a good life; they need to do what they can to assure that their conception is reasonable and that the resolution they reach is free of error. They are fallible, and they will make mistakes. The mistakes, however, can be corrected if they are sufficiently critical of themselves and open enough to learn from the criticisms of others. Nevertheless, the resolution they reach in any one occurrence of the conflict will not carry over to the next because of individual variations in the identity, characters, and circumstances of the agents. That, however, does not stop a particular resolution from being reasonable. The conflict will recur, and it will have to be resolved again and again. It is a tempting illusion to suppose that the conflict could be dissolved once and for all, if only the universal principle were found, but, however tempting, it remains an illusion. The pluralistic approach sees it as such; those who are unconvinced by it continue—futilely—to chase it.

8

The Art of Life

> The delicate and difficult art is to find, in each new turn of experience, the *via media* between two extremes: to be catholic without being characterless; to have and apply standards, and yet to be on guard against their desensitizing and stupefying influence, their tendency to blind us to the diversities of concrete situations and to previously unrecognized values; to know when to tolerate, when to embrace, and when to fight. And in that art, since no fixed and comprehensive rule can be laid down for it, we shall doubtless never acquire perfection.
>
> ARTHUR O. LOVEJOY, *The Great Chain of Being*

I

The three preceding chapters were meant to resolve philosophical problems involved in specifying some of the conditions of good lives. But the resolutions raise the closely connected question of what people should do to meet the specified conditions. It is one thing to know that good lives must be meaningful, free, personally satisfying, and morally commendable, and quite another to know how to make one's life conform to these conditions. The second kind of knowledge—the application of knowledge of the first kind to individually variable lives and circumstances—is the art of life.

The question of whether there is an art of life, therefore, may be understood as the question of whether there is some general prescription which, if followed, would enable individuals to make their lives good, even though it is acknowledged that there are great differences among individuals and among the contexts in which the prescription ought to apply. It is widely assumed that the answer to this question is in the affirmative. The great religions, the poetic visions of Homer, Lucretius, Virgil, Dante, Milton, and

Goethe, the philosophies of life of the Stoics, Epicurians, and Skeptics, of Kierkegaard, Schopenhauer, and Nietzsche, of the romantics, psychoanalysts, and existentialists, all prescribe a general form that the art of life must take. Salvation, rationality, authenticity, faith, self-realization, and good works, freedom from illusion, self-deception, neurosis, false consciousness, bad faith, and slavish adherence to phony authorities or to one's own bad self are some of the names under which arts of life are on offer. The reason, therefore, why the art of life presents a philosophical problem is not that there is much doubt about its existence but that there are deep disagreement about its nature.

One main source of this philosophical problem is the conflict between the moral and aesthetic modes of reflection. According to the moral mode, the key to the art of life is morality. According to the aesthetic mode, the key is the agents' creative development of themselves. Moral reflection regards the art of life as a primarily moral art in which the agents' creativity typically plays only a minor role. Aesthetic reflection regards the art of life as an essentially creative art in which the agents' morality may have only negligible significance.

The moral and the aesthetic approaches to the art of life reflect the ambiguity of the meaning of "art". Art always aims at some product, but producing it may depend either on the agents' skills or on their creative efforts. This difference, of course, is not absolute because skill and creative effort may go together, but they nevertheless pull in different directions. Skill is typically the possession of a technique that is learned from other practitioners. Those who have it are usually artisans, craftsmen, or performers. They need to be competent at some traditional practice, but they need not break new ground. Creative efforts, on the other hand, are often successful if they are in some way novel or original, if they change the traditional way of doing or looking at things. It is typical of artists that they make such efforts. The moral approach interprets the art of life as a skill. The aesthetic approach interprets it as a creative effort.

The ideal for the moral approach is Aristotle's *phronimos*, the honorable agent with practical wisdom. The skill of such agents is to apply their knowledge of good and evil in the often complex circumstances of everyday life. The products of their skill are their own lives and actions that, in the variety of their characters and circumstances, reflect the requirements of morality. These lives are exemplified by Homer's Hector, Livy's Cincinnatus, Shakespeare's Horatio, and Henry James's Isabel Archer.

The ideal for the aesthetic approach is the creative life. The effort it requires centers on making oneself into a certain kind of person. The medium of the art of life is the life of the artist. The aim of their creative efforts is to develop their potentialities and give their lives such form, direction, and value as their characters and circumstances make possible. This may lead to a life dedicated to art, power, conquest, honor, or the making of a new world. The corresponding lives may be like those of Wagner, Julius Caesar, Napoleon, Brutus, or Nietzsche.

Both the moral and the aesthetic approaches to the art of life require justification. The justification of the moral approach is in terms of practical reason. Practical reason is the aspect of reason that guides human lives and actions, and it is to be contrasted with the theoretical aspect of reason that aims at knowledge of the world independently of its effect on human lives and actions. The basic assumption underlying the moral approach is that it is by living in accordance with practical reason that people can make their lives good. The justification of the aesthetic approach is in terms of ideals of human excellence. Such ideals lead people to break out of the mold of everyday life, to free themselves from custom, convention, tradition, and the shackles of history, to leave behind conventional wisdom about what is possible and impossible, aim high and give their creative best to achieve their ideals. The extent to which people succeed in living in this manner is the extent to which their lives will be good.

Much more will be said about both approaches and their justifications, but even the little that has been said is sufficient to make clear that there is a conflict between them. The motivational source of the moral approach is practical reason; of the aesthetic one it is the will. Since the requirements of practical reason apply to everyone impartially and impersonally, the moral approach is universalistic. Since the will is employed to develop the potentialities of individual agents, to overcome their limitations, and since potentialities and limitations vary with individuals and circumstances, the aesthetic approach is essentially connected with individual differences, with different levels of achievement, excellence, and consequently of merit, and it is thus individualistic.

Being guided by either practical reason or the will does not, of course, exclude the other, but it does relegate it to a subordinate position. It is well if practical reason aids the creative effort of the will, but if it does not, then it is but another confining limitation that good lives must overcome. And the contrary is true as well: it is good if doing what practical reason dictates coincides with what the agents happen to will, but if it does not, then the will must be altered so as to follow the dictates of practical reason. In the first case, led by aesthetic reflection, the agents do what they do, not because it is practically reasonable, but because they will it. In the second case, following moral reflection, the agents do what they will, not because they will it, but because practical reason dictates it.

Reflection on this conflict in the moral mode leads to subordinating the striving for excellence to the requirements of practical reason. The claims of excellence are not denied, but their significance is made secondary. This seems unjustified from the aesthetic mode of reflection because privileging the claims of practical reason appears to be arbitrary unless it can be shown to constitute the kind of excellence that makes lives good. The rejoinder prompted by moral reflection is that the supposition that the pursuit of any kind of excellence will contribute to good lives needs to be justified, and only reliance on practical reason can justify it. To which aesthetic reflection suggests the reply that justification in terms of practical reason is the means to the pursuit of excellent ends, and the justification of any means can only be the excellence of the ends to which it leads. But that justification presupposes that some people have striven successfully to achieve the excellence and thus have led good lives. And so the argument goes perennially back and forth among reflective people who are committed to there being an art of life but disagree whether its primary requirement is universalistic practical reason or individualistic will.

The critical aim of this chapter is to show, first, that the claims of universalistic practical reason lead to an indefensible absolutism that, among its many defects, makes an art of life impossible, and, second, that the claims of individualistic will lead to an equally indefensible relativism with its own multiple defects, one among which is that it endangers the conditions in which the art of life can be practiced. The chapter's constructive aim is to show how the pluralistic approach resolves the philosophical problem about the art of life by combining the salvageable components of the moral and aesthetic approaches, discarding the rest, and adding something of its own.

II

The art of life and the problems involved in its interpretation are well illustrated by John Stuart Mill's work. The art of life, according to Mill, has "three departments, Morality, Prudence or Policy, and Aesthetics; the Right, the Expedient, and the Beautiful or Noble." "To this art," says Mill, "all other arts are subordinate; since its principles are those which must determine whether the special aim of any particular art is worthy and desirable, and what is its place in the scale of desirable things." The art of life, then, combines factual propositions derived from what Mill calls science and general principles that "enjoin or recommend that something should be." These general principles taken together may be called "the Doctrine of Ends;

which, borrowing the language of the German metaphysicians, may also be termed, not improperly, the principles of Practical Reason."

The art of life must have "a *Philosophia Prima*" peculiar to it, and it comprises "the first principles of Conduct," for "there must be some standard by which to determine the goodness or badness, absolute and comparative, of ends." But this is not all: "Whatever that standard is, there can be but one: for if there were several ultimate principles of conduct, the same conduct might be approved by one of these principles and condemned by another; and there would be needed some more general principle as umpire between them."

"If that principle be rightly chosen, it will be found, I apprehend," says Mill, "to serve quite as well for the ultimate principle of Morality, as for that of Prudence, Policy, or Taste." Mill then says that "the general principle to which all rules of practice ought to conform, and the test by which they should be tried, is that of conduciveness to the happiness of mankind, or rather, of all sentient beings: in other words . . . the promotion of happiness is the ultimate principle." For the "discussion and vindication of this principle" Mill refers the reader to the "volume entitled *Utilitarianism*."[1] And in *Utilitarianism* Mill says that the "greatest happiness principle" is "the foundation of morals," "the standard of morality," and "the criterion of morality."[2]

If this were all, we could simply conclude that Mill follows the moral approach to the art of life. In doing so, he opts for absolutism over pluralism, for universality over individuality, for reason over will. He recognizes that aesthetic and prudential ideals of excellence, two of the three "departments" of the art of life, may conflict with moral considerations, which form the third "department," but these conflicts are settled by "the ultimate principle of Morality," namely, the greatest happiness principle. If ideals of excellence conflict with what is morally right, the right should prevail. The art of life then is a moral art, and its aim is the greatest happiness possible for all sentient beings.

Mill thinks that the art of life is moral, and that means that people trying to live a good life are required "to be as strictly impartial [between their own happiness and that of others] as a disinterested and benevolent spectator," that each person should form "an indissoluble association between his own happiness and the good of the whole," that "their ends are identified with those of others," and that the "feeling of unity . . . be taught as a religion, and the whole force of education, of institutions, and of opinion [be] directed, as it once was in the case of religion, to make every person grow from infancy surrounded on all sides both by the profession and the practice of it."[3] Even Mill's sympathizers must be embarrassed by the oppressive priggish voice of moralistic hectoring that is expressed in these lamentable lines. Mill simply does not face the consequence of his position that the extent to which the right prevails is the extent to which agents must act contrary to their ideals of excellence. There may be good reasons for acting in this way, but these reasons, if they exist, cannot alter the fact that the art of life, in Mill's interpretation, requires the denigration of elements whose necessity to good lives Mill himself recognizes. If the art of life is the kind of moral art that Mill takes it to be, then its universal, impartial, and impersonal claims prescribe that individuals ought to subordinate the goodness of their own lives to the goodness of other people's lives. Since the art of life is the art that enables individuals to make good lives for themselves, Mill's moralistic interpretation dooms it to failure.

The moralizing voice, however, is not Mill's only one. A quite different voice is heard in *On Liberty*: "The cultivation of an ideal nobleness of will and conduct should be to individuals an end, to which the specific pursuit of either of their own happiness or of that of others . . . should, in any case of conflict, give way."[4] Mill thinks that "the free development of individuality is one of the leading essentials of well-being," and he paraphrases Wilhelm von Humboldt with great approval: "the end of man . . . is the highest and most harmonious development of his powers . . . that for this there are two requisites, 'freedom, and variety of situations'; and . . . 'individual vigor and manifold diversity,' which combine themselves in 'originality.'"[5] And he says: "He who lets the world, or his own portion of it, choose his plan of life for him has no need of any other faculty than the ape-like one of imitation. . . . What will be his comparative worth as a human being? It really is of importance not only what men do, but also what manner of men they are that do it. Among the works of man which human life is rightly employed in perfecting and beautifying, the first importance surely is man himself."[6]

As these passages make obvious, there is a deep conflict in Mill's work about the nature of the art of life. He rightly sees that morality, prudence, and aesthetics must be part of the art of life and that they conflict. But whereas in *Utilitarianism* he attempts to resolve their conflict in favor of the moral approach, in *On Liberty* he does so in favor of the aesthetic. He is pulled one way by the universalistic claims of practical reason and in another by the individualistic claims of the will. His case illustrates not only the philosophical problem about the art of life, but also the predicament of reflective agents who find themselves participating in both of the modes of reflection whose conflict gives rise to the problem.

It must be acknowledged, of course, that Mill was aware of the conflict between the claims of practical reason and morality, on the one hand, and individual will and ideals of excellence, on the other. It is generally conceded that even if a utilitarian resolution can be found, Mill has not found it. So we shall leave him in his state of conflict and turn to what is perhaps the most powerful attempt to resolve the conflict in favor of the moral approach: the one proposed by the greatest of those "German metaphysicians" to whom Mill refers and who think that the art of life consists in living according to "the principles of Practical Reason."

III

Perhaps the central idea of Kant's moral thought is that the claims of practical reason and individual will come to the same thing: "the will is nothing but practical reason."[7] Kant denies, therefore, that they conflict. He certainly does not deny that they often appear to conflict, but that appearance, he thinks, comes from a deficiency either of practical reason or of the will. He also thinks, for reasons central to his position, that these two sources of mistaken beliefs about there being a conflict are really one.

Kant thinks that practical reason must be understood as a command. It tells how reason requires that one should act. It is, therefore, a command whose force rational agents, insofar as they are rational, cannot fail to recognize. As a result, what they are commanded to do is what they will to do. For rational agents, there cannot be a conflict between practical reason and their will. Kant thinks that if it is understood what practical reason and the will consist in, then it becomes apparent why there cannot be a conflict between them, nor between either of them and morality. Practical reason and the will coincide because of their nature. Their coincidence, therefore, is a necessary, not a contingent, matter. Practical reason and the will are but two aspects of rational agency. The cement, so to speak, that holds them together is the freedom of rational agents. If agents act freely, then they act according to practical reason, their actions reflect their will, they act autonomously, and their actions conform to the requirements of morality. In order to understand Kant's reason for thinking that these implications hold, it is necessary to understand the internal relations that connect practical reason, will, freedom, autonomy, and morality.

Kant says that "will is a kind of causality belonging to living beings so far as they are rational. *Freedom* would then be a property this causality has of being able to work independently of determination by alien causes."[8] The will is thus a power individuals have to produce changes in themselves and their environment. This power may be exercised heteronomously or autonomously. In the first case, its exercise depends on alien causes, that is, on causes not within, or fully within, the agent's control. The laws of nature, events in their environment, physiological and psychological needs, and so forth may determine or influence the agents' will independently of their own choices. In the second case, the exercise of the will depends wholly on the agents' choices, and this is what makes it free. The freedom of the will thus means, negatively, that it is not dependent on alien causes, and, positively, that it is subject only to its own control, that, as Kant puts it, it is a law to itself. If the will is free in this sense, then it is autonomous. The "freedom of the will . . . [is] autonomy—that is, the property which the will has of being a law to itself."[9]

Kant thinks that autonomous agents will give themselves the law that he calls the categorical imperative: "Act only on that maxim through which you can at the same time wish that it should become a universal law."[10] That is, act according to a principle that you would want all agents to follow if they were in your position. The categorical imperative, Kant claims, expresses the requirements of autonomy, practical reason, and morality. It does so for autonomy because it is a law that agents choose to be guided by. If they are guided by their needs, desires, feelings, or ideals of excellence, then they are not acting autonomously, they are not in full control of what motivates them, because causes independent of their will determine or influence what needs, desires, feelings, or ideals of excellence they have. Autonomous agents, guided by the categorical imperative, thus *must* act in abstraction of all contingent features of their characters and circumstances, otherwise they would stop being autonomous.

If agents act autonomously, then they also act according to practical reason because they act in accordance with a law that anyone and everyone who abstracted from contingencies would also choose. For practical reason just is to act in accordance with a principle that one thinks that all agents ought to act on if they were in one's situation. The task of practical reason, therefore, is to find a principle that applies universally, impartially, and impersonally to all agents in a particular situation. The categorical imperative tells agents how they must think in order to find that principle. They must ask themselves how they think anyone ought to act, and then act according to the answer they give to themselves. Rational agents *must* be guided by the categorical imperative because if they were not, they would act contrary to how they themselves think that everyone ought to act. To act contrary to the categorical imperative, therefore, would be inconsistent, and thus irrational.

In acting according to practical reason and the categorical imperative, however, agents are also acting morally. For they act according to a universal, impartial, and impersonal principle that states how people ought to act in a particular situation. If agents are guided by the categorical imperative, then they must have some reason for thinking that the way they have concluded that everyone ought to act is right. For otherwise they would not think that everyone ought to act that way. So that when it comes to their own actions, they would be inconsistent if they were to act contrary to the way they think that everybody ought to act. If they were inconsistent in this way, they would also be immoral, because they would be acting in violation of how they themselves think that everyone ought to act.[11] Rational agents, therefore, *must* act morally, because if they did not, they would not be rational agents.

It is for these reasons that Kant thinks that the categorical imperative embodies the requirements of autonomy, practical reason, and morality; that violating one involves violating the others; and that meeting the requirements of one involves meeting the requirements of the others. As he puts it: "An absolutely good will, whose principle must be the categorical imperative, will . . . contain only the *form of willing*, and that as autonomy. In other words, the fitness of the maxim of every good will to make itself a universal law is itself the sole law which the will of every rational being spontaneously imposes on itself without basing it on any impuls[e] or interest."[12] Kant, of course, does not think that everybody actually acts according to the categorical imperative. Those who fail do so because they are wanting in autonomy, practical reason, or morality. If they were not wanting in these ways, then they would act as they themselves would realize that they ought to act, if they had not been prevented from reasoning well enough about it.

Kant's position has far-reaching moral, political, legal, and educational implications. But the implication that is of immediate relevance to the art of life is that, like Mill, Kant supposes that it is a moral art, that if nonmoral ideals of excellence conflict with morality, then practical reason requires that morality should prevail and that nonmoral ideals of excellence should be subordinated to it. Ideals of excellence are unavoidably heteronomous. Holding their claims to be higher than or equal to those of morality is unavoidably irrational and immoral because nonmoral ideals express contingent aspirations, whereas morality expresses an aspiration that all rational agents must have insofar as they are rational. The crucial difference, according to Kant, is that the aspirations expressed by ideals of excellence are to realize various ends that rational agents *may* aim at, but the aspiration expressed by morality is to *be* a rational agent. That is why morality is a precondition of the pursuit of nonmoral ideals of excellence, and why it must always prevail over them if they conflict.

"The practically *good*," says Kant, "is that which determines the will by concepts of reason, and therefore not by subjective causes, but objectively— that is, on grounds valid for every rational being as such." Such objective determination by practical reason is expressed by the categorical imperative. By contrast, hypothetical imperatives express subjective causes that are "concerned with art . . . [and] with well-being." Hypothetical imperatives thus express what Kant calls counsels of prudence and of art, and he says that such counsels are only "subjective and contingent," having to do with whether "this or that man counts this or that as belonging to his happiness." And he goes on, "As against this, a categorical imperative is limited by no condition and can quite precisely be called a command, as being absolutely, although practically, necessary."[13]

The implication of Kant's view for the art of life is that when the counsels of prudence, art, happiness, and well-being—in other words, ideals of excellence—conflict with the command of the categorical imperative, then rational agency requires obeying the command and disregarding the counsel. And the reason he gives is that obeying the command is necessary for rational agency, and hence for morality, whereas following the counsel is not. If the art of life is informed by Kant's views, then its practitioners must resign themselves to the fact that practical reason and morality often conflict with and take precedence over their ideals.

IV

There are numerous reasons for doubting Kant's position, but only two will be discussed here. The first emerges if it is remembered why Kant supposes that morality often requires agents to act contrary to their ideals of excellence. His reason is that these ideals are contingent aims, whereas the requirements of morality are necessarily binding on all rational agents. They are, as Kant thought, the preconditions of pursuing any contingent aims. But why should this be so? Why cannot people be moved by ideals of excellence and rank them higher than the requirements of morality? Kant accepts that this can be done, that it often is done, but he claims that practical reason provides no support for such ranking. It is, he thinks, always contrary to practical reason to act contrary to morality. And the reason is that morality comes to people in the form of a universal, impartial, and impersonal command, namely, the categorical imperative. People could not consistently make it a universal law that everyone should be motivated by the same ideals of excellence because rational agents need not be motivated by them at all and because those who are motivated differ widely in the ideals of excellence that motivate them. It must be asked, however, Why must moral commands be universal, impartial, and impersonal? Why could there not be moral commands that are binding on some agents but not on others? Kant's answer is that there could not be such *moral* commands because moral commands are requirements of practical reason, and reason must be universal, impartial, and impersonal; otherwise it is not reason. And with this, we have reached the heart of the matter.

It is easy to see that if reason is theoretical, then the conclusions reached by its means will hold universally, impartially, and impersonally. Theoretical reason yields factual truths that do not depend on the subjective preferences of anyone. Kant, however, takes great pains to avoid basing morality on theoretical reason because that is his way of avoiding unjustifiable metaphysical claims. Practical reason, however, is not theoretical reason. Its conclusions are not factual truths but, as Kant says, commands. Why should it be supposed that it is reasonable for a particular agent to act only on a command that it is reasonable for all agents to act on? That there are *some* such commands may be acknowledged. There may be situations is which all reasonable agents ought to act in the same way. Kant's claim, however, is much stronger than this. It is that *all* commands, insofar as they are reasonable and moral, require *all* agents to follow them, and that if the agents fail to do so, then they are acting irrationally and immorally.

The force of Kant's claim depends on his assimilation of practical reason to theoretical reason. Kant, however, gives no reason to suppose that they are assimilable, and there is a good reason to suppose that they are not. This reason is that the factual truths that theoretical reason yields are not attached to any individual, but commands are. Commands always tell individual agents what it is that they ought to do. What they ought to do, however, often depends on their history, character, relationships, circumstances, on how they conceive of their self-interest, on what ideals of excellence they hold, and these considerations vary with individuals. So it is the exception, not the rule, for commands to apply universally, impartially, and impersonally.

It is useless to try to avoid this central difficulty in Kant's position by saying that if individual agents reasonably decide what they ought to do, then they must make the universal, impartial, and impersonal claim that everyone in their situation ought to do the same thing. For, in the first place, there is often no one else who could be in the agents' situation because the agents' history, character, and so forth are unique. In the second place, the agents may reasonably decide that when the very possibility of living according to their crucially important ideals of excellence is at stake, it is justifiable to violate some relatively unimportant moral command and fail to keep a lunch date, return a borrowed book on time, tell a harmless lie, or not be as helpful to strangers as they might be. They may rightly think that anyone in their position ought to do the same, so that they do make a universal, impartial, and impersonal claim, but it is contrary to morality. So moral commands need not be universal, impartial, and impersonal; and universal, impartial, and impersonal commands need not be moral. In that case, however, the ground falls out from under Kant's argument that practical reason requires that, if they conflict, morality must take precedence over the agents' ideals of excellence because moral claims are universal, impartial, and impersonal whereas the claims of ideals of excellence are not.

The second reason for doubting Kant's position is also connected with the differences between theoretical reason and practical reason as a command. The factual truths that theoretical reason yields are expressible as propositions, and true propositions are consistent with one another. One true proposition cannot contradict another because if it did, one of them would have to be false, which true propositions cannot be. But it is otherwise with commands. There is no reason why one command of practical reason could not require agents to do something that is incompatible with another command of practical reason. This is true of all commands of practical reason, even of universal, impartial, and impersonal ones. If Kant is right, practical reason commands universally, impartially, and impersonally that one should not lie, cheat, steal, or murder; that one should help others, be kind, save endangered innocent lives, keep promises, pay debts, and so forth. But it is a plain fact of everyday life that such commands often conflict and call for incompatible actions. Helping someone may involve telling a lie, saving an innocent life may involve breaking a promise.

The significance of such commonplace conflicts is that even if Kant's account of practical reason and morality is correct as far as it goes, it does not go far enough. It is not enough to know that one ought to be guided by the universal, impartial, and impersonal commands of the categorical imperative, one must also know how to resolve conflicts among such commands. If there is some principle that helps one to do that, then practical reason must include it. In that case, however, Kant's claim that the categorical imperative expresses the requirements of both practical reason and morality is mistaken. On the other hand, if there is no such principle, then the categorical imperative is an inadequate guide to conduct.

Kant's position cannot be rescued by arguing that the occurrence of conflicts among the bona fide commands of practical reason shows only that it is the agents' reasoning and not the categorical imperative that is at fault. For even if the agents conclude that it ought to be a universal law that one of the two conflicting commands ought to be acted on, the other command remains universal, impartial, and impersonal. In disobeying it, the agent is violating an absolute moral requirement. If, to avoid this difficulty, commands are watered down to allow for not following them in case of conflicts, then their absoluteness is abandoned. Commands, then, become toothless prescriptions to the effect that one should not lie, steal, cheat, and so forth unless there is a good reason for it. Practical reason, then, must include an account of what makes particular reasons good or bad, but Kant gives no such account. And it is hard to see how such an account, if one were given, could deny that a good reason for overriding a relatively unimportant moral command is that some ideal of excellence that agents regard as vital to their living a good life requires it. If this is conceded, however, then everything that Kant means to deny is conceded.

The problem that underlies both of these objections is that Kant does not realize how far-reaching are the implications of his reinterpretation of practical reason. If practical reason is a command, and not the application of knowledge gained by theoretical reason, then it is illegitimate to suppose, as Kant does, that the commands of practical reason have the features that the knowledge gained by theoretical reason has. That knowledge is of factual truths and the propositions that express them must hold universally, impartially, and impersonally, and cannot conflict. But commands are addressed to individuals whose characters and circumstances differ and who have, therefore, very different reasons for obeying or disobeying them. And quite apart from these individual differences, commands, unlike propositions expressing factual truths, can and often do conflict and thus lack the absoluteness that Kant attributes to them. It must be concluded then that Kant's argument that the moral approach to the art of life ought to dominate over the aesthetic approach fails.

V

Two distinctions will help to understand the aesthetic approach to the art of life.[14] The first is between the aesthetic attitude and its objects. The attitude involves the appreciation of some object for being what it is. The appreciation, therefore, is not instrumental. Its object is not valued because of some end beyond itself that it helps to achieve or to constitute, but because the object is fine, admirable, or great in itself. The object may make people happier, societies more just, nations more civilized, and lives more uplifting. The aesthetic appreciation of it, however, is not on account of its contribution toward achieving valuable aims but for its intrinsic excellence, which is unaffected by the good or bad uses that it may have.

The object toward which the aesthetic attitude is directed may be found in nature, such as a landscape, a sunset, a human body, or it may be a human achievement, such as a work of art, an imaginative discovery, the ingenious surmounting of a formidable obstacle, or the elegant solution of a recalcitrant problem. But since we are interested in the aesthetic approach to the art of life, the objects that concern us here are human lives that merit appreciation because of their intrinsic excellence. Such lives are outstanding human achievements. They may be lives of artists or scientists: creative, brilliant, original, penetrating, and imaginative; lives of heroes: magnificent, confident, impressive, daring, adventurous, and charismatic; lives of conscientious protesters: noble, honorable, constant, steadfast, and incorruptible; lives of connoisseurs: refined, discriminating, elegant, sensitive, and graceful; lives of athletes: disciplined, energetic, competitive, robust, and determined; or lives of sages: wise, deep, profound, calm, serene, judicious, and learned. All such lives involve significant human achievements, accomplished in the face of obstacles that daunt others, made possible by the outstanding qualities of their agents. Their achievements are rare because most people lack the required qualities and cannot overcome the obstacles. These lives, of course, are the ideals of nonmoral excellence that, according to Kant, ought to be subordinated to morality.

The second distinction is between two perspectives from which ideals of excellence may be viewed: those of the actor and the spectator.[15] Both appreciate the intrinsic excellence of the ideals, regardless of their moral standing, but they appreciate them in different ways. The spectators merely appreciate them from the outside for being admirable, fine, and great, but they are not moved to model their own lives on them. The actors are so moved. They adopt these lives as ideals of how they themselves want to live. Their attitude is not like that of knowledgeable amateurs visiting a museum but like the attitude of artists toward the master from whom they want to learn. The actors are inspired by these ideals of excellence to become more like the agents who lived the lives. In order to succeed, they have to make great efforts to transform themselves from what they are in their more or less ordinary state to approximate as closely as they can the extraordinary state represented by the ideals of excellence that inspire them.

The required creative efforts depend on their will, but it is their individual will that takes an individual form and has an individual object, rather than Kant's abstract and formal will that is the same for all rational agents. The object of the will is individual because it involves the transformation of agents from what they happen to be, given their contingent characters and circumstances, into what their ideals of excellence inspire them to be. The form of the will is also individual because it involves the development of the contingent individually variable potentialities of the agents so that they could become what they want to be. According to the aesthetic mode of reflection, the art of life is to effect this transformation. It is barely a metaphor to describe agents who are thus engaged as artists who work in the medium of their own lives.

It seems clear that many lives are meaningful, free, and personally satisfying because of the agents' mastery of the art of life thus understood. What is not clear, however, is how successful engagement in the art of life is related to morality. Mill in *Utilitarianism* and Kant, representing the moral mode of reflection, think that the art of life must be practiced in conformity to the requirements of morality, and if they conflict, then morality must prevail.

There are two deep reasons that tell against this view. One is that there are great problems with Mill's and Kant's justifications of their incompatible conceptions of morality. Quite independently of the art of life, reasonable people may reasonably reject both the greatest happiness principle and the categorical imperative to which Mill and Kant appeal in order to justify what they take to be the requirements of morality. The other reason is the grotesque indifference to human psychology that permeates both types of moral reflection. They both require reasonable people to act contrary to the ideals of excellence that inspire them and to which they have dedicated their lives; to go against the very dictates of their will that they have with much effort trained themselves to follow; and to violate their hard-won sense of what makes their lives meaningful, free, and personally satisfying. If reasonable people even pause to ask why they should do such violence to their most cherished values, then the answer, that some universal, impartial, and impersonal principle requires it, will seem to them to carry no conviction unless it can be shown how it bears on living the lives they have reasonably decided they want to live. This is not to say, of course, that they will be indifferent to morality. Morality has an important place in many ideals of excellence, and some place in any reasonable one. The aesthetic mode of reflection will lead them, however, to rank the significance of moral claims lower than the claims of their ideals of excellence, if they come into conflict.

The philosophical problem presented by the conflict between these two modes of reflection was old even when Plato took formal notice of it as the "ancient quarrel between philosophy and poetry."[16] Although the quarrel is ancient, in the eighteenth and nineteenth century in Germany it recurred in a new form, and this constitutes a momentous event in the history not just of this problem but of reflection on the nature of good lives. This "great turning-point—it seems to me the greatest yet," says Isaiah Berlin, "is well enough known under the name of 'romanticism,'"[17] It is the product of numerous artists, poets, playwrights, novelists, and philosophers, but perhaps the pivotal figure in struggling with its implications is Nietzsche. Romanticism, in Nietzsche's hand, is a particular interpretation of the aesthetic approach to living meaningful, free, and personally satisfying lives. This interpretation has a critical and a constructive aspect.

Its critical aspect is encapsulated in Nietzsche's notorious claim: "God is dead. God remains dead. And we have killed him."[18] This is Nietzsche's typically perfervid way of saying that the idea that there is an objective truth about values that can be known and that reasonable actions aim to reflect is no longer tenable. Values do not exist independently of our will; values are what we make them. The question is what values we should make. In the critical aspect of his thought, Nietzsche takes for granted Kant's argument against the possibility of a metaphysical foundation for values, but he rejects Kant's argument for the coincidence of practical reason and morality. One should seek a "new immoral, or at least unmoralistic . . . anti-Kantian . . . 'categorical imperative' . . . which will articulate this *new demand:* we need a critique of moral values, *the value of these values themselves must first be called in question.*"[19] Nietzsche thus sees human beings, or, as he would put it, the human beings that matter, as possessing autonomy and having to decide what to do with it. They must make a decision about the values that should guide how they live without the illusion that theoretical or practical reason can help them. The constructive aspect of Nietzsche's romantic version of the aesthetic approach is concerned with how that decision should be made, how autonomous lives should be lived.

Nietzsche thinks that "This is at bottom a question of taste and aesthetics,"[20] and not of morality. It is "precisely morality" that is "to blame if the highest power and splendor actually possible . . . was never in fact attained."[21] "The subtle tricks of old moralists and preachers of morals," the "stiff and decorous Tartuffery of the old Kant as he lures us on the dialectical bypaths that lead to his 'categorical imperative'—really lead astray and seduce,"[22] and all of it ought to be rejected. Its rejection, however, has the positive goal of "clearing the way for new ideals, for *more robust* ideals."[23] "We immoralists . . . make it a point to be *affirmers.*"[24] But what ideals do immoralists affirm? Nietzsche answers: they affirm the "Ego . . . this creating, willing, evaluating Ego, which is the measure and value of things,"[25] The "noble type of man experiences *itself* as determining values; it does not need approval; it judges 'what is harmful to me is harmful in itself'; it knows itself to be value-creating. . . . [It has] feeling of fullness, of power that seeks to overflow, the happiness of high tension, the consciousness of wealth that would give and bestow. . . . Noble and courageous human beings who think that way are furthest removed from that morality which finds the distinction of morality precisely in pity, or in acting for others, or in *desinteressement.*"[26]

The question still remains, however, of what these affirmers of the ego have to do to create their own values. Nietzsche thinks that they should ask themselves: "What does your conscience say?" And they will hear the answer if they listen well and honestly: "You must become who you are." People who follow their consciences become "human beings who are new, unique, in-comparable, who give themselves laws, who create themselves." The way to accomplish that is "To 'give style' to one's character—a great and rare art! It is practiced by those who survey all the strengths and weaknesses of their nature and then fit them into an artistic plan until every one of them appears as art and reason and even weaknesses delight the eye. . . . In the end, when the work is finished, it becomes evident how the constraints of a single taste governed and formed everything large and small. Whether this taste was good or bad is less important than one might suppose, if only it was a single taste!"[27] This is what people whose lives have become ideals of excellence have accomplished. Those who want to become themselves ought not, of course, imitate them; they should learn from them to do for themselves what these "highest exemplars" of humanity have done for themselves.[28]

VI

Any attempt to assess Nietzsche's views is fraught with danger. This is partly Nietzsche's doing, because he writes to provoke his opponents and sympathizers alike, and he succeeds. He is a fervent hater and lover. Being the intellectual that he is, it is ideas that he hates and loves with the deep passions of his brilliant and unsteady mind. Everything is either profoundly base or profoundly noble. This makes measured response difficult. Apart from this, however, there is the further problem that it is practically irresistible not to read Nietzsche in the light of subsequent history. The Nazis honored him. Numerous mass murderers imagined themselves to be Nietzschean *Ueber-menschen* with the strength, vision, and determination to rid the world of vermin and thereby create the postmoral world that Nietzsche prophesied. We know, as Nietzsche could not, about the terrible uses to which some of his ideas have been put. If these dangers are avoided, hard as that is, there is still the most serious one of all: his fertile mind has produced an amazing array of unsystematic and unsupported aphoristic dicta, many of which contain important kernels of truths obscured by exaggeration, bombast, and self-aggrandizement. This being said, let us now attempt an assessment of the implications of Nietzsche's views for the art of life.

Nietzsche rightly sees that if morality has no metaphysical foundation and if its principles are commands rather than propositions about values, if, that is, morality is what Kant thinks that it is, then there is no convincing reason why autonomous agents should subordinate their pursuit of ideals of excellence to universal, impartial, and impersonal moral commands. Nietzsche thinks that autonomous agents ought to exercise their autonomy in pursuit of ideals of excellence, and if morality stands in their way, then they should see through its sham imperatives. The art of life is to choose one's ideals of excellence well and to train one's will to pursue them uncompromisingly. Anything else is a weakness that jeopardizes the meaning, freedom, and satisfactions of one's life.

One of the things that Nietzsche does not see is that morality need not be understood either as a Kantian system of commands or as a Platonic system of knowledge of the good obtained by means of metaphysics. Morality may be seen as a system designed to protect some requirements that all good lives have, regardless of how their goodness is conceived. The basis of the system, understood in this third way, is the factual, but not metaphysical, claim that all human beings have some physiological, psychological, and social needs that must be satisfied if they are to live meaningful, free, and satisfying lives. The satisfaction of these needs is a minimum requirement of all good lives, and one purpose of morality is to create the conditions in which they can be satisfied. Reasonable people pursuing ideals of excellence have good reasons, therefore, to conform to these requirements, since doing so protects the system on which their own pursuits depend.

More needs to be, and will shortly be, said about this conception of morality. What has already been said, however, is surely sufficient to cast doubt on Nietzsche's claim that a stark choice must be made between Kant's moral absolutism and Nietzsche's immoralism. Nietzsche is right to reject Kant's view of practical reason and morality, but he is wrong to take that to be the rejection of practical reason and morality. It is a consequence of Nietzsche's tendency to see things in terms of extremes that the rejection of Kant's moral absolutism leads him to embrace radical relativism. He recognizes no constraints—moral, rational, or other—on the pursuit of ideals of excellence. Autonomous agents create their own values, make their own laws, and that is what is important, rather than what their values and laws happen to be. This is how Nietzsche could come to regard as admirable moral monsters like Cesare Borgia, the treacherous murderer, and Napoleon, who pursued his ideal of excellence by orchestrating the slaughter of hundreds of thousands of people. Nietzsche is so obsessed with saying an understandable no to "old moralists and preachers of morals" that he fails to see that ideals of excellence can be pursued only within the constraints of practical reason and morality that protect the conditions in which individuals can follow their pursuits.

Another blind spot of Nietzsche's is that he led by his romanticism to an unacceptably narrow view, first, of the ends whose pursuit may make lives meaningful, free, and satisfying and, second, of the motivational sources for pursuing them. Consider the ends, ideals of excellence, whose pursuit Nietzsche advocates. Let us agree that the lives of creative artists and scientists, heroes, honorable protesters, refined connoisseurs, disciplined athletes, and wise sages do indeed represent the "highest exemplars," that they are admirable, and that their lives are meaningful, free, and satisfying. These lives, in effect, exemplify one of the "departments" of the art of life, namely, the aesthetic one, having to do with the beautiful and the noble, that, we have seen earlier, Mill discusses. But what about the other two: morality and prudence? Why does Nietzsche not recognize that moral and prudent lives may also be meaningful, free, and satisfying? Why could not principled, conscientious, dutiful, loving moral lives—or moderate, judicious, cautious, industrious, well-planned prudent lives—not be as meaningful, free, and satisfying as noble and beautiful lives? Nietzsche regards them with contempt. But this is nothing but a romantic prejudice in favor of Promethean lives of *Sturm und Drang*, full of strife, passion, excess, ecstasy, risk, and suffering—lives amazingly similar to Nietzsche's. If the ends that make life worth living are created, not discovered, if the key to such lives is the law that autonomous agents make for themselves, then it ought to be possible for them to value ends other than the romantic ones that Nietzsche is led by his predilection to advocate. Romantic absolutism is only a little less absolutistic and no less arbitrary than moral absolutism.

There is also the problem created by the narrow view Nietzsche takes of the motivation on which the successful practice of the art of life depends. It is a truism that the sources of human motivation are many: reason, emotion, ambition, imagination, love, duty, need, honor, shame, and so on routinely move people to action. Of all the sources of motivation, Nietzsche focuses on one, the will, and claims for it a controlling role in the pursuit of ideals of excellence. Why should one accept this?

There is no doubt that the will is normally involved in human actions, because agents must move from intention to performance. The same, however, is true of reason, emotion, and imagination. Normal human beings normally need to reason about what they want and how to get it; they have various feelings on that subject; and they have to envisage what it would be like to achieve what their reasons and feelings prompt them to seek. Doubtless the pursuit of ideals of excellence is difficult, and the agents must make efforts of will to succeed. But, as before, the same difficulties call for careful reasoning, authentic feelings, and lively and accurate imagination of the ends they aim at. Nietzsche nevertheless insists on the overriding importance of the will, and denigrates the rest. The explanation, but not the justification, is once again the romantic prejudice that meaningful, free, and satisfying lives are lives of strife. In those lives the will *is* primary. But this romantic prejudice rests on the arbitrary identification of the preferences of German writers and artists in

the eighteenth and nineteenth centuries with lives worth living. It is to Nietzsche credit that he rejects the absolutism of principles, but he has not left behind the absolutistic frame of mind: instead of being dogmatic about principles, he is dogmatic about motives and about the ends that he thinks are
worth pursuing.

VII

It follows from Kant's identification of practical reason and morality that
if the pursuit of nonmoral ideals of excellence conflicts with morality, then
reason requires that morality should prevail. Nietzsche's reaction is to accept
Kant's understanding of practical reason and morality but reject them as
guides to good lives. The pluralistic reaction is to reject Kant's understanding of practical reason and morality but accept them as guides to good lives,
provided they are rightly understood. Their right understanding must allow
that many moral requirements are not universal, impartial, and impersonal
and that many requirements of practical reason are not moral. There are
moral requirements that vary with societies and individuals, and there are requirements of practical reason that concern the pursuit of nonmoral ideals
of excellence. The right understanding, therefore, rejects two of Kant's basic assumptions: that the requirements of practical reason and morality are
universal, impartial, and impersonal, and that their requirements are identical. It must be emphasized that this pluralistic understanding allows that
some requirements of practical reason and morality may be universal, impartial, and impersonal, and that *some* of their requirements may be identical. It
is only the absolutist claim that is rejected by the pluralistic approach.

The pluralistic approach is similarly circumspect about Nietzsche's insistence on the central importance of the pursuit of nonmoral ideals of excellence in lives that are meaningful, free, satisfying, and thus good. Good lives
certainly involve their pursuit, and there certainly is a plurality of such ideals,
but their pursuit must be reasonable, and morality often aids rather than hin-
ders their pursuit. The aim of the pluralistic approach to the art of life may
be expressed, therefore, as that of making room for a plurality of nonmoral
ideals of excellence in practical reason and morality.

This approach, of course, raises the question of how to resolve conflicts
between morality and ideals of excellence. If the simple and general answers
of both Kant and Nietzsche, namely, that one should always override the
other, are rejected, then what is the answer? The pluralistic approach provides an answer, but it is neither simple nor general. There is a reasonable
resolution of these conflicts, but what it is depends on how important the

conflicting moral requirements and ideals of excellence are to the goodness of a particular agent's life. In order to explain this answer, it is necessary to distinguish between three levels on which such conflicts may occur: the universal, the social, and the individual.

The universal level includes the satisfaction of basic physiological, psychological, and social needs that all normal human beings normally have simply because they are human: the need for nutrition and rest, some pleasure and appreciation in one's life, security and order, and so forth. All societies must have and enforce rules that aid the satisfaction of basic human needs. These rules protect the minimum requirements of all good lives; they are the basic moral rules. They are, therefore, universal because human beings are alike in having these needs, benefiting from their satisfaction, and being harmed by their prolonged frustration. If these rules are systematically violated in a society, then it is on the way toward disintegration because it loses the allegiance of the people who are prevented from making good lives for themselves.

The social level is characterized by two kinds of rules. One is concerned with the application of the universal rules. For instance, all societies must protect the lives of the people living in them, so they must all have a rule prohibiting murder. But this prohibition leaves open whether murder can ever be justified and how far its prohibition extends. Does it end at the borders or does it include outsiders? How inclusive is its prohibition in the society itself? What is the status of suicide, abortion, capital punishment, war, euthanasia, infanticide, revenge, feuds, and other forms of killing? What is recognized as a mitigation or an excuse for murder? These are difficult questions that all societies must answer, and not just in the case of murder but in the application of the whole range of universal rules that concern the satisfaction of basic needs. Different societies, of course, may answer them perfectly reasonably but differently, as history and anthropology testify.

Another kind of social rule is concerned with the protection of some possibilities whose realization would contribute to good lives. These possibilities go beyond the minimum requirements in respect to which good lives are alike. That there be such possibilities is necessary for good lives, but there are great variations both within and among societies in what they are. Ideals of excellence are among these possibilities, but there are others: desirable occupations, accepted modes of intimacy, recognized private pastimes, ways of participating in political affairs, and conventional forms of competition, love affairs, social protest, child rearing, paying respect, and so forth.

Societies, then, must have social rules that protect the local interpretations of universally required rules, as well as the locally recognized possibilities that good lives may aim to realize. These rules are general but not universal.

They apply to everyone, but only within a particular society. Outsiders living in their own societies are not blamed for having different interpretations and valuing different possibilities. The violation of such social rules is still prohibited, but less strongly than the violation of universal rules. For the universal rules protect conditions necessary for good lives, whereas the social rules protect only interpretations and possibilities to which recognized alternatives exist.

The individual level is the context in which people are engaged in trying to make a good life for themselves. They pursue various ideals of excellence, understood broadly enough to include both those favored by romantics and those that are prudential or aesthetic without Promethean strife. One task that individuals have in this context is to try to coordinate their pursuit of ideals of excellence with the pursuits of others. They want minimal interference with their own pursuits and maximum protection of the conditions on which their pursuits depend. They have good reasons, therefore, to adopt ideals of excellence that are likely to avoid interference and secure protection. One of the purposes of universal and social moral rules is to coordinate the pursuits of individuals. Individuals have good reasons, therefore, to conform to moral rules because they aid rather than hinder their pursuits. Thus individuals will also have rules that regulate their own pursuits by adjusting their ideals of excellence to the universal and social rules. These individual rules, of course, vary from person to person, since the kind of adjustment that they call for depends on what forms the universal and social rules take and on what the agents' ideals of excellence.

The justification of the rules on all three levels is that they create the conditions in which individuals can pursue their ideals of excellence and thus make good lives for themselves. The ideal case is when this justification holds. In real life, however, the ideal case rarely holds because public and private reasons often diverge. Universal, social, and individual moral rules frequently conflict with ideals of excellence. These conflicts raise for individuals the question of how they should live. If individuals reflect on such conflicts in the moral mode, they will resolve them one way; if they reflect on them in the aesthetic mode, they will resolve them in another. But since both modes embody considerations that they have good reasons to value, whichever resolution they opt for, they will lose something that their conceptions of a good life require. The art of life is to resolve such conflicts in nonideal cases in a way that minimizes the unavoidable loss.

The essential claim of the pluralistic approach to the art of life is that these conflicts have a reasonable resolution, but what it is depends on the details of the conflicting public and private reasons. Their details vary, and so, therefore, reasonable resolutions vary from case to case. These variations, however, do not exclude a general approach to the reasonable resolution of these conflicts. To begin with, it needs to be borne in mind, contra Kant, that unlike theoretical reason, practical reason is always reason for particular agents to act in particular way in particular circumstances.

There are two types of practical reason that could guide actions in this particular manner: private and public. Private reasons lead agents to perform an action because it makes their particular lives better. Public reasons lead agents to perform an action because it strengthens the particular conditions in which all agents in a particular society could live good lives. Private reasons, of course, may include the agents' concern with good lives for others, because reasonable ideals of excellence are not exclusively self-centered. Similarly, public reasons take into account good lives for the agents because the agents are among those who benefit from strengthening the conditions that make good lives possible for everyone in that context. By and large, public reasons are endorsed by the moral and private reasons by the aesthetic mode of reflection.

As we have seen, in the ideal case public and private reasons coincide because the conditions of good lives that are supported by public reasons are also conditions of good lives that their agents have private reason to want. And among the conditions that agents have private reasons to want are those that are endorsed by public reasons that make good lives possible for them. In nonideal situations, public and private reasons conflict. Their conflict may be described from the point of view of public reasons as being caused by ideals of excellence that violate reasonable conditions of all good lives. They may also be described from the point of view of private reasons as being caused by unreasonable conditions that prevent the pursuit of reasonable ideals of excellence. However described, these are the conflicts that concern us. The pluralistic approach depends on the recognition that their resolutions take different forms depending on whether the conflicts occur on the universal, social, or individual levels.

On the universal level, the question is whether the universal rules that public reason endorses do indeed protect the conditions of all good lives, regardless of what form they may take. This is a plain factual question that has a factual answer. The question is whether the satisfaction of some particular physiological, psychological, or social need is basic to good lives. People in a society may believe that it is, and be mistaken; or they may believe that it is not, and be mistaken about that. If the conflict between private and public reasons occurs because agents are correct in thinking that the public reasons are mistaken in these ways, then the conflict should be resolved in favor of private reasons. In all other cases, however, public reasons ought to prevail against private ones on the universal level. For the conditions public reasons protect are also the conditions of the good lives of the agents whose private reasons lead them to oppose the conditions, consequently their opposition cannot be reasonable, since they want to live good lives. If the universal rules they oppose do really protect the conditions of all good lives, then their private reasons for opposing them must be mistaken.

On the social level, the question is whether it is right to exclude ideals of excellence when these conflict with the social rules that govern both the application of the universal rules in a particular society and the possibilities of good lives beyond the satisfaction of basic needs. These excluded ideals of excellence conform to the universal rules but conflict with some of the social rules. The public reason in favor of these social rules is that the universal rules must be interpreted in one way or another and some possibilities of good lives must be provided beyond the satisfaction of basic needs, and the social rules embody conventional ways in which a particular society has provided these necessities. The private reason for opposing these social rules is that they exclude ideals of excellence simply because they are unconventional, and that is a poor reason for interfering with people's pursuit of them.

The reasonable resolution of the conflict on the social level depends on whether the conventions that prevail in a society do indeed offer justifiable interpretations of the universal rules and a sufficient variety of possibilities among which people may choose to make some their own. The mere fact that there are interpretations and possibilities other than conventional ones is not a sufficient reason for opposing the conventional ones. A sufficient reason would be that these other interpretations and possibilities do not interfere with ideals of excellence that are already recognized on the social level and that they make possible hitherto unrecognized ideals of excellence that some people in the society wish to pursue. Since both public and private reasons aim to secure the conditions of good lives, if unconventional ideals of excellence are opposed by public reason on the ground that they do interfere with these conditions, then the burden of proof rests on advocates of public reason. They need to make a case justifying the interference. If the case is made, private reason ought to give way. If the case is not made, private reason ought to prevail. Making and contesting such cases is, of course, difficult. But the difficulty results from the uncertainties of the details of particular cases, not from doubts about what would count, on the social level, for and against public and private reasons.

On the individual level, the question is whether there could be public reasons for excluding ideals of excellence that conform to the universal and social rules and that individuals have private reasons to pursue. Here the presumption is overwhelmingly in favor of private reasons and against public ones. For if an ideal of excellence does not interfere with the satisfaction of basic needs, if it conforms to the local interpretations of universal rules, and if it does not endanger the pursuit of conventionally recognized ideals of excellence, then it is difficult to see what public reason there could be against pursuing it.

Ideals of excellence may be imprudent because they carry great risks for those who pursue them. Or they may be aesthetically displeasing because they violate the sense of decorum, style, beauty, or hygiene of others. Or they may be morally condemned, from the point of view of some other ideal of excellence, for violating moral rules other than the universal and social ones, such as those of religious, ethnic, or aristocratic codes. But the cost, if there is one, of imprudence, bad taste, and moral failure will be borne by the agents who pursue the ideals of excellence that are open to such objections. They have private reasons to run these risks, and, for reasons Mill gives in *On Liberty*, it is better to let them act on their private reasons, even if they seem weak, than to interfere to save them from their own folly, if it is that. On the individual level, therefore, if private and public reasons conflict, the presumption is in favor of resolving the conflicts by letting private reasons prevail. The presumption can be defeated, but only by adducing public reasons to show why an ideal of excellence that conforms to universal and social rules ought nevertheless to be excluded.

This pluralistic approach to the art of life resolves the philosophical problem resulting from the conflict between the public reasons that follow from the moral mode of reflection and the private ones that follow from the aesthetic mode by distinguishing between three levels on which the conflict may occur. On the universal level, the presumption is in favor of morality and public reasons. On the individual level, the presumption is in favor of ideals of excellence and private reasons. On the social level, there is no clear presumption in either direction because everything depends on the adequacy of the local interpretations of universal rules and on the richness of available possibilities. Which way the presumption falls depends on the details, and these vary from context to context. On all three levels, however, the resolution of the conflict is particular, not general. For the resolutions always depend both on private reasons derived from a variety of ideals of excellence and on public reasons derived from social rules that differ, change, and undergo constant revision in particular contexts.

It must be acknowledged, however, that this approach to resolving the conflicts may not succeed in all cases because there may be people whose commitments to their ideals of excellence are so strong as to give them private reasons that defeat any public reason that may conflict with them. Devout religious believers, uncompromising revolutionaries, dedicated artists, and others may just want to pursue their ideals even if they violate universal and social rules. Such people are not irrational because they act on private reasons; they are aware of the public reasons they reject; so they know what they are doing and why. They are not indifferent to the moral considerations that the universal and social rules embody, but they are sincerely convinced that their private reasons are weightier than the public reasons. If, however, these people are reasonable, they realize that those who do not share their ideals of excellence do not think as they do about the respective weights of public and those particular private reasons. These other people have excellent public reasons to prohibit the violations of universal and social rules by those who pursue ideals of excellence they themselves do not share. Both sides, therefore, will persist in their incompatible rankings of public versus private reasons.

According to the pluralistic approach, when such conflicts occur, defenders of public reason have good reasons to prohibit the pursuit of ideals of excellence that violate universal and social rules. And those who are committed to their pursuit must take this into account as part of what their commitments entail. If they are reasonable, they know that their commitments make them liable to moral sanctions and to its consequences. They cannot, therefore, reasonably protest if these consequences catch up with them. Such people may be described as conscientious objectors to morality who are willing to pay the price of their commitments.

It is in everybody's interest in a society that conflicts of this kind be avoided. In general it is better not to have people who pursue ideals of excellence that interfere with the pursuit of other ideals of excellence. And it is better for individuals not to pursue ideals of excellence that put agents at odds with the society in which they live. Better or not, however, such conflicts may occur. The pluralistic approach is to recognize them, allow them to occur, and let the contest between defenders of public and private reasons decide the case. It must be emphasized, however, that this contest is not between morality and ideals of excellence but between, on the one hand, universal and social rules that protect the conditions in which ideals of excellence can be pursued and, on the other, ideals of excellence that violate these rules.

It will perhaps be apparent by now how the pluralistic approach can accommodate some of the important concerns of both Kant and Nietzsche. Kant is right: the art of life is a moral art; universal, impartial, and impersonal rules do have an important place in it; and practical reason is the appropriate guide to participation in it. But Kant is also wrong: the art of life is not only a moral art but also a prudential and an aesthetic one; the place of universal, impartial, and impersonal rules is on the universal level, but there are also rules on the social and individual levels, which are particular; and practical reason is a guide to action on all three levels, but many of its requirements are particular, not universal or general, and its requirements, as expressed by private reasons deriving from ideals of excellence, may conflict with its requirements, as expressed by public reasons deriving from morality. Kant's approach to the art of life is thus most at home on the universal level and least on the individual level.

The opposite is true of Nietzsche's approach: it is most at home on the individual level and least on the universal one. The art of life is essentially concerned with the pursuit of ideals of excellence; moral rules may hinder their pursuit; living good lives often requires the rejection of the universal, impartial, and impersonal rules of the Kantian conception of morality and practical reason. Nevertheless, the pursuit of ideals of excellence should be constrained by morality and practical reason because they protect the conditions that make their pursuit possible; the art of life is not just an aesthetic art but also a moral and a prudential one; and the rejection of Kant's requirement that the rules of morality and practical reason must be universal, impartial, and impersonal is not the rejection of morality and practical reason because there are many moral rules and practical reasons that are particular and none the worse for that.

VIII

In closing, it needs to be made clear how the dispute about the art of life illustrates the pattern of philosophical arguments and the pluralistic approach to resolving them that is one central topic of this book. To begin with, the problem originates in everyday life because it is in that context that people have to answer the practical question of what they can do to make their lives meaningful, free, and satisfying. The resources of everyday life, however, are insufficient because the answers they afford are conflicting. People normally feel the force of moral constraints that hold in their context and they are attracted by their ideals of excellence, but they are moved by them in incompatible directions. This forces them to reflect. If they reflect in the moral mode, they are led to subordinate their ideals of excellence to moral constraints. If they reflect in the aesthetic mode, they arrive at the opposite conclusion. Each mode of reflection suggests the inadequacy of the other, for each rightly recognizes that the other underestimates the significance of its own concerns. Kant's absolutist moral reflection has no convincing answer to the question of why reasonable people would constrain the pursuits that make their lives meaningful, free, and satisfying by adhering to universal, impartial, and impersonal moral rules. Nietzsche's relativist aesthetic reflection has no convincing answer to the question of why reasonable people would cooperate to provide the conditions others need for their pursuits of ideals of excellence if these pursuits interfere with their own pursuits.

Moral reflection inflates the significance of moral constraints. Aesthetic reflection inflates the significance of ideals of excellence. Each struggles to accommodate the other, but in the last analysis each must remain committed to the general answer that in the inevitable conflicts its own favored values should always prevail over the values favored by the other. If either did otherwise, it would be inconsistent.

The pluralistic approach resolves this conflict by rejecting the assumption common to both modes of reflection that a reasonable resolution must be general. It is true that when moral constraints and ideals of excellence conflict, then one must prevail over the other. But it is not true that the one that reasonably prevails in a particular context is the one that should always prevail in all contexts. The question of which one should prevail is answered differently on each of the three levels, and, within each level, it may be answered differently in different societies, depending on the identity both of the social and individual rules and of the ideals of excellence. There will always be a reasonable answer to the question of what the optimal balance is, but it will not always be the same.

The pluralistic approach recognizes that such conflicts can only be resolved, not dissolved, for moral constraints and ideals of excellence exist in a state of tension. People want to live meaningful, free, and satisfying lives, but they need the cooperation of others, which can be secured only if they accept moral constraints on what they do to make their lives meaningful, free, and satisfying. The key is to have as few moral constraints and as much meaning, freedom, and satisfaction as possible. What that turns out to be, however, varies. In each context moral constraints and ideals of excellence must be balanced against each other, and in each context the reasonable balance is likely to be different. The art of life, according to the pluralistic approach, is to find the reasonable balance in one's own context. But, as the epigraph to this chapter says, "in that art, since no fixed and comprehensive rule can be laid down for it, we shall doubtless never acquire perfection."

9

The Nature of Human Self-Understanding

I can see no evidence to suggest that human life is not something self-contained. There are properly many patterns and purposes within life, but there is no general and as it were externally guaranteed pattern or purpose of the kind for which philosophers and theologians used to search. We are what we seem to be, transient mortal creatures subject to necessity and chance. This is to say that there is, in my view, no God in the traditional sense of the term. . . . Equally, the various metaphysical substitutes of God—Reason, Science, History—are false deities. Our destiny can be examined but it cannot be justified. . . . We are simply here. And if there is any kind of sense or unity in human life, and the dream of this does not cease to haunt us, it is of some other kind and must be sought within human experience.

IRIS MURDOCH, "The Sovereignty of Good over Other Concepts"

I

The search for human self-understanding is the search for the right way to understand the human situation in the world. If we understand it, we can cope with the disruptions of everyday life better. We can form a more realistic conception of our possibilities and limits, adopt and pursue projects more reasonably, and have a better chance of succeeding at them. The attempt at human self-understanding, however, should not be conceived in terms of a simple distinction between human beings as subjects who aim at understanding and the world constituted of the forces that we aim to understand. Human beings are part of the world, and the forces to which we are subject are often human forces, for instance, those that operate in politics, economics, morality, medicine, and the law. We are thus not merely passive subjects but often active agents of the forces that we aim to understand. Understanding them, therefore, is not just understanding what there is in the world external to us, but also forces that are internal to us. The beliefs that constitute our understanding may be true or false, and we need them to be true if we are to achieve our purposes. Consequently, we need standards of criticism and justification for evaluating them. But these standards are themselves fallible and should be held open to criticism and justification. We must, therefore, continually evaluate both our standards in the light of our purposes and our purposes in the light of the beliefs that our standards entitle us to regard as true. The attempt to understand the forces to which we are subject, thus, must be directed both inward, toward the evaluation of our beliefs, standards, and purposes, and outward, toward the world external to us. We need to know what forms these two kinds of understanding should take and how they are connected. Two influential modes of reflection, however, suggest incompatible answers to these questions, and they make it unclear how we should understand ourselves and our situation in the world. This gives rise to the philosophical problem that is the subject of the present chapter.

II

One of these answers is suggested by the scientific mode of reflection: what needs to be understood are the laws of nature. This should be the aim of our internal understanding of ourselves, of our beliefs, standards, and purposes, and of our external understanding of everything else. The disruptions of everyday life in the forms of chance, accidents, good and bad fortune, unpredictable occurrences, and so forth are merely the epiphenomena of our failure to understand the laws of nature that govern these events. They betoken our ignorance, not any haphazardness in the scheme of things. Nothing is unpredictable; what stands in the way is only our inability to predict it.

The general strategy of the scientific mode of reflection is to seek to understand the world and ourselves in it from the point of view of the world. The understanding, therefore, is external to us. It acknowledges that there are human beliefs, standards, and purposes and that it is human beings who seek the understanding, but it regards us and our beliefs, standards, and purposes, as natural events to be understood, if at all, in the same way as all other natural events. That it is *we* who are trying to understand and that *we* are guided by our beliefs, standards, and purposes is only incidentally connected with the content of the understanding that we seek. Scientific reflection, therefore, treats our internal understanding of what we are about as just another natural event to be understood externally. It can readily acknowledge that our internal understanding of ourselves matters to us, but it denies that how we understand ourselves has any bearing on what external understanding reveals.

No one can reasonably doubt the power and coherence of the scientific mode of reflection. If doubts about it nevertheless linger, they can be laid to rest by the undeniable benefits that the various sciences have provided. Chief among which benefits is the greatly increased control we have over the forces that affect human lives. It is one thing, however, to acknowledge the importance of the understanding that scientific reflection yields, but quite another to accept it as the only legitimate mode of reflection. The historical mode of reflection is a legitimate alternative. In trying to understand historical reflection, it must be borne in mind that just as scientific reflection is not reflection *in* the various sciences, but reflection *about* the cumulative implications of the general outlook that the various sciences taken together suggest, so historical reflection is to be distinguished from the reflections of historians on the segments of history that interest them. Historical reflection is reflection *about* the cumulative implications of the general outlook that the various historical writings suggest. It is reflection on what human history suggests about the human prospect in general.

It has often been supposed in the past that the aim of historical reflection is to discern a pattern in human history. The enactment of divine providence, the self-realization of the Absolute, the spread of civilization, the interplay between challenge and response, the progress toward a classless society or toward the greatest happiness of the greatest number have been some of the proposed patterns. It is safe to say, however, that this way of conceiving historical reflection has been discredited by the works of historians themselves, who have shown again and again that the past cannot be made to fit into the oddly shaped Procrustean beds constructed on the basis these speculations.

Historical reflection, therefore, is *not* an alternative to scientific reflection in the sense that it offers a set of historical laws in place of the laws of nature that scientific reflection favors. The alternative is to understand human history internally, from the human point of view, rather than externally, from the point of view of the world in which human beings and prospects have no privileged position. Historical reflection, therefore, aims at understanding sub specie humanitatis, whereas scientific reflection aims at understanding sub specie aeternitatis. As we shall shortly see, these are not merely alternative but incompatible modes of reflection, and that is why they lead to the philosophical problem that is the topic of this chapter.

Historical reflection can and should accept all that the various sciences discover about the laws of nature and their effects on human beings. But that is not where its interest lies. Its interest is in how we conceive of ourselves, in our beliefs, standards, and purposes, and in how they affect our actions. What matters from its point of view is not whether the beliefs, standards, and purposes that guide us are reasonable, but the fact that, reasonable or not, they are what guide us, and that understanding our actions requires understanding our intentions behind them. The beliefs may be false, the standards may be misguided, and the purposes may be misconceived, but it is to them that we must look if we wish to understand why people act as they do.

Historical reflection permits us to conclude in some cases that human actions were the executions of human intentions, and this is taken to support the claim that the extent to which this was so was the extent to which the agents were in control of their actions. They were, then, not controlled by forces external to them, for they were the authors of their deeds. It is, of course, true that the beliefs, standards, and purposes in the background may themselves have been formed by external forces over which the agents had no control. It is also true, however, that they may not have been so formed. External forces may continue to dominate agents through the intentions they cause them to have, but whether this is true can be settled only by further historical investigation. The agents may have been conditioned, indoctrinated, prejudiced, stupid, ill-informed, or brutalized, and, although their actions executed their intentions, the intentions themselves may have been the unintentional products of adverse conditions. If that is the truth, then they were not in control of their actions.

Historical reflection, however, supports the conclusion that it is possible for people in favorable circumstances to be in control of many of their intentions and actions. There may be legitimate differences of opinion about how frequently circumstances were favorable to this control, but there can be little doubt that many people have critically examined their beliefs, standards, and purposes and successfully acted on those that passed their scrutiny. Critics who doubt this need look no further than at themselves to find reason to believe that this possibility is at least sometimes realized. Historical reflection, therefore, leads to a different conclusion about the possibilities and limits of control than scientific reflection. According to historical reflection, control is made possible by the deliberate cultivation of both a critical frame of mind that tests the authenticity of one's intentions and a practical wisdom that translates authentic intentions into appropriate actions.

From the point of view of scientific reflection, the possibility of control appears to be either obscurantist or shallow. The laws of nature govern all there is and all that happens, including the extent to which some people can sometimes cultivate a critical mentality and practical wisdom. That they can do so under certain conditions is just a further instantiation of the laws of nature, not a way of being exempt from them. The rejoinder from the perspective of historical reflection is to grant that this is how it appears sub specie aeternitatis, but to deny that it accurately reflects what is important sub specie humanitatis. What matters to us is that sometimes we can control our intentions and actions, that to some extent we can shape our lives. Presumably, there is a law of nature in the background whatever happens. What matters, however, is that some laws are favorable to us, whereas others are not.

This conflict between scientific and historical reflection presents a philosophical problem because what is at stake is not the facts but their significance. Historical reflection would be indefensible if it did not acknowledge the laws of nature that the various sciences have discovered. Scientific reflection would be equally indefensible if it denied the historical evidence about the different degrees of control that different historical arrangements have made possible. The problem occurs because historical reflection finds the possibility and degrees of control significant, whereas scientific reflection finds significant the causes of which the possibility and degrees of control are effects. This conflict cannot be resolved by appealing to not-yet-considered facts because the two modes of reflection will attribute conflicting significance to the new facts, just as they have done to the old ones. If the conflict is to be resolved, it must be done by evaluating the attributions of conflicting significance.

III

Having seen the nature of the conflict between the scientific and the historical modes of reflection, we need now to see how their champions attempt to justify their position and criticize that of their opponents. Wilfrid Sellars makes a case for the scientific mode of reflection.[1] He distinguishes between three levels of understanding in the cognitive history of humanity. The first is the mythic one, on which both the natural and the human worlds are understood in terms of agency and purpose. Natural events are personified and seen as the effects of purposive personal agency. The appropriate explanation of all events is thus supposed to be teleological. On the second level, a distinction is drawn between how natural and human events are to be explained. Causal explanation is taken to be appropriate for natural events, whereas teleological explanation is retained for human events. On this level, a dualism is supposed to exist between the natural and the human worlds. The resulting self-understanding of humanity roughly coincides with the commonsense view of the world. Sellars calls this the "manifest image of man" to imply that from its perspective the world and human beings are by and large as they appear to human observers. According to Sellars, we are now in the process of transition from the second to a third level, from the manifest to the scientific image of man. On the third level, the dualism between the natural and the human worlds is abandoned, and the appropriate explanation of all events, both natural and human, is recognized to be causal. The teleological explanation in terms of beliefs, standards, and purposes that is typical of historical reflection is seen, therefore, as superseded by the vastly more powerful causal explanation that characterizes the sciences and provides the means for greatly improved prediction and control.

Sellars recognizes that there is a conflict between the manifest and the scientific images. He thinks that "this difference in level appears as an irreducible discontinuity in the *manifest* image" between the natural and the human worlds, but as "a reducible difference in the *scientific* image."[2] The conflict seems to be irreducible, given the manifest image, because human events are taken to be explainable only teleologically and natural events only causally, whereas the difference seems reducible in the scientific image because on that level teleological explanations are seen as imperfect forms of causal explanations. Sellars, of course, thinks that the scientific image is a great advance over the manifest image. The basic reason he gives for this is that the manifest image yields an understanding only of appearances, whereas the scientific image yields the understanding of reality that is responsible for the appearances being what they are. It is a consequence of Sellars's view that the causal explanations of science are deeper than the teleological explanations of history. When the two kinds of explanation conflict, scientific explanation should take precedence because historical explanation is an inferior form of scientific explanation.

Sellars deepens his view by making clear that the causal explanation that he takes to characterize thinking on the third level is of a particular kind. It is the explanation of perceptible events, both natural and human, in terms of imperceptible entities and processes. The reason why the manifest image is of appearances and the scientific image is of reality is that the perceptible events that constitute the manifest image are reducible to the imperceptible entities and processes that constitute the scientific image. The world is not really composed of the middle-sized objects that human sense organs have grown accustomed to in the course of evolution, but of subatomic particles and forces that are the ultimate constituents of everything that exists. The manifest image serves us well enough for ordinary purposes. If, however, we want deeper understanding and better prediction and control, if we are interested in why the world appears as it does, if we want to cope with the disruptions of everyday life, then we must look past the surface of perceptible events for the imperceptible causes whose effects they are.

In a series of articles, Carl Hempel applies essentially the same view to historical explanation.[3] He argues that all genuine explanations must conform to what has been called "the covering law model." According to this model, the explanation of any event whatsoever consists in showing that the statement referring to the event is the conclusion of a deductive argument whose premises are statements that refer to certain antecedent events, to certain conditions roughly simultaneous with the event to be explained, and to certain empirically testable universal laws of nature. The argument shows that, given the truth of the premises, the conclusion necessarily follows. Or that, given the antecedent events, the surrounding conditions, and the relevant laws, the event to be explained had to occur. The explanation of the event, then, is taken by the covering law model to be a matter of finding the events, conditions, and laws that make its occurrence inevitable.

Hempel presents this model as an ideal. He stresses that actual explanations conform to it only imperfectly because the specification of the relevant events, conditions, and laws is frequently incomplete. The purpose of the explanation may make a complete specification unnecessary and pedantic (for example, why did I pick up the menu in the restaurant?); or there may be practical difficulties in the way of a complete specification (why did the hurricane destroy this house but not the one next to it?); or knowledge of the relevant events, conditions, and laws may be lacking (why do only some people exposed to the same conditions develop cancer?). That we are often content with or settle for incomplete explanations does not, however, call the ideal into question.

Hempel thinks that historical explanations are typically incomplete. "What the explanatory analyses of historical events offer is . . . in most cases not an explanation . . . but something that might be called an *explanation sketch*. Such a sketch consists of a more or less vague indication of the laws and initial conditions considered as relevant, and it needs 'filling out' in order to turn into a full-fledged explanation. The filling out requires further empirical research."[4] If the further research is done, the resulting explanation will conform to the covering law model, and becomes indistinguishable from scientific explanation. If the further research is not done, the explanation "amounts to a pseudo-explanation which may have emotive appeal and evoke vivid pictorial associations, but . . . does not further our theoretical understanding of the phenomena under consideration."[5]

The mode of reflection from which this view follows approaches the human situation in the world from the outside, from the perspective of the world, rather than internally, from the perspective of those who dwell in the world with their vested interests in how life will go for them. Viewed sub specie aeternitatis, our concern with good lives has no more significance than the concern of members of any other natural kind would have for their well-being, if they could have such a concern. Scientific reflection, therefore, suggests a view of humanity that is as impartial, impersonal, and disinterested as the view would be of an omniscient observer who beholds the natural course of events and the fortunes of all the various natural kinds, but remains totally neutral and uninvolved. Scientific reflection thus aims to be resolutely non-anthropocentric. The better it succeeds, the closer it comes to the ideal of omniscience and neutrality that motivates it.

Champions of that ideal, however, hold it not merely as one ideal among many but as the ideal that all reasonable inquirers will aim at insofar as they seek understanding. They take the ideal to define what rationality consists in, how truth is best pursued, and they take scientific explanation to be the model to which all other kinds of explanation must conform if they aim at rationality and truth. This absolutist claim has provoked an avalanche of critical responses.[6]

IV

These critical responses represent a variety of philosophical orientations.[7] They all agree in rejecting the absolutist claim on behalf of scientific explanation, in claiming autonomy for historical explanation, and in recognizing the importance of understanding human events internally, sub specie humanitatis. William Dray may be taken to speak for all of them in the following passage: "When a historian sets out to explain a historical action, his problem is usually that he does not know what reason the agent had for doing it. To achieve understanding, what he seeks is information about what the agent believed to be the facts of his situation, including the likely results of taking various courses of action considered open to him, and what he wanted to accomplish: his purposes, goals, or motives. Understanding is achieved when the historian can see the reasonableness of a man's doing what the agent did, given the beliefs and purposes referred to; his action can then be explained as having been an 'appropriate' one. The point I want to emphasize is that what is brought out by such considerations is a conceptual connection between understanding a man's action and discovering its rationale."[8]

The relevance of this conception of historical explanation to the covering law model is that an explanation that conforms to this model is neither necessary nor sufficient for historical explanation thus conceived. It is not necessary because it is not the aim of historical explanation to establish that, given specifiable antecedent events, surrounding conditions, and a law of nature, agents will always do what the agent on the spot did. The aim of historical explanation is to make it understandable why *that* agent performed *that* action. This aim is achieved by finding the agent's reasons for performing the action. It is irrelevant to the achievement of this aim whether or not there is a law that the action instantiates.

Nor is an explanation that conforms to the covering law model sufficient for this conception of historical explanation, because the establishment of a lawful connection between the agent and the action is insufficient to explain why the agent found it reasonable to perform that action. The agent's reason for performing the action may be, and usually is, quite different from the law, if there is one, that governs the agent's action. This becomes obvious if it is recognized that the law may not have been discovered at the time of the action, or, if discovered, the agent may have been ignorant of it, and yet the agent may have had perfectly good reasons for performing the action.

That conformity to the covering law model is neither necessary nor sufficient for historical explanation does not, of course, mean that explanations of human action that do conform to that model could not be given. There may, or may not, be excellent scientific explanations of human actions. The point about historical explanations is that they are different from and irreducible to scientific explanations. This is not because there are no such laws as the scientific explanation of human action requires; whether there are such laws is a question which defenders of the irreducibility of historical explanation are not obliged to answer. The reason why historical explanation is irreducible is that it seeks a kind of understanding that is different from the kind that scientific explanation seeks. Dray puts the point with admirable clarity: "What drives to the study of history, as much as anything else, is . . . an interest is discovering and imaginatively reconstructing the life of people at other times and places. To discover and understand their life, we need to be able to do more than regularize, predict, and retrodict their actions; we need to apply to those actions the categories and concepts of *practice;* we need to take a view of them . . . *from the inside*. Even if . . . we accept the possibility and usefulness of covering law explanations for some purposes, we may still share the desire to extend such understanding and evaluation of human life *from the standpoint of agency*."[9]

To pass from historical explanation to historical reflection, two qualifications need to be added. The first concerns the motivation for seeking historical explanation. It may be the love of truth, but human motivation is rarely so simple and pure. We often want to understand and evaluate human lives by imaginatively reconstructing the beliefs, standards, and purposes of people at other times and places because of the light they shed on our lives and on our beliefs, standards, and purposes. We are often interested in them because we want to compare how they tried to cope with their circumstances to how we try to cope with ours. We often view other lives as experiments in living from which we may learn, whether by adapting them to our context (if they are successful), by avoiding their mistakes (if they are not), or, as is most likely, by sorting out the good and bad in them in order to improve our own experiments.

Such comparisons, of course, call for reflection on how others have attempted to control their lives, how they coped with their circumstances, and how successful they were in realizing their hopes. When we reflect in this manner, we are interested in *them*, but we are interested in *ourselves* too and in what we can learn from them. This interest gives historical reflection a practical point, in addition to the theoretical point that it undoubtedly also has. Historical reflection helps us to cope with the disruptions of our everyday life. When Dray and others speak about understanding others in terms of "practice," "from the inside," and "from the standpoint of agency," it is this possibility that is in the background.

This practical aspect of historical reflection is one of the reasons why historical and scientific reflections are incompatible. The aim of scientific reflection is understanding sub specie aeternitatis, to which the consideration of human interests is not only irrelevant but a serious handicap, for it undermines the impartiality, impersonality, and disinterestedness that science seeks. The aim of historical reflection, however, is understanding sub specie humanitatis, to which the consideration of human interests is central. The deep objection that defenders of the autonomy of historical reflection have to the absolutist claim that all genuine explanations must conform to the covering law model is that explanations that do that are committed to ignoring human interests, and they treat human beings as objects to be understood rather than as agents in whose good lives we, including champions of the covering law model, have a vested interest. The objection is not to scientific explanation, whose legitimacy and importance are unquestionable, but to the absolutist claim that leads scientific reflection to denigrate historical explanation either as an inferior mode of scientific explanation, or as a pseudo-explanation.

A second qualification of this account of the irreducibility of historical explanation emphasizes its social aspect.[10] The agents whose actions are to be explained are usually of interest because they have influenced in some manner the fate of their society. They were rulers, commanders, ambassadors, gray eminences, revolutionaries, judges, explorers, scientists, poets, charismatic figures, heretics, and so forth. They interest us because they have left their marks on the course of events. Understanding their actions, therefore, is not merely a matter of understanding why they did what they did, but also of understanding the social and political institutions and arrangements that their actions represented or against which they were directed.

Furthermore, the beliefs, standards, and purposes in terms of which actions are explained are rarely the unique possessions of individual agents. They are usually derived, by way of education, indoctrination, habituation, imitation, and so forth, from the social context in which the individuals live. But they are not derived piecemeal for particular purposes; they are parts of a system of beliefs, standards, and purposes that jointly form an overall outlook. The constituent parts of this outlook are connected in countless ways with each other. They form a mutually reinforcing whole whose parts are understandable only by understanding their place in the overall outlook, which may be identified as an ideology, a world-view, the spirit of an age, a mentality, a philosophy, a frame of mind, and so forth. Call it what we may, the point is that understanding the beliefs, standards, and purposes of individuals depends on understanding this outlook in the background. That, however, requires the understanding to have a social aspect. This remains true even when the beliefs, standards, and purposes of the individual whose action is to be explained are contrary to the prevailing outlook. For understanding the significance of an agent's dissent requires understanding what it is from which the agent dissents.

Lastly, actions are only exceptionally discrete events like a sudden whim, a flash of insight, or an act of motiveless malignity. Usually actions are responses to the actions of others. There are provocations, treaties, favors, injustices, threats, overtures, lies, and promises in the background. There are also familial, ethnic, national, racial, and religious ties or conflicts. Actions usually derive part of their significance from their nexus with a long chain of actions that extends far into the past, often beyond the life of the agent. Actions, therefore, are social also in the sense that understanding them requires understanding the actions to which they are responses.

The social aspect of historical explanation leads to the recognition of how difficult it would be to apply the covering law model to historical explanation. The model requires the specification of both the relevant law and the antecedent events and surrounding conditions in conjunction with which the law would explain a particular action. So long as the antecedent events and surrounding conditions are taken to be the agent's beliefs, standards, and purposes, specifying them does not seem to be particularly difficult. But if the specification includes, as it should, the social and political arrangements and the prevailing outlook in the background, as well as the past and present actions of others to whom the agent is responding, then its difficulty will rightly seem to be formidable.

It is at this point that the historian's skill enters. That skill is to identify and select from the multitude of past and present events and conditions just those that would be sufficient to explain why a particular agent performed a particular action. Historians look for events and conditions that were significant for agents, whose influence agents felt, and then propose explanations of the agents' actions. These explanations, however, are not just explanations *of* the agents' reasons for acting, they are also explanations *for* the historians' audience. Historians aim to make intelligible for their contemporaries the considerations that have led agents at different times and places, with different outlooks, living under different political and social arrangements, to act as they did. Historians can assume that some features of the agents' contexts were sufficiently similar to the audience's so as to require little explanation. But it is bound to be otherwise with features that have influenced the agents and differ from the features with which the historians' audience is familiar. Part of the skill of historians is to identify and select the features that require explanation and those that do not. Historical explanations, therefore, need to take into account not just the agent's point of view but also that of the audience, and they must establish a bridge between these two viewpoints. Because these viewpoints continually shift as the context of explanation changes, historical explanations, unlike scientific ones, can be both true and fail as explanations, both interpret the facts accurately and stand in need of reinterpretation.

Historians, of course, often disagree with one another's explanations. But what they disagree about is whether or not the events and conditions that were taken to be significant in an explanation were the truly significant ones from the agent's and the audience's point of view. Scientific explanation has no use for this skill and for this kind of explanation, it is indifferent to the shifting points of view of the agents and the audiences, because it aims to discover the lawful connection between the antecedent events, surrounding conditions, and the agents' action regardless of what the agent, the audience, or the historian regards as significant among those events and conditions. And this, of course, requires successful scientific explanations to specify all of those countless events and conditions that constitute the social aspect of actions. Historical explanations are designed to cope with this difficulty, but it is unclear that scientific explanations can do so. At any rate, no scientific explanation has hitherto done so, whereas numerous historical explanations have.

If historical explanation is irreducible to scientific explanation, if it is an autonomous form of explanation whose aim is to explain the actions of individuals from the inside, in terms of their beliefs, standards, and purposes, if it explains by exhibiting the reasonableness of an action given the intention of the agent and the situation of the audience, then historical reflection has genuine content. It is reflection on the significance of historical explanations for the human prospect. That significance emerges from the many contexts and the many ways in which human agents in the past have tried to control the course of events. The conclusion historical reflection permits us to draw is that the possibility of control depends on the extent to which actions are successful executions of the intentions of their agents. The case for the autonomy and importance of historical reflection is that it proceeds sub specie humanitatis and it addresses this abiding human concern. Scientific reflection, by contrast, proceeds sub specie aeternitatis and it is, therefore, indifferent to this concern.

V

Defenders of the absolutist claim for scientific explanation will not be convinced by this case for the autonomy of historical explanation. One of their predictable responses may be to object to the relativist implications of historical explanation conceived in this manner. Historical explanations aim to explain actions from the point of view of their agents by exhibiting the reasons the agents had for performing their actions. But the agents' reasons may not be the causes of their actions because they may be rationalizations, the result of self-deception, ignorance of themselves, or indoctrination, the symptoms of neurosis, false consciousness, corruption, stupidity, or wishful thinking. The reasons agents suppose themselves to have for their actions may just be stories they tell themselves or to others. The question is whether the stories are true. The only way of discovering that, however, is to find the real causes of their actions and then see whether the stories do justice to them.

The search for the real causes of actions, these critics argue, is of course, the search for scientific explanations that proceed in terms of the imperceptible entities and processes that constitute the scientific image, and from which the perceptible effects that compose the manifest image follow. This search unavoidably goes beyond the question that historical explanation concentrates on, namely, what was the agent's reason for performing the action. If historians aim to tell true stories, then they must rely on scientific explanations that account for perceptible actions in terms of imperceptible causes. If they are not interested in the truth beyond finding out or reconstructing the agents' reasons for their actions, then they must resign themselves to a blatant form of relativism that disqualifies historical explanations from being taken seriously.

Defenders of the autonomy of historical explanation will reply that they aim to tell true stories and that historical explanation is quite adequate for evaluating their truth. Historical explanation aims to exhibit the plausibility of the stories that connect the agents' beliefs, standards, and purposes to their actions by asking whether it is reasonable to suppose that they were what formed the agents' intentions. So the stories the agents construct, or those that may be constructed for them, are not just taken for granted but are tested for reasonableness.

This reply, however, does not escape the dilemma that historical explanation must either become scientific or lose its claim to serious attention through relativism. For historical explanations exhibit the reasonableness of the stories in terms of vague generalizations, commonsense expectations, and supposed correlations that are the currency of the manifest image and which historians and their audience share. If historians are serious about getting at the truth, they must subject to rigorous testing the generalizations, expectations, and correlations that they use to test the reasonableness of the stories they tell. And that, of course, means that they must subject them to scientific testing. Otherwise, they evaluate questionable appearances by equally questionable appearances.

In short, scientific reflection leads to the conclusion that historical reflection is unreliable because it is confined to the context of the manifest image of man. It lacks the resources and the intention to search for the imperceptible causes of perceptible phenomena. If it remains in that context, it is doomed to a relativism that cannot adequately test its own explanations. If it leaves that context, it can overcome relativism, but only by moving to the context of the scientific image, and thus abandoning historical for scientific explanation.

The reply is to accept the fallibility of any one of the particular generalizations, expectations, and correlations with which the manifest image is replete, to recognize that they should be accepted only if they withstand sustained critical scrutiny, but to deny that there is an alternative to accepting the *system* of beliefs that constitutes the manifest image. The findings of various sciences may falsify particular beliefs of the manifest image, but it is impossible that the scientific image could falsify and replace the system of beliefs of the manifest image *in its totality* because the scientific image presupposes the correctness of that system. The reason for this is that the manifest image is both chronologically and epistemologically prior to the scientific image.

The chronological priority of the manifest image is the result of the fact that when beings like us, with our sensory and motor capacities, with our genetic makeup and the physical conditions of our lives, form an image of the world, it will be the manifest image. To beings like us, the world will manifest itself in that way. This is not to say that the manifest image could not be a totally false picture of the world. It could be, but that is most unlikely, since we have responded to the world throughout human history on the assumption that the picture is true, and we have done well enough. Nor is it to say that the manifest image is anything like a complete picture of the world. The world undoubtedly has aspects inaccessible to our unaided perceptions and commonsense beliefs. These aspects may be closed to the manifest image, but not to the scientific image, which relies on theories, instruments, and calculations that go beyond the capacities of the manifest image. It should also be granted that the scientific image can explain and elaborate what the manifest image merely accepts. The most powerful explanations and elaborations of the perceptible entities and processes of the manifest image are in terms of the imperceptible entities and processes of the scientific image. None of this means, however, that the scientific image falsifies the manifest image in its totality. The explanations, elaborations, and new knowledge that the scientific image provides explain, elaborate, and enlarge the manifest image. These scientific achievements go beyond the manifest image, but they do not replace it.

The epistemological priority of the manifest image explains why the scientific image cannot replace the manifest image. Scientific explanations must rely on and employ the resources of the manifest image at several points. For scientific explanations are explanations designed and tested by human beings who have no alternative to using the resources of the manifest image.

One of these points is observation. Scientific explanations in terms of imperceptible objects derive their data from and are tested by the observation of perceptible objects. The observation is performed by human beings who must begin with sensory observation of the perceptible objects of the manifest image. We can certainly extend the reach of the senses with which we are bound to begin by developing instruments that greatly enlarge our observational capacities. But not even with the help of the most sophisticated instruments can we leave behind the unavoidable human starting point in the manifest image. Another closely related point is the testing of scientific explanations. Scientific explanations must be tested, if their acceptance of rejection is to be reasonable. Testing consists in deriving predictions that can be verified or falsified by observation. Even if, with the aid of mathematics, powerful explanations were constructed that range far beyond the reach of the human senses and the manifest image, we would have reason to accept them only if they could be verified or falsified. And that means that the predictions derived from them must fall within the range of what we could observe given the resources of the manifest image. Although the truth of the scientific explanations that constitute the scientific image does not depend on our senses and the manifest image, our reasons for believing that they are true does ultimately depend on them, for the reasons must count as such for beings who are constituted as we are, with our observational and testing capacities. The scientific image, therefore, presupposes the reliability of the manifest image.

To this defense of the autonomy of historical explanation, defenders of the absolutist aspiration of scientific explanation will reply that the transformation of the manifest into the scientific image is a gradual process. It involves the slow transformation of the prevailing cognitive outlook, and it brings with it a changed way of seeing the world, new expectations, and thus a radical alteration of the background. As the transformation occurs, so we accustom ourselves to understand the world and our place in it on the basis of the best information that the science of the day can provide. Defenders of the autonomy of historical explanation will, then, reply that no matter how slow the transformation is and how astonishing are the achievements of science, the manifest image cannot be replaced by the scientific image because that would require changing the physiological constitution of human beings and their relation to their physical environment. If that could be done, unlikely as it is, it would result in changes so radical as to make the prediction of how the world would appear to us (are these changed beings us?) then impossible. And so the debate goes back and forth. The time has come to step outside of it and reflect on it.

VI

Underlying the debate is a conflict between two modes of reflection regarding how we should understand ourselves and our position in the world. The scientific mode of reflection stresses the importance of understanding the world. The historical mode of reflection stresses the importance of understanding in the achievement of human purposes. Scientific reflection is sub specie aeternitatis. It abstracts from human concerns and offers an external approach to our self-understanding that leads to an impartial, impersonal, and disinterested understanding of ourselves from the outside. Historical reflection is sub specie humanitatis. It is inseparable from its practical concerns. It offers an internal approach to our self-understanding that is centrally concerned with ourselves as agents who try to control their lives.

The facts that matter for either mode of reflection are not denied by the other. What they disagree about is the significance of the facts. The scientific mode of reflection regards as significant that we are natural entities, that we are subject to laws, and that we have no privileged position in the world. The historical mode of reflection regards as significant that we are sometimes able to control our actions, that we can to some extent shape our lives, and that the goodness of our lives depends on our privileging human concerns. Each mode of reflection can accommodate the other as a special case of itself. Scientific reflection interprets historical reflection as an inferior mode of itself; a mode that is vitiated by a relativism unable to evaluate the truth of its own explanations. Historical reflection interprets scientific reflection as one of the several approaches to understanding the world that we have developed in the course of our history, a mode vitiated by an absolutism that fails to recognize the legitimacy of other modes of explanation and is indifferent to good lives for human beings.

The result of this conflict is an impasse about how we should understand ourselves. Both modes have legitimate and important aims. It matters whether we understand the world, and it matters what social and political arrangements have shown themselves conducive to our achievement of greater control over our lives. Both modes are defective, however, as the defenders of each rightly charge the other. This impasse may be summed up thus: in the search for human self-understanding, scientific reflection concentrates on understanding the world at the expense of good human lives, whereas historical reflection concentrates on good human lives at the expense of understanding the world. Each is right in what it stresses and wrong in what it overlooks. The result is the philosophical problem about the right way of understanding ourselves in the world.

The pluralistic approach proposes a way out of the impasse. Its strategy is to recognize the legitimacy of the aims of both the scientific and historical reflection and to avoid the absolutism of the one and the relativism of the other. The pluralistic approach, therefore, is critical of certain aspects of both scientific and historical reflection. But it is crucial that the targets of this criticism are *not* science and history, whose explanations are just fine from the pluralistic point of view. The targets are the conclusions regarding human self-understanding that scientific and historical reflections draw from the rightly valued explanations of science and history. The criticism calls for the revision of both scientific and historical *reflection*, but it leaves science and history just as they are. The dispute between the pluralistic approach and scientific and historical reflection is about the significance of scientific and historical explanations, not about their acceptability.

Let us now approach this dispute by considering a concrete case. The last great battle in the Pacific during the Second World War was in Okinawa. The battle, which was the final stage of the island-hopping strategy of the Allies before the planned invasion of Japan, was exceptionally bloody: it cost over 12,000 American and about ten times as many Japanese lives. The Japanese rejected repeated offers of surrender, and they fought to the death. In the last hours of the battle, when the Japanese defeat was final and the Allies were about to enter the caves where the Japanese headquarters were, all the high-ranking Japanese officers committed suicide by hara-kiri. All that is, but one Colonel Hiromichi Yahara, who escaped, reached Japan, and lived to tell the story of the battle from the Japanese point of view. The present discussion is derived from his remarkable book.[11] It will concentrate on the question, Why did Yahara not commit hara-kiri?

Yahara was a professional soldier. He was trained at the Japanese equivalent of West Point, played an important role in the strategic planning of the war, had a distinguished military record, demonstrated his courage and willingness to die on numerous occasions, was much decorated, and was indeed one of the best officers in the Japanese army. Given the Japanese military code, honor required that Yahara should commit hara-kiri together with his fellow officers. Honor was the highest value of that code, and acting contrary to it was the worst thing that a Japanese officer could do. Yet that is just what Yahara had apparently done. Why? The point of asking this is to bring out the way in which the pluralistic approach to trying to answer it leads to a conception of human self-understanding that differs from that of either scientific or historical reflection. The key to the pluralistic approach is a distinction between three different kinds of possibilities and limits that establish the framework within which human actions are to be understood.

The first of these possibilities and limits are *physical*. They are set by the physical conditions within which agents have to proceed. The limits are defined by the laws of nature, the immediate environment, and the sensory, motor, and physiological capacities of the agents. Actions within these limits are physically possible. It was physically impossible for Yahara to escape by flying, conquer the Allied forces single-handedly, or commit hara-kiri and live. But it was physically possible for him to commit hara-kiri, surrender, desert, escape by boat, or die fighting.

The second of these possibilities and limits are *social*. They are set by the institutions, conventions, and moral, political, aesthetic, and religious arrangements that prevail in the agents' context. They are established by what *could* be a live option, or unthinkable, for typical agents born, raised, and living in that context. The qualification expressed by the *could* is important because the social background is usually much richer and varied in possibilities and limits than what *would* apply to typical agents. The Japanese social background during the Second World War comprised different social possibilities and limits for monks, peasants, geishas, artists, enlisted men, army officers, the emperor, and so forth. For a monk or for a geisha, hara-kiri would not have been a live option, just as, for Yahara, asking for mercy or changing sides would have been unthinkable.

The third kind of possibilities and limits are *psychological*. They depend on the agents' character and personal circumstances, out of which emerge the important beliefs, standards, and purposes that partly constitute their identity. Certain physically and socially possible actions are impossible for some agents because performing them would be a violation of their identity. Not committing hara-kiri was obviously a psychological possibility for Yahara, since he acted on it, but it was probably not for many of his fellow high-ranking officers for whom it was unthinkable, given their characters, circumstances, and identities.

It may then be said that physical possibilities and limits hold universally for all human agents with only a narrow range of variations. Social possibilities and limits hold for agents immersed in the same social context. Psychological possibilities and limits hold only for individual agents. In a primitive setting, where people live close to the subsistence level, these three kinds of possibilities and limits tend to coincide. For survival requires that the society and individuals in it should realize their meager physical possibilities and not waste their energies on refining them. It is, however, otherwise in civilized settings, where societies and individuals have escaped from primitive necessities, enjoy the luxury of choosing among their physical possibilities, and have introduced political, moral, aesthetic, and religious refinements. These refinements at once enlarge and restrict their possibilities, not by denying their physical limits, but by introducing a variety of alternative ways in which physical possibilities may be realized and in which social and psychological limits may put some possibilities beyond the pale.

Understanding the physical, social, and psychological possibilities and limits of agents is a necessary, but not a sufficient, condition for understanding their actions. For the actions are only indirect consequences of their agents' possibilities and limits. What actions are direct consequences of are the agents' *beliefs* about their possibilities and limits. The agents' beliefs mediate between their actual possibilities and limits and their actions. These beliefs can be true or false, reasonable or unreasonable. The possibilities and limits agents believe themselves to have may not be their actual possibilities and limits, and the agents, in taking them to be actual when they are not, may or may not be reasonable. It may be that, given the evidence at their disposal, it is reasonable for them to regard some possibilities and limits as actual even though they are not. Understanding the actions of agents thus requires understanding, first, their actual physical, social, and psychological possibilities and limits; second, the possibilities and limits they believe themselves to have; and third, whether or not they are reasonable in holding their beliefs about their possibilities and limits.

The first two requirements are perhaps clear enough, but the third needs further explanation. Why do agents hold and act on unreasonable beliefs? The explanation may be psychological: they are stupid, stubborn, neurotic, blinded by passion or ideology, self-deceiving, and so forth. Or the explanation may be social: the institutions, conventions, and arrangements in the agents' context interfere with holding reasonable beliefs because they are dogmatic, discourage critical thinking, repress dissent, brutalize numerous people, and so on.

The next point to note is that understanding whether or not the agents are reasonable in holding their beliefs about their possibilities and limits requires understanding not just the beliefs they end up holding and acting on, but also the beliefs they might have held and acted on, but did not. Adequate understanding requires not just understanding which of their possibilities agents accept, but also which of them they reject. Part of understanding their actions is to go beyond understanding their beliefs, standards, and purposes in order to understand the beliefs, standards, and purposes that were rejected possibilities for them.

If we take this pluralistic approach to understanding why Yahara did not commit hara-kiri, the following picture emerges. As a result of his training as an army officer, his expertise in military strategy and tactics, and his thorough knowledge of the terrain in Okinawa, Yahara formed beliefs about his physical possibilities and limits that were in all likelihood reasonable and true. It was clear to him that he could commit hara-kiri or that he could take the risky course of trying to escape in mufti by mingling with the civilian population, commandeering a boat, and making his way to Japan. But these beliefs, of course, are insufficient to make it understandable why he chose escape rather than hara-kiri.

There were also his beliefs about his social possibilities and limits. Among them were beliefs characteristic of Japanese army officers of his time and training. The military code of conduct was his code, and it was quite clear to him that, given that code, the honorable action was hara-kiri, and that action, indeed, was what his fellow officers took. If Yahara had done the same, then his true and reasonable beliefs about his physical and social possibilities and limits would have been sufficient to understand why he had committed hara-kiri. The fact remains, however, that he did not. That shows that his true and reasonable beliefs about his physical and social possibilities and limits are still insufficient for understanding why he escaped. The weight of understanding thus rests on Yahara's beliefs about his psychological possibilities and limits.

In trying to understand those beliefs, it is necessary to distinguish between the question of what his beliefs were and the question of whether his beliefs were true and reasonable. What Yahara's beliefs were may be reconstructed from the story he tells in the book. Yahara believed that it was his duty to escape because he was ordered to do so by his commanding officer. He was to report the outcome of the battle to the Japanese high command in Tokyo. Yahara admits that the order was implied rather than direct, but high-ranking officers rarely gave direct orders to other high-ranking officers. If this belief of Yahara were reasonable and true, then it would explain why he escaped rather than committed hara-kiri. But there are good, although not conclusive, reasons for doubting Yahara's belief.

To begin with, after he had reached Tokyo and reported on the battle, his fellow officers at the Japanese high command doubted that he had received the order that he claimed to have received, and Yahara was disgraced. Then, it is hard to see why it would have been thought important by his commanding officer that Yahara should report the outcome of the battle, since its outcome would have reached the high command long before Yahara could have been supposed to make his way to Tokyo. Moreover, it was clear to everybody that the war was lost, and that Yahara's report would be utterly pointless. But this is not to say that there is reason to doubt Yahara's sincerity, courage, and willingness to die. There is good reason to accept that Yahara really did believe that it was his duty to escape. Part of that reason is Yahara's book, published more than thirty years after the war, long after the Japanese military code had been discredited, when Yahara lived in obscurity, and both he and his supposed disgrace were forgotten. In the book Yahara nevertheless insists that his story is true, even though he, and just about everybody else, had repudiated the military code from which his supposed disgrace followed.

If we understand that Yahara had acted on a sincere but false belief, we are closer to understanding why he did not commit hara-kiri, but we still do not understand it fully, because we do not understand how he came to hold that false belief. If he had not really received an order to escape, why did he believe that he had received it? Here we can only speculate. There are many hints in the book that Yahara had doubts about the war and about the Japanese military code before the battle of Okinawa. He soldiered on as he was supposed to, but he did not do so wholeheartedly. His mind was divided, not evenly perhaps, but divided nevertheless. Part of the reason for this may be that he was exceptional among Japanese officers in speaking English and in having spent a two-year tour of duty in America in the 1920s. Maybe he came to be of a divided mind because he recognized that there were military codes other than his own, and maybe he could see how his own code, with hara-kiri and so forth, would seem from the point of view of that other code. Maybe. But if this speculation has anything to it, it would make it more understandable why Yahara would have been much more likely than his fellow officers to mistakenly regard as an order the aside or the expression of a forlorn wish of his commanding officer that the Japanese stand not be forgotten (there was much saki drunk in the headquarters in Okinawa). What had led him to hold a false belief may have been his half-suppressed doubts about the military code that had brought the horrors of the war upon the Japanese. If this speculation is correct, we can understand both why Yahara did not commit hara-kiri and why his own belief about it was sincere but false. Let us assume that the speculation is correct, and let us see how the pluralistic approach, whose product it is, differs from and is preferable to both scientific and historical reflection on the significance of Yahara's not committing hara-kiri.

VII

The fundamental difference between the pluralistic approach, on the one hand, and scientific and historical reflection, on the other, may be expressed by taking overdue notice of the ambiguity of the phrase "human self-understanding." It can be understood either in a general or in a particular sense. In both senses, it is *self*-understanding because it is we who are trying to understand something about ourselves. In the general sense, human self-understanding involves trying to understand the collective situation of humanity in the world, rather than the situation of any individual. To be sure, this understanding is the result of generalizing from the situations of particular individuals, which involves the recognition of substantial differences in their characters and circumstances. But the aim of general self-understanding is to abstract from individual differences and to understand features of the human situation that are the same for everyone. In the particular sense, human self-understanding involves trying to understand the situations of specific individuals. Particular self-understanding recognizes that in important respects the situations of individuals are alike. But its aim is to reach an understanding of the situations of individuals that includes both general human similarities and particular individual differences. Scientific and historical reflection aim at human self-understanding in the general sense, whereas the pluralistic approach aims at the particular.

According to scientific reflection, human beings are to be understood as one natural kind among others, subject to the laws of nature and explainable by them. Individual differences are seen as the results of differences in antecedent events and surrounding conditions. Scientific reflection, therefore, attributes primary significance to the laws that establish physical possibilities and limits. It regards social and psychological possibilities and limits as variations in the events and conditions in which the laws of nature operate. A metaphor for understanding the human situation, as scientific reflection sees it, is that we are like actors in a play who enact their roles in accordance with a script that has been written for them.

According to historical reflection, human beings are to be understood in terms of the institutions, conventions, and arrangements from which they derive their beliefs, standards, and purposes that make their actions understandable. Human beings are social, and they are to be seen as the products of their societies. Individual differences are largely the results of the different institutions, conventions, and arrangements that exist in different social contexts. Historical reflection, therefore, attributes primary significance to the social context that establishes social possibilities and limits. It regards physical limits as simply the boundaries within which a society must function and the physical possibilities as the repository of the possibilities among which a society tries to realize some. And it regards psychological possibilities and limits as the products of the influences of the various institutions, conventions, and arrangements in which individuals participate. A metaphor for understanding the human situation, as historical reflection sees it, is that we are like spiders sustained by the webs they have spun.

According to the pluralistic approach, human beings are to be understood as individuals who try to make the best of their lives in the context that is partly, but only partly, composed of their physical and social possibilities and limits. The pluralistic approach attributes primary significance to the psychological possibilities and limits that make it understandable why different individuals act differently even though their physical and social limits and possibilities are the same. Individual differences reflect the different ways in which individuals respond to their physical circumstances and to the social influences that surround them. The pluralistic approach acknowledges that physical and social possibilities and limits establish the range of psychological possibilities and limits, but it regards it as the central aim of human self-understanding to understand what individuals make of their possibilities and limits within that range. A metaphor for understanding the human situation, as the pluralistic approach sees it, is that we are like pioneers who carry their earthly goods in their covered wagons, pick their different destinations, and make of them what they can, given the terrain, their goods, their skills, and their good or bad fortune.

Scientific reflection leads to understanding individuals as the *loci* where the laws of nature, antecedent events, and the surrounding conditions bring about certain effects. Historical reflection leads to understanding individuals as *representatives* of the social institutions, conventions and arrangements that have influenced them most strongly. The pluralistic approach leads to understanding individuals as *agents* who have some control over their lives. Scientific and historical reflection are thus not interested in human beings as individual agents; they are interested in them generally, as the subjects through which physical or social forces happen to act. The pluralistic approach is interested in human beings as the particular agents that they are, not just as the loci of physical forces or as the representatives of social forces, but as the particular agents who respond in their particular ways to their physical and social limits and possibilities.

When scientific reflection tries to understand the significance of Yahara not killing himself, it relies on the relevant laws of nature, chief among which are the ones having to do with the information-processing capacities of the human brain, in conjunction with the antecedent events and surrounding conditions of Yahara's action. The laws, events, and conditions jointly explain why they caused a different effect in Yahara's case from that which they caused in the cases of his fellow officers. In all this, Yahara is a mere placeholder. And that is precisely what scientific reflection takes to be the general human significance of Yahara's case: we are all placeholders; we are direct causes that result from many indirect causes that come together in us to produce certain effects, which are our actions. In this mode of reflection, the custom of killing oneself by hara-kiri, Yahara's two-year immersion in an alien society, his growing doubts, and his flagging loyalty to his country and caste all appear in the script in small print. What matters is having yet another striking confirmation of the laws of nature by showing that an apparently anomalous case is the result of variations in the antecedent events and the surrounding conditions.

Historical reflection on the significance of Yahara's case will accept the scientific explanation of his not killing himself. It will deny, however, that scientific reflection correctly interprets its human significance. Yahara had been acted on by many causes, but the human significance of some of them is much greater than that of others. Historical reflection concentrates on the social institutions, conventions, and arrangements that have formed Yahara's beliefs. But it does not concentrate on them in order to find out whether these beliefs were true or reasonable, or whether the social forces that shaped his beliefs were pernicious. Historical reflection locates the significance of Yahara's action in the beliefs that led to it, and it locates the significance of his beliefs in the social background that formed them. The puzzle of why he did not kill himself is resolved by finding the social influences that affected him but not his fellow officers. The significance of Yahara's action for human self-understanding is that we are all to be understood as the products of our societies, and individual differences among us are the effects of different social influences.

The pluralistic approach accepts that it is possible to give a scientific explanation of Yahara's action and that in order to understand his action it is necessary to single out the social forces that historical explanation stresses. But the pluralistic approach denies that scientific and historical reflections are adequate for understanding the human significance of his action. The reasons for this are twofold: the scientific and historical modes of reflection are both deficient, and the pluralistic approach contributes an essential component that its competitors cannot.

Scientific reflection is deficient because of its absolutism. It claims that human self-understanding is the understanding of ourselves as denizens of the natural world whose actions are explainable by natural laws. Nonscientific explanations are bad explanations either because they are inferior attempts at scientific explanation or because they are pseudo-explanations. This claim is false. It is true that we are part of the natural world and that our actions are explainable by natural laws. But it is not true that human self-understanding based only on these truths is adequate.

The explanation of very many human actions in terms of natural laws sheds meager light on human self-understanding. For scientific explanations depend not only on natural laws but also on the antecedent events and surrounding conditions that define the context in which the laws operate. In the case of human actions, these events and conditions are extremely varied, often so much so as to render the context of particular actions unique. This was certainly true of Yahara's not killing himself. Even if we suppose that there is some law in the background that specifies that agents with brain states similar to Yahara's will act in a certain way, the variety of antecedent events and surrounding conditions allows only one agent to be in that brain state, namely, Yahara.

In fact, the job of explanation is done by the specification of events and conditions, and not at all by a law, which, of course, has not been found. To be told that Yahara did not kill himself because his brain was in a certain state is to add very little to our understanding of the human significance of his action. But to be told that familiarity with social possibilities different from his own made it psychologically possible for him to question, however hesitantly, the social possibilities and limits that he had hitherto accepted is to understand something important about how human beings can achieve greater control over their lives. The absolutism of scientific reflection marginalizes precisely those elements of scientific explanation on which human self-understanding depends, namely, antecedent events and surrounding conditions. This being so does not cast doubt on the importance of scientific explanations, but it does call into question the absolutist claim that scientific reflection makes on their behalf.

Historical reflection is deficient because of its relativism. Its claim is that human self-understanding is the understanding of ourselves as social beings whose actions are explainable by our beliefs, standards, and purposes, which are themselves explainable by the social institutions, conventions, and arrangements that have formed them. Historical explanations, therefore, exhibit the reasons agents have for their actions. Historical reflection is relativist because it claims that historical explanations are sufficient for human self-understanding. It assumes that by understanding the agents' social possibilities and limits we understand the significance of their actions. This claim is false.

The claim rests on the mistaken supposition that actions are reasonable if their agents have reasons to perform them. Historical explanations provide these reasons, first, in terms of the beliefs, standards, and purposes of the agents, and, second, in terms of their social backgrounds. This is fine for historical explanations, but it will not do for historical reflection. Human self-understanding is incomplete if it fails to consider whether the reasons agents have for their actions are good reasons. The reasons are not made good by being derived from the agents' social background, for human self-understanding requires an answer to the question of whether the social institutions, conventions, and arrangements that ultimately supply the agents' reasons are themselves reasonable. We do not merely want to know why Yahara did not commit hara-kiri. We want to know also whether committing hara-kiri in the circumstances judged appropriate for it is reasonable. And what we want to know is not whether it is reasonable given the Japanese military code in the Second World War, but whether it is reasonable.

According to historical reflection, what is reasonable for human beings is what counts as reasonable in the social background whose products they are. This is why historical reflection is relativist. And because it is relativist, it lacks the resources to account for the human significance of historical explanations. Surely it matters to human self-understanding whether the institutions, conventions, and arrangements that explain our actions enhance, diminish, or remain indifferent to the goodness of our lives. But whether they are one or the others cannot be determined by additional historical explanations because the same question arises for all historical explanations, if, but only if, they are treated as data for historical reflection on human self-understanding.

Historical reflection on human self-understanding, therefore, faces a dilemma it can neither satisfactorily resolve nor avoid. Either it considers the effects of social influences on the goodness of human lives or it does not. If it does not, it cannot claim even to approximate an adequate approach to human self-understanding. If it does, then it must go beyond its own concern with social possibilities and limits and evaluate their effects on the goodness of human lives. It may do so by calling on the resources of science or by considering the goodness of the lives of individuals who conformed to or have gone against their social background. In either case, it must appeal to considerations that lie beyond its limits.

These deficiencies of scientific and historical reflection provide part of the motivation for the pluralistic approach. Another part is provided by the combination of two constructive considerations that the pluralistic approach regards as crucial, but to which scientific and historical reflection, because of their very nature, cannot do justice. The first is that human self-understanding must be particular, not general. The second is that human self-understanding must be evaluative, and its evaluation must proceed from the point of view of the goodness of the lives of individual human beings.

The claim that human self-understanding must be particular does not mean that it has no general aspects. There certainly are general truths the understanding of which is necessary for human self-understanding. Nor can there be any doubt that scientific and historical explanations are important sources of these general truths. We are subject to the laws of nature and social influences do affect our actions, so understanding them is part of understanding ourselves. But it is only a part, and if that were all we had, we would not understand ourselves. It is also a necessary part of human self-understanding that our physical and social possibilities and limits do not exhaust our possibilities and limits. We can often take account of our physical and social possibilities and limits, think about them, try to realize some of our possibilities and ignore others, test our limits, approve or disapprove of some. We can, that is to say, often have some control over our lives. This possibility of control is a highly significant fact about us, and no adequate attempt at human self-understanding can fail to take account of it.

Taking account of it, however, requires the consideration of individual agents, for the account is necessarily an attempt to answer the question of how individual agents have responded to the physical and social conditions of their lives. The account must be of why *Yahara* did not commit hara-kiri, not of how people in certain brain states will act, nor of how Japanese officers will act. Human self-understanding is understanding the different ways in which individuals could respond and the reasons why specific individuals do respond in particular ways. The possibility of self-understanding in this sense is of prime significance because it shows that we are not completely at the mercy of our physical and social conditions that undoubtedly influence how we live. If scientific and historical reflection fail to recognize this, they must be held to be seriously incomplete. If they do recognize it, each must hold itself to be seriously incomplete. Their incompleteness is the result of their basic theoretical commitment to an understanding of human actions as the results either of natural laws or of social influences.

The second constructive consideration that distinguishes the pluralistic approach from scientific and historical reflection is its insistence that human self-understanding must be evaluative and its point of view must be the goodness of the lives of individual human beings. This consideration follows from the preceding claim that human self-understanding must be particular. If we ask why it is so important for human self-understanding that we can have some control over our lives, the obvious answer is that the physical conditions are indifferent to the goodness of our lives, the social influences upon us may benefit or harm us, and the more control we have over them, the more we can shape them to our advantage. We seek self-understanding and control to make our lives better. We can certainly adopt modes of reflection in which the goodness of human lives has no significant place. But we can do that only because we are well enough off to afford the luxury of reflection that ignores how well off we are. And being well enough off is partly the result of our control over the conditions of our lives, a control that must be exercised in the interest of our living good lives. This is another reason why scientific and historical reflections aiming to understand, but not to evaluate, the physical and social conditions of our lives are seriously incomplete.

In closing, it needs to be said why the approach to human self-understanding that has been defended is pluralistic. It is pluralistic, first, because it rejects the view that adequate human self-understanding is general. It must be particular because there is a vast plurality of ways in which particular agents respond to the physical and social conditions of their lives. It is pluralistic, secondly, because it recognizes the importance of a plurality of modes of reflection for human self-understanding. It embraces not only scientific and historical reflection but also aesthetic, moral, religious, and subjective reflection that can contribute in important ways to our understanding of ourselves. It is pluralistic, thirdly, because it denies that it is possible to justify the absolutist claim of any mode of reflection. Such claims always depend on the assimilation of other modes of reflection to a favored mode, and this always leads to missing the significance of the assimilated modes. And it is pluralistic, fourthly, because it denies that its position leads to relativism. Conformity to logic, explanation of the relevant facts, openness to criticism, and consistency of beliefs and actions are the tests by which the reasonability and the truth of beliefs can—fallibly—be judged.

Conclusion: The Human World

To say more than human things with human voice,
That cannot be; to say human things with more
Than human voice, that also, cannot be;
To speak humanly from the height or from the depth
Of human things, that is acutest speech.

WALLACE STEVENS, "Chocorua to Its Neighbor"

The human world is the world we have made. It is the world of tools, machines, books, and buildings; of customs, conventions, values, institutions, and rules; and of beliefs, jokes, ideals, theories, works of art, and hobbies. We have made it out of the resources we found inside and outside ourselves. The human world, with all that is good and bad in it, is a small part of the natural world. From the perspective of the natural world, the human world is an insignificant episode in a small segment of the temporal and spatial vastness of the scheme of things. From the human perspective, the human world is of great significance because it is the context in which we try to make good lives for ourselves.

The history of human reflection is the history of our attempts to understand the world and our situation in it. These attempts have been made in two directions. One stresses understanding the world and seeks what the Greeks have called *sophia*. It is an understanding that an omniscient God would have, if there were such a God. The other stresses understanding our situation in the world and seeks what the Greeks have called *phronesis*. It is an understanding of how we can make good lives for ourselves. One seeks theoretical wisdom, the other practical wisdom. One is incidentally human, the other is essentially so.

The problems that we have been discussing occur in the context of the human world. They have to do with essential conditions of good lives; they are problems of practical wisdom. They occur because there is a plurality of modes

199

in which we can reflect on our situation in the world. Each of these modes is believed to be valuable and irreducibly different from the others, and they provide conflicting accounts of the significance of the facts on which good lives depend. This creates philosophical problems, but it should not be supposed that all philosophical problems are like those that have been discussed.

There are also philosophical problems that arise when we try to understand the world independently of our situation in it; these are problems of theoretical wisdom. Their existence must be acknowledged, but the focus of the argument has been directed elsewhere. It would be a mistake, however, to attempt a sharp separation of the two kinds of problems. Because we seek to understand our situation *in the world*, we must have some understanding of the world; and because it is *we* who seek that understanding, we must have some understanding of the human world from which we derive the means of any understanding that we may have. Still, our attempts at understanding go in different directions and encounter different problems.

The difference between these two directions of human understanding is central to this book. The absolutist tradition in the history of human reflection regards the difference as a result of human failing. The thought is that if we understood the world as it really is, then our situation in it would become obvious. We would not, then, have problems concerning how to live good lives, for the nature of good lives would follow from the nature of the world. That we have such problems is a symptom of our imperfect understanding of the world. It is an intellectual, and perhaps also a moral, failing in us. If we could transcend our limitations, if we could understand ourselves from the outside, as one natural kind among others, then we would shed our biases, prejudices, and self-serving and self-limiting anthropocentrism. Through transcendence, and only through it, as the absolutist tradition has it, the nature of good lives would become clear. Our past and present unclarity is the result of our failure to achieve this transcendence, or so it has been thought by some of the greatest minds.

These great minds unfortunately differed both about the means whereby transcendence could be achieved and about the sort of conclusions that would be reached if the right means were employed. Some thought that religious reflection would lead to transcendence, others that the reflection should be scientific, poetic, mathematical, mystical, or metaphysical. Some thought that transcendence would reveal a benign cosmic order; others that it would be indifferent and impersonal forces; yet others that it would be a steady progress toward perfection; and others still that it would be a battlefield on which good and evil forces eternally clash. But underlying these and other great disagreements has been the shared assumption that the key to good lives is the transcendence of the human perspective.

   The pluralistic approach rejects this assumption, as well as its implication that the human perspective is an obstacle to true understanding. It does not reject, indeed it insists, that the right way to understand the natural world is by transcending the human point of view. The natural world is what it is, independently of how it affects the goodness of our lives. Curiosity, wonder, attachment to truth, and self-interest motivate us to seek this kind of understanding. The great benefits and dangers of the growth of scientific knowledge and technological expertise are the results. Nor does the pluralistic approach reject the search for answers to religious questions about what, if anything, may lie beyond the natural world. What it rejects is the assumption that the pattern of good lives would be given to us once we have achieved whatever turns out to be the right kind of transcendence. *The* pattern of good lives could not be given because good lives do not have a single pattern. There are countless patterns for good lives, and they are not given to us but made by us. No doubt, the understanding of the world that the transcendence of the human point of view gives us has an important bearing on good lives. For the natural world provides a range of physical limits and possibilities within which good lives must be lived. Good lives, however, depend also on social and psychological limits and possibilities, of which there are many. Societies and individuals adopt some and reject others, and which they adopt or reject varies. The existence of a single pattern to which good lives must conform is thus precluded. The pluralistic approach therefore rejects the absolutist search for such a single pattern, or small number of patterns, for good lives.

   The rejection of the absolutist idea that the key to good lives is the transcendence of the human point of view is not the rejection of reason. The pluralistic view, that the human world is the context in which we can make our lives good, does not mean that the human world could be whatever we want to make it, nor that the goodness of lives depends simply on being thought good by those who live them. Good lives take a plurality of forms, but they cannot take just any form. The human world is much richer in possibilities and limits than those determined by the natural world, but the human world remains part of the natural world. The natural world thus imposes restrictions on the forms good lives can take and on the possibilities and limits that can be developed in the human world. The pluralistic approach recognizes, therefore, that there are restrictions that reason requires us to observe. But it also recognizes that the requirements of reason are not exhausted by the recognition of physical constraints on good lives. There are also social and psychological constraints, and reason requires that they should also be recognized. The rejection of absolutism, therefore, does not lead pluralists to a relativism that regards the requirements of reason as arbitrary. That the nature of good lives cannot be specified by a list of universal requirements derivable from the transcendence of the human world does not mean that good lives need not conform to the requirements of reason. It means rather that reason has requirements that are not derived from the transcendence of the human world and are not universal. These requirements are particular and concrete, and they take different forms in different societies and in different lives. It is because pluralists recognize these differences and deny that all requirements of reason must be universal that they have been mistakenly thought of as relativists.

The source of this mistake is the absolutist view that if it is reasonable to believe that something is true of a particular thing, then it must also be reasonable to believe that it is true of all other relevantly similar particular things. This is why the requirements of reason are thought to be connected with universality. The connection does hold in the natural world, but only if the human world has been excluded from it. Our theoretical interest in the natural world is in finding similarities among particular objects in order to explain and predict their behavior. But the connection between reason and universality does not hold in the human world, where our interest is primarily practical, and theoretical only to the extent to which it contributes to good lives. What matters in the human world is not merely how we are alike, but also how we are different. Our differences matter because they have a crucial bearing on what would make our lives good. The range of physical possibilities and limits within which good lives must fall is roughly the same, but the range of social and psychological possibilities and limits is much more extensive than what can be incorporated in a single good life. Good lives are formed of particular subsets of physical, social, and psychological limits and possibilities. It is in terms of these subsets that we must understand good lives, but they are different for different people because people have different combinations of physical, social, and psychological possibilities and limits. The universal requirements of reason, therefore, can give us only a meager understanding of the requirements of good lives. They can tell us about physical possibilities and limits that are alike for all good lives, but there is much more to good lives than these similarities. If the requirements of reason had to be universal, then relativists would be right in believing that the social and psychological aspects of good lives could not be subject to its requirements. But since the requirements of reason need not all be universal, relativists are mistaken, and all aspects of good lives can be subject to its requirements, even though many of them will not be universal.

It may be said against this that the universality of the requirements of reason is not impugned by the fact that they happen to apply only to some lives. Their universality holds because they would apply to all relevantly similar lives, if there were any. That there are not is a contingent fact that affects only the number of cases covered by the requirements, but not the nature of the requirements themselves. This defense, however, is a surrender. For it is the nature of good lives that there will be, at most, only a few relevantly similar other lives, given the essential differences among the social and psychological possibilities and limits of different people. As a result, universal requirements beyond physical possibilities and limits do not obtain. Hence, all good lives cannot be relevantly similar, and hence the search for a pattern by means of transcendence to which all good lives must conform is not only not required but actually opposed by reason.

The rejection of the transcendence of the human world as the key to good lives imposes the obligation on pluralists to provide an alternative approach. The alternative is to rely on the resources of the human world. The creation of the human world is the great evolutionary achievement of our species. For that world is the small segment of the natural world over which we have gained control. The significance of control is that it alleviates the necessity that governs the natural world. The human world contains the possibilities we have created for ourselves, possibilities that open up ways of living and acting that are unavailable in the natural world. They enrich our lives not merely by increasing our options, but also by allowing us to choose between them. Control thus makes it possible to shape our lives.

To be sure, our control is imperfect in several ways. It remains subject to contingency, to the intrusion of natural forces beyond our control. Galactic events, deadly viruses, volcanic eruptions, climatic changes, epidemics, and so forth may resist our control and undo the world we have made for ourselves. The human world is also threatened by forces that exist in us and yet often escape our control: human destructiveness, aggression, hostility, greed, hatred, cruelty, and similar vices often lead to conflicts that endanger civilized life. But the forces that threaten us from the inside need not be fratricidal; they may just be limitations of our ability to understand the complexities that we have created, the different forms human lives may take, or the nature of the conflicts among incompatible elements that constitute the human world. Our control is thus imperfect, and the human world is always at risk. The going so far has been good; there is no reason to panic about the future, but there is no reason either to anticipate Utopia just around the corner.

The human world, then, with our imperfect control of it, is still rich enough to provide the resources we need for good lives. These resources are social and psychological possibilities and limits. Lives are made good by the realization of the right possibilities and by conformity to the right limits. Reason plays a central role in good lives because it enables us to identify the right possibilities and limits, and to distinguish them from the wrong ones.

The human world contains many different societies, and each society contains many different individuals. The possibilities and limits are right or wrong for particular societies and individuals. But being right or wrong for them does not mean that it is the judgment of that society or individual that makes a possibility or a limit right or wrong. Such judgments may be reasonable or unreasonable. A society can be wrong even if its members are unanimous in judging otherwise, and individuals can be wrong even in their best-considered judgments.

The standard by which the reasonableness of such judgments can be determined is the contribution of the judged possibilities and limits to good lives. This, of course, requires an account of what lives are good. The pluralistic view is that all good lives must meet certain conditions, but there is a plurality of ways of meeting them. The first of these conditions is that the individuals are satisfied with their lives overall. They have no regrets about the major decisions they have taken; they do not have bad feelings about their lives; they want their lives to go on by and large in the same way. This satisfaction is necessary but not sufficient for good lives, because the overall satisfaction of individuals may be misguided. This can happen in two ways. First, people may sincerely believe that they are satisfied with their lives overall when in fact they are not. They disguise the truth from themselves because it is too painful, too threatening, or has consequences they are unwilling to face. Their satisfaction is thus based on self-deception. Second, individuals may be truly satisfied with their lives overall but ought not to be. Their overall satisfaction could be the result of stupidity, laziness, lack of imagination, indoctrination, low expectations, traumatic experiences, or repressed feelings, which obscure from them the possibilities of life that they are missing. If they knew about their missed possibilities, they would recognize the impoverishment of their lives. Their satisfaction is thus based on ignorance. Could we say, then, that if individuals are satisfied with their lives overall, and if their satisfaction is not vitiated by self-deception or ignorance, their lives are good?

We cannot because there may be moral grounds for denying that lives that meet these necessary conditions are good. We need to eliminate the possibility that the satisfactions that make a life good are enjoyed at the expense of other people. We need to recognize, that is, that lives are made good not just by the realization of satisfying possibilities but also by conformity to moral limits. Moral limits are derived from the moral conventions of the society in which the individuals live. The purpose of these conventions is to protect the conditions that enable all people in that society to live good lives. The moral conventions of a society may be faulty, of course, if they ill-serve their purpose. They can be criticized, changed, or abandoned for that reason. But if the conventions by and large serve their purpose, and if individuals conform to the limits that the conventions impose on the satisfactions that they may legitimately seek, then the moral condition of good lives is also met.

The pluralistic standard, then, for determining the reasonableness of judgments about the rightness or wrongness of particular possibilities and limits is their contribution to good lives. And the goodness of lives, according to pluralists, is judged on the basis of the agents' overall satisfactions with their lives, the elimination of erroneous satisfactions that result from self-deception and ignorance, and conformity to moral conventions that protect the conditions of good lives for all those who live together in a society. This standard, of course, allows for a wide plurality of reasonable good lives because the agents may derive overall satisfactions from very many different combinations of social and psychological possibilities and limits, because there are very many forms of self-deception and ignorance and very many ways of overcoming them, and because the moral conventions of societies may protect the conditions of good lives in very many different ways. The pluralistic standard, therefore, is a standard expressing the requirements of reason, but its requirements are particular and plural, not universal and singular.

One consequence of the pluralistic approach to good lives is that many of the requirements of reason cannot be expressed in terms of universal or even general principles or rules. They must be judged on a case-by-case basis. The judgments must be particular and they must be based on the concrete details of individual lives. How this can be done has been shown in the pluralistic resolution of the problems connected with the meaning of life, the possibility of free action, the place of morality in good lives, the art of life, and the nature of human self-understanding. These proposed resolutions thus performed a dual role in the argument of this book: they showed why the pluralistic approach to these perennial problems is preferable to the various absolutist alternatives, and they showed how the pluralistic approach to the requirements of reason avoids the arbitrariness of relativism.

The pluralistic approach, therefore, changes *us* by changing our understanding of the nature of the good lives that we seek; it changes *philosophy* by proposing a better approach to some perennial problems than those of absolutism and relativism; and it changes the perennial *problems* that beset good lives by interpreting them in a way that makes their resolution possible.

Notes

Chapter 1. Everyday Life

1. Beginning in this way is not new. Aristotle's methodological precept was: "We must, as in all other cases, set the phenomena [*phainomena*] before us and, after first discussing the difficulties, go on to prove, if possible, the truth of all the reputable opinions [*endoxa*] about these . . . or, failing this, of the greater number and most authoritative; for if we both resolve the difficulties and leave the reputable opinions undisturbed, we shall have proved the case sufficiently." The phenomena that Aristotle thinks we must set before us are the elements of everyday life, and the reputable opinions are the considered beliefs about them. Aristotle, *Nicomachean Ethics*, trans. W. D. Ross, rev. J. O. Urmson, in *The Complete Works of Aristotle*, ed. Jonathan Barnes (Princeton: Princeton University Press, 1984), 1145b1–8.

For an account of Aristotle's method and some of its implications, see Martha C. Nussbaum, *The Fragility of Goodness* (Cambridge: Cambridge University Press, 1986), chap. 8. The method has been rediscovered and named "reflective equilibrium" by John Rawls, *A Theory of Justice* (Cambridge: Harvard University Press, 1971), pp. 20, 48–51. Rawls's use of the method has spawned a vast literature, which is usefully reviewed and evaluated by Christine Swanton, *Freedom* (Indianapolis: Hackett, 1992), chap. 2.

2. David Hume, *Enquiries concerning the Principles of Morals*, ed. L. A. Selby-Bigge (Oxford: Clarendon Press, 1961), p. 209.

3. Jane Austen, *Sense and Sensibility* (Harmondsworth, England: Penguin, 1969), chap. 46, p. 338.

4. It has been rightly observed that "social life would be psychologically intolerable if each of its moments required from us full attention, deliberate decision, and high emotional involvement. . . . Triviality is one of the fundamental requirements of social life. . . . If we understand this . . . we shall see that there are limits not only to disorder and discontinuity, but also to the frequency of 'significant events.' We will then become very careful how we view . . . 'mere routines' in social life—simply because we will recognize that if social life in its entirety were charged with profound meaning, we would all go out of our minds." Peter L. Berger, *Facing Up to Modernity* (New York: Basic Books, 1977), pp. xvi–xvii.

5. How this contingency has played out historically is traced by Charles Taylor, *Sources of the Self* (Cambridge: Harvard University Press, 1989), part 3. Taylor shows how the significance

attributed to what he calls ordinary life, and what is called here everyday life, has changed historically, and how these changes have affected Western identity, morality, and politics. The present argument, unlike Taylor's, is not historical. It is about the significance everyday life has, not about what it is seen as having or about the changing beliefs regarding its significance.

6. The necessity of everyday life is supported by three different lines of argument. One is anthropological. See Robin Horton, "African Traditional Thought and Western Science," in *Rationality*, ed. Bryan R. Wilson (Oxford: Blackwell, 1970), pp. 131–171; "Tradition and Modernity Revisited," in *Rationality and Relativism*, ed. Martin Hollis and Steven Lukes (Oxford: Blackwell, 1982), pp. 201–260; and "Material-Object Language and Theoretical Language: Towards a Strawsonian Sociology of Thought," in *Philosophical Disputes in the Social Sciences*, ed. Stuart C. Brown (Sussex: Harvester Press, 1977), pp. 99, 197–224.

Another is an interpretation of Hume's view of the nature of philosophy. See Donald W. Livingstone, *Hume's Philosophy of Common Life* (Chicago: University of Chicago Press, 1984), especially the introduction and chaps. 1–3, and *Philosophical Melancholy and Delirium* (Chicago: University of Chicago Press, 1998).

The third is an approach to descriptive metaphysics. See Peter F. Strawson, *Individuals: An Essay in Descriptive Metaphysics* (London: Methuen, 1959), part 1.

7. George Edward Moore, "Some Judgments of Perception," in *Philosophical Studies* (London: Routledge, 1922), p. 228.

Chapter 2. Modes of Reflection

1. W. B. Gallie memorably describes the concepts that stand for these approaches as "essentially contested"; see his *Philosophy and the Historical Understanding* (London: Chatto & Windus, 1964), p. 158.

2. "Modes of reflection" and various cognate notions have of course historical roots. The *fons et origo* is probably Georg W. F. Hegel, *The Phenomenology of Mind*, trans. J. B. Baillie (New York: Harper, 1967); Robin G. Collingwood, *Speculum Mentis of the Map of Knowledge* (Oxford: Clarendon Press, 1924), employs the notion of "scale of forms"; Michael Oakeshott, *Experience and Its Modes* (Cambridge: Cambridge University Press, 1933), uses "modes of experience"; Ernst Cassirer, *Philosophy of Symbolic Forms*, trans. Ralph Mannheim (New Haven: Yale University Press, 1955), concentrates on "symbolic forms"; Nelson Goodman, *Ways of Worldmaking* (Indianapolis: Hackett, 1978), puts it in terms of "worlds that we make"; Clifford Geertz, *Local Knowledge* (New York: Basic Books, 1983), calls them "cultural forms"; Gallie, as we have seen above, regards them as "essentially contested concepts"; Wittgensteinians refer to them as "language games" or as "forms of life"; some other expressions are "perspective," "linguistic framework," "conceptual scheme," and "universe of discourse."

Two distinction are important to this body of work. One is between Hegel and Collingwood, on the one hand, who organize what is here called modes of reflection hierarchically, and Oakeshott, Cassirer, Gallie, Goodman, and Geertz, on the other hand, who deny that modes of reflection can be ranked hierarchically. The other distinction is between Cassirer, Goodman, Gallie, and Geertz, who are led to relativism by their recognition of the plurality of modes of reflection, and Hegel, Collingwood, and Oakeshott, who are not. The view that will be defended here is pluralistic and antirelativist. It aims to avoid two grave defects that run through this historical tradition. One is the failure to distinguish clearly between a pluralistic and a relativistic view of modes of reflection. The other is the failure to explain how modes of reflection can be distinguished from other ways of thinking, and the failure to avoid arbitrariness in what is regarded as a mode of reflection.

3. "Rationality is not *just* a concept *in* a language like any other; it is this too, for, like any other concept it must be circumscribed by an established use: a use, that is, established in the language. But I think it is not a concept which any language may not have, as is, for instance, the concept of politeness. It is a concept necessary to the existence of any language: to say of a

society that it has a language is also to say that it has a concept of rationality. . . . This, however, is so far to say nothing about what in particular constitutes rational behaviour in that society; that would require particular knowledge about the norms they appeal to in living their lives." Peter Winch, "Understanding a Primitive Society," in *Ethics and Action* (London: Routledge, 1972), pp. 33–34.

4. The early Wittgenstein provides one example of this mistake: "We feel that even when all *possible* scientific questions have been answered, the problems of life remain completely untouched. Of course there are then no questions left, and this is the answer. The solution of the problem of life is the vanishing of the problem." Ludwig Wittgenstein, *Tractatus Logico-Philosophicus*, trans. D. F. Pears and B. F. Guinness (London: Routledge, 1961), 6.52 and 6.521. The later Wittgenstein had second thoughts about this: "Philosophers constantly see the method of science before their eyes, and are irresistibly tempted to ask and answer questions in the way science does. This tendency . . . leads the philosopher into complete darkness." *The Blue and Brown Books* (Oxford: Blackwell, 1969), p. 18. Wittgenstein is right in his second thoughts. It is important to add, however, that the darkness would not be lightened if philosophers followed the method of any other mode of reflection. Darkness falls if any mode of reflection is regarded as a model that other modes of reflection ought to follow.

Other examples of this mistake are: "To suppose . . . that we possess criteria of rationality which are independent of our understanding of the essentials of the scientific process is to open the door to cloud-cuckoo land" (Thomas S. Kuhn, "Reflections on My Critics," in *Criticism and the Growth of Knowledge*, ed. I. Lakatos and A. Musgrave [Cambridge: Cambridge University Press, 1970], p. 264); "The natural sciences with their critical methods of problem-solving . . . have represented for quite a long time our best efforts at problem-solving" (Karl R. Popper, "A Realist View of Logic, Physics, and History," in *Objective Knowledge* [Oxford: Clarendon Press, 1972], p. 290); from science, with the help of logic, "a canonical idiom can be abstracted and then adhered to in the statement of one's scientific theory. The doctrine is that all traits of reality worthy of the name can be set down in an idiom of this austere form if in any idiom. . . . It delimits what counts as scientifically admissible construction, and declares that whatever is not thus constructible . . . must either be conceded the status of one more irreducible given term or eschewed" (Willard Van Orman Quine, *Word and Object* [Cambridge: MIT Press, 1960], pp. 228–229).

5. An illuminating discussion of this point is Anthony O'Hear's *Beyond Evolution* (Oxford: Clarendon Press, 1997), especially chap. 3.

6. "There often arises quarrels between theories, or, more generally, between lines of thought, which are . . . irreconcilable with one another. A thinker who adopts one of them often seems to be logically committed to rejecting the other, despite the fact that the inquiries from which the theories issued had, from the beginning, widely divergent goals. In disputes of this kind, we often find one and the same thinker—very likely oneself—strongly inclined to champion both sides yet, at the very same time, strongly inclined to repudiate one of them just because he is strongly inclined to support the other. He is both satisfied with the logical credentials of each of the points of view, and sure that one of them must be totally wrong if the other is even largely right." Gilbert Ryle, *Dilemmas* (Cambridge: Cambridge University Press, 1956), p. 1.

7. The history of philosophy shows that "philosophers, more than any other type of investigator, persistently work at what appear to be the same unchanging problems. . . . [A]lthough these problems appear not only to be unchanging but to admit of rational or even necessary solutions, yet the history of philosophy presents them as the centres of unending conflicts and debates, punctuated briefly from time to time by claims that a revolution has taken place and that philosophical problems will now be speedily wound up—after which things go on again very much as before." Gallie, *Philosophy and the Historical Understanding*, p. 7.

8. One is "compelled to philosophize by problems which arise outside philosophy. . . . Genuine philosophical problems are always rooted in urgent problems outside of philosophy, and they die if these roots decay." Karl R. Popper, "The Nature of Philosophical Problems and Their Roots in Science," in *Conjectures and Refutations* (New York: Harper, 1963), pp. 71–72.

9. The closest view to the one defended here is Thomas Nagel's in *The View from Nowhere* (New York: Oxford University Press, 1986). Nagel says on pp. 3, 6, and 10: "This book is about a single problem: how to combine the perspective of a particular person inside the world with the objective view of that same world, the person and his viewpoint included. It is a problem that faces every creature with the impulse and the capacity to transcend its particular point of view and conceive of the world as a whole." This "tension pervades human life, but it is particularly prominent in the generation of philosophical problems." And "I believe that the methods needed to understand ourselves do not yet exist."

The present view differs from Nagel's in three fundamental ways. First, Nagel recognizes only two modes of reflection: the subjective and the objective, whereas there are many more. Consequently, Nagel has an unnecessarily restricted account of the origin of philosophical problems. Second, Nagel does not distinguish between understanding facts and understanding the significance of facts. As a result, Nagel fails to see that many philosophical problems are not about understanding facts but about understanding their significance. Third, Nagel thinks that the method for resolving philosophical problems does not yet exist, but it does, as it will be argued later.

10. "Let us remind ourselves of how philosophical perplexities typically arise, and the form they are apt to take. Common sense commits itself to various assertions about the world. . . . Then, because we are self-reflective creatures, we turn back on our commonsense assumptions and find them to be . . . puzzling and problematic. . . . The concepts we habitually employ raise the kinds of disturbing questions we call 'philosophical'. A characteristic expression of this puzzlement asks how what we had hitherto taken for granted is actually so much as possible." Colin McGinn, *Problems of Philosophy* (Oxford: Blackwell, 1993), p. 8.

Chapter 3. Philosophical Problems

1. "But if I am asked whether absolute goodness exists; or whether the material world is real; or what infinity is; or why I cannot go back into the past, or be in two places at once; or whether you can ever know fully what I think or feel as I know these things; or whether freedom is better than happiness, or justice, and what justice is—when questions of this type are asked . . . the principal difficulty is to know where to look for the answers at all; to know how even to begin to set about looking for a satisfactory solution. . . . It is when we are in this kind of perplexity, when it is clear that the problem is not empirical, at however sophisticated a level, nor one to be solved by the application of deductive techniques . . . that we are in the presence of a genuine philosophical problem." Isaiah Berlin, "Philosophy and Government Repression," in *The Sense of Reality*, ed. Henry Hardy (London: Chatto & Windus, 1996), pp. 57–58. "Philosophical problems . . . are, of course, not empirical problems." "Philosophy . . . leaves everything as it is. It also leaves mathematics as it is, and no mathematical discovery can advance it. A 'leading problem of mathematical logic' is for us a problem of mathematics like any other." Ludwig Wittgenstein, *Philosophical Investigations*, trans. G. E. M. Anscombe (Oxford: Blackwell, 1968), pp. 109, 124.

2. "A philosophical problem has the form: 'I don't know my way about.' " Wittgenstein, *Philosophical Investigations*, p. 123.

3. René Descartes, *Discourse on the Method of Rightly Conducting the Reason and Seeking the Truth in the Sciences*, in *The Philosophical Works of Descartes*, trans. Elizabeth S. Haldane and G. R. F. Ross (Cambridge: Cambridge University Press, 1970), pp. 85–86.

4. David Hume, *A Treatise of Human Nature*, ed. L. A. Selby-Bigge (Oxford: Clarendon Press, 1960), pp. xvii–xviii.

5. Immanuel Kant, *Prolegomena to Any Future Metaphysics*, rev. and trans. Lewis White Beck (New York: Liberal Arts, 1950), p. 4.

6. John Stuart Mill, *Utilitarianism* (Indianapolis: Hackett, 1979), p. 1.

7. Ludwig Wittgenstein, *Tractatus Logico-Philosophicus*, trans. David F. Pears and Brian F. McGuinness (London: Routledge, 1961), p. 5.

8. David Hume, *Enquiries Concerning Human Understanding and Concerning the Principles of Morals*, ed. L. A. Selby-Bigge (Oxford: Clarendon Press, 1961), p. 165.

9. Colin McGinn, *Problems in Philosophy* (Oxford: Blackwell, 1993), pp. vii, 2.

10. Thomas Nagel, *The View from Nowhere* (New York: Oxford University Press, 1986), p. 12.

11 Bertrand Russell, *The Problems of Philosophy* (London: Oxford University Press, 1967), p. 90.

12. The main source of our knowledge of this ancient view is Sextus Empiricus, *Outlines of Scepticism*, trans. Julia Annas and Jonathan Barnes (Cambridge: Cambridge University Press, 1994). The secondary literature is too large to be listed here, but some of the more important works are Julia Annas, *The Morality of Happiness* (New York: Oxford University Press, 1993), chap. 8; Julia Annas and Jonathan Barnes, *The Modes of Scepticism* (Cambridge: Cambridge University Press, 1985); Jonathan Barnes, *The Toils of Scepticism* (Cambridge: Cambridge University Press, 1990); Myles Burnyeat, ed., *The Skeptical Tradition* (Berkeley: University of California Press, 1983), see essays 1–9; Michael Frede, *Essays in Ancient Philosophy* (Minneapolis: University of Minnesota Press, 1987); Benson Mates, *The Skeptic Way* (New York: Oxford University Press, 1996); Martha C. Nussbaum, *The Therapy of Desire* (Princeton: Princeton University Press, 1994), chap. 8.

The skeptical relativist challenge to philosophy has had a continuous history beginning almost as soon as philosophy and thriving to this day. Protagoras and the Sophists began it. Pyrrho, Sextus Empiricus, and other ancient skeptics continued it. From them, it was taken over by Michel de Montaigne, "Apology for Raymond Sebond," in the *Essays* in *The Complete Works of Montaigne*, trans. Donald M. Frame (Stanford: Stanford University Press, 1948). It was carried on by Hume in the *Treatise* and the *Enquiries*, on which see Donald W. Livingstone, *Hume's Philosophy of Common Life* (Chicago: University of Chicago Press, 1984) and *Philosophical Melancholy and Delirium* (Chicago: University of Chicago Press, 1998). From Hume we may jump to present-day deconstructionists in France, Heidegger in Germany, and, in America, Richard Rorty, *Philosophy and the Mirror of Nature* (Princeton: Princeton University Press, 1979), *Consequences of Pragmatism* (Minneapolis: University of Minnesota Press, 1982), and *Philosophical Papers*, vols. 1–2 (Cambridge: Cambridge University Press, 1991). David R. Hiley, *Philosophy in Question* (Chicago: University of Chicago Press, 1988), has an admirable discussion of the skeptical challenge to philosophy.

The version of skeptical relativism that is presented here is a reconstruction of this position. It is not to be identified with the thought of any particular skeptic. Other reconstructions are, of course, possible. The point of the present one is to make as strong a case for the position as possible.

13. Wittgenstein, *Philosophical Investigations*, p. 109. The interpretation of Wittgenstein as a skeptical relativist is controversial. This is not the place to settle this question. Nothing substantive in skeptical relativism depends on whether Wittgenstein really held it.

14. Ibid., p. 133.

15. Ibid., p. 255.

16. This doubt has entered into contemporary philosophy as "the problem of the criterion." See, e.g., Roderick Chisholm, *The Problem of the Criterion* (Milwaukee: Marquette University Press, 1973).

17. Hume, *Enquiries*, p. 160.

18. Hume, *Treatise*, p. 183.

19. Sextus, *Outlines of Scepticism*, I.vii.

20. Ibid., I.xi.

21. Hume, *Enquiries*, p. 44.

22. Wittgenstein, *Philosophical Investigations*, p. 226.

Chapter 4. The Pluralistic Approach

1. For metaphysical pluralism, see, e.g., William James, *A Pluralistic Universe*, in *William James: Writings 1902–1910*, ed. Bruce Kuklick (New York: The Library of America, 1987). For

epistemological pluralism, see, e.g., Nicholas Rescher, *Pluralism* (Oxford: Clarendon Press, 1993). For moral pluralism, see, e.g., John Kekes, *The Morality of Pluralism* (Princeton: Princeton University Press, 1993). For axiological pluralism in general, see Joel J. Kupperman, *Value . . . and What Follows* (New York: Oxford University Press, 1999). For anthropological pluralism, see, e.g., Clifford Geertz, *The Interpretation of Cultures* (New York: Basic Books, 1973). It is not always clear whether Geertz is in favor of pluralism or relativism.

2. Friedrich Nietzsche, *The Gay Science*, trans. Walter Kaufmann (New York: Vintage, 1974), p. 125.

3. "The conversation . . . may suffer damage, or even for a time come to be suspended, by the bad manners of one or more of the participants. For each voice is prone to *superbia*, that is, an exclusive concern with its own utterance, which may result in its identifying the conversation with itself and its speaking as if it were speaking only to itself. And when this happens, barbarism may be observed to have supervened." Michael Oakeshott, "The Voice of Poetry in the Conversation of Mankind," in *Rationalism in Politics*, new and expanded edition, ed. Timothy Fuller (Indianapolis: Liberty Press, 1991), p. 492. And again, "There are some minds which give us the sense that they have passed through an elaborate education which was designed to initiate them into the traditions and achievements of their civilization; the immediate impression we have of them is an impression of cultivation, of the enjoyment of an inheritance. But this is not so with the mind of the . . . [absolutist]. If . . . we glance below the surface, we may, perhaps, see in the temperament . . . of the [absolutist] a deep distrust of time, an impatient hunger for eternity, and an irritable nervousness in the face of everything topical and transitory." Oakeshott, "Rationalism in Politics," in *Rationalism in Politics*, p. 7. The original "rationalist" has been replaced by "absolutist," which accords with Oakeshott's meaning.

Chapter 5. The Meaning of Life

1. John Stuart Mill, *Autobiography* (New York: Columbia University Press, 1924), chapter 5.

2. Thomas Nagel, "The Absurd," in *Mortal Questions* (Cambridge: Cambridge University Press, 1979), p. 13.

3. Nagel, "The Absurd," pp. 14–15.

4. Ludwig Wittgenstein, *Tractatus Logico-Philosophicus*, trans. D. F. Pears and B. F. McGuinness (London: Routledge, 1961), 6.41.

5. Wittgenstein, *Tractatus*, 6.421.

6. Ludwig Wittgenstein, "A Lecture on Ethics," *Philosophical Review* 74 (1965): 5.

7. William Faulkner, *A Fable* (London: Chatto & Windus, 1955), p. 267.

8. Albert Camus, *The Myth of Sisyphus*, trans. Justin O'Brien (London: Hamish Hamilton, 1955).

9. Richard Taylor, *Good and Evil* (New York: Macmillan, 1970), p. 259.

10. Plato, *Euthyphro*, trans. Lane Cooper, in *Plato: The Collected Dialogues*, ed. Edith Hamilton and Huntington Cairns (Princeton: Princeton University Press, 1961).

11. Wittgenstein, *Tractatus*, 6.421.

12. Friedrich Waismann, "Notes on Talks with Wittgenstein," *Philosophical Review* 74 (1965): 15.

13. David Wiggins, "Truth, Invention, and the Meaning of Life," *Proceedings of the British Academy* 62 (1976): 348–349.

Chapter 6. The Possibility of Free Action

1. Some recent defenses of libertarianism are Roderick Chisholm, *Person and Object* (La Salle, Ill.: Open Court, 1976); Robert Kane, *The Significance of Free Will* (New York: Oxford University Press, 1995); Robert Nozick, *Philosophical Explanations* (Cambridge: Harvard University Press, 1981), pp. 291–397; Richard Taylor, *Action and Purpose* (Englewood Cliffs, N.J.:

Prentice-Hall, 1966); and Peter van Inwagen, *An Essay on Free Will* (Oxford: Oxford University Press, 1983).

2. Some recent defenses of determinism are Ted Honderich, *How Free Are You?* (Oxford: Oxford University Press, 1983); Galen Strawson, *Freedom and Belief* (Oxford: Clarendon Press, 1986); and Bruce Waller, *Freedom Without Responsibility* (Philadelphia: Temple University Press, 1990).

3. Some recent defenses of compatibilism are several essays in Harry G. Frankfurt, *The Importance of What We Care About* (New York: Cambridge University Press, 1988); Stuart Hampshire, *Thought and Action* (London: Chatto & Windus, 1960), and *Freedom of the Individual*, expanded edition (Princeton: Princeton University Press, 1975); and Abraham I. Melden, *Free Action* (London: Routledge, 1961).

4. For overviews and bibliographies, see Richard Double, "Misdirections in the Free Will Problem," *American Philosophical Quarterly* 34 (1997): 357–366; John M. Fisher, introduction to *Moral Responsibility*, ed. John M. Fisher (Ithaca: Cornell University Press, 1986), and "Freedom and Determinism," in *Encyclopedia of Ethics*, ed. Lawrence C. Becker (New York: Garland, 1992); Gary Watson, introduction to *Free Will*, ed. Gary Watson (Oxford: Oxford University Press, 1982), and "Free Action and Free Will," *Mind* 96 (1987): 145–172.

5. The distinction between these two modes of thought has been discussed by Colin McGinn, *The Subjective View* (Oxford: Clarendon Press, 1983); Thomas Nagel, "Subjective and Objective," in *Mortal Questions* (New York: Cambridge University Press, 1979), and *The View from Nowhere* (New York: Oxford University Press, 1967); Wilfrid Sellars, "Philosophy and the Scientific Image of Man," in *Science, Perception and Reality* (London: Routledge, 1963); and Bernard Williams, *Descartes: The Project of Pure Enquiry* (Atlantic Highlands, N.J.: Humanities Press, 1978).

6. Nagel, *View from Nowhere*, p. 112.

7. Richard Taylor, "Determinism," in *Encyclopedia of Philosophy*, ed. Paul Edwards (New York: Macmillan, 1967), 2:372.

8. Watson, "Free Action and Free Will," p. 169.

9. This line of thought extends from the Stoics through Spinoza to our own days. For some contemporary explorations of it, see Bernard Berofsky, *Liberation from Self* (New York: Cambridge University Press, 1995); David C. Dennett, *Elbow Room* (Cambridge: MIT Press, 1984); and Stuart Hampshire, *Thought and Action* and *Freedom of the Individual*.

10. Some explorations of this idea are Frankfurt, "Freedom of the Will and the Concept of a Person," in *Importance of What We Care About*; Charles Taylor, "Responsibility for Self," in *The Identities of Persons*, ed. Amelie Rorty (Berkeley: University of California Press, 1976); Gary Watson, "Free Agency," in *Free Will*; and Susan Wolf, *Freedom within Reason* (New York: Oxford University Press, 1991).

11. On the nature of this kind of reflection see John Kekes, *Moral Wisdom and Good Lives* (Ithaca: Cornell University Press, 1995), chaps. 4–8.

Chapter 7. Morality in Good Lives

1. Some of the issues involved in this conflict are discussed in W. David Falk, "Morality, Self, and Others," and "Morality, Form, and Content," both in *Ought, Reasons, and Morality* (Ithaca: Cornell University Press, 1986); Philippa Foot, "Are Moral Considerations Overriding?" in *Virtues and Vices* (Oxford: Blackwell, 1978); John Kekes, *The Morality of Pluralism* (Princeton: Princeton University Press, 1993), chap. 9; Thomas Nagel, *The View from Nowhere* (Oxford: Oxford University Press, 1985), chap. 10; Samuel Scheffler, *Human Morality* (New York: Oxford University Press, 1992); and Gregory Vlastos, *Socrates, Ironist and Moral Philosopher* (Ithaca: Cornell University Press, 1991), chap. 8.

2. This seems to be the view of Ayn Rand and her followers. See Ayn Rand, *The Virtue of Selfishness* (New York: Signet, 1964), and Tibor R. Machan, *The Libertarian Alternative* (Chicago: Nelson-Hall, 1974).

3. See David Gauthier, *Morals by Agreement* (Oxford: Clarendon Press, 1986); and Bernard Williams, "Persons, Character and Morality" and "Moral Luck," both in *Moral Luck* (Cambridge: Cambridge University Press, 1981), and *Ethics and the Limits of Philosophy* (London: Collins, 1985), especially chap. 10.

4. This is the dominant view in past and present moral philosophy. All consequentialists and deontologists hold it. Some of the few dissenters are Machiavelli, Hobbes, and Nietzsche, and perhaps also Aristotle in some passages.

5. See Neil Cooper, *The Diversity of Moral Thinking* (Oxford: Clarendon Press, 1981), and Richard M. Hare, *The Language of Morals* (Oxford: Clarendon Press, 1952) and *Moral Thinking* (Oxford: Clarendon Press, 1981).

6. This is the Kantian view. Some contemporary versions of it are Christine M. Korsgaard, *The Sources of Normativity* (New York: Cambridge University Press, 1996) and *Creating the Kingdom of Ends* (New York: Cambridge University Press, 1996), and Thomas Nagel, *The View from Nowhere*, and *Equality and Partiality* (New York: Oxford University Press, 1991).

7. See Kurt Baier, *The Moral Point of View* (Ithaca: Cornell University Press, 1957), and Lawrence C. Becker, *Reciprocity* (London: Routledge, 1986).

8. See Kekes, *Morality of Pluralism*, chap. 9.

9. See Philippa Foot, "Morality as a System of Hypothetical Imperatives," in *Virtues and Vices*.

10. See W. David Falk, "Morality, Self, and Others" and "Morality, Form, and Content," in *Ought, Reasons, and Morality*, and William K. Frankena, "The Concept of Morality," *Journal of Philosophy* 63 (1966): 688–696.

11. Versions of this argument are to be found in Alan Gewirth, *Reason and Morality* (Chicago: University of Chicago Press, 1978), and John Rawls, *A Theory of Justice* (Cambridge: Harvard University Press, 1971).

12. See Kekes, *The Morality of Pluralism*; Charles Taylor, "The Diversity of Goods," in *Philosophy and the Human Sciences* (Cambridge: Cambridge University Press, 1985); and Williams, "Persons, Character and Morality," and *Ethics and the Limits of Philosophy*.

13. See Susan Wolf, "Moral Saints," *Journal of Philosophy* 79 (1982): 419–439.

14. Immanuel Kant, *Groundwork of the Metaphysics of Morals*, trans. H. J. Paton (New York: Harper, 1964), p. 66.

15. For an exploration of this line of thought, see the essays collected in *Anti-Theory in Ethics and Moral Conservatism*, ed. Stanley G. Clarke and Evan Simpson (New York: State University of New York Press, 1989).

16. This is the conclusion that emerges from Henry Sidgwick's *The Methods of Ethics* (Indianapolis: Hackett, 1981) and from Isaiah Berlin's lifelong meditations on this topic; see, for instance, Berlin, "John Stuart Mill and the Ends of Life," in *Four Essays on Liberty* (London: Oxford University Press, 1969). See also Stuart Hampshire's essays in *Morality and Conflict* (Cambridge: Harvard University Press, 1983) and *Innocence and Experience* (Cambridge: Harvard University Press, 1989).

Chapter 8. The Art of Life

1. All quotations are from John Stuart Mill, *A System of Logic* (London: Longmans, 1872), bk. 6, chap. 12, sec. 6–7.

2. These phrases occur so frequently in Mill's *Utilitarianism* that it would be pedantic to document their uses.

3. John Stuart Mill, *Utilitarianism* (Indianapolis: Hackett, 1979), pp. 16, 17, 31, 32.

4. Mill, *System of Logic*, bk. 6, chap. 12, sec. 7.

5. John Stuart Mill, *On Liberty* (Indianapolis: Hackett, 1978), pp. 54–55.

6. Ibid., p. 56.

7. Immanuel Kant, *Groundwork of the Metaphysics of Morals*, trans. H. J. Paton (New York: Harper, 1964), p. 80.

8. Ibid., p. 114.

9. Ibid.

10. Ibid. Kant gives several formulations of the categorical imperative, and relations among them are exceedingly complicated. These complications are irrelevant for the present purposes, so they will be ignored. For a discussion of them, see H. J. Paton, *The Categorical Imperative* (London: Hutchinson, 1947), bk. 3.

11. The precise nature of the inconsistency involved in violating the categorical imperative is a controversial question. Perhaps the most convincing account of it is given by Christine M. Korsgaard, *Creating the Kingdom of Ends* (New York: Cambridge University Press, 1996), essays 3 and 5.

12. Kant, *Groundwork*, p. 112.

13. Ibid., pp. 81, 84.

14. For a very interesting discussion of the aesthetic approach to the art of life, see Alexander Nehamas, *The Art of Living* (Berkeley: University of California Press, 1998). See also Robert E. Norton, *The Beautiful Soul: Aesthetic Morality in the Eighteenth Century* (Ithaca: Cornell University Press, 1995), for part of the history of this idea. For a contemporary defense of the aesthetic approach, see Richard Shusterman, *Pragmatist Aesthetics* (Oxford: Blackwell, 1992) and *Practicing Philosophy* (New York: Routledge, 1997).

15. See Friedrich Nietzsche, *On the Genealogy of Morals*, trans. Walter Kaufmann, in *Basic Writings of Nietzsche*, ed. Walter Kaufmann (New York: Modern Library, 1966), essay 3, sec. 6.

16. Plato, *The Republic*, trans. Robin Waterfield (New York: Oxford University Press, 1993), 607b.

17. Isaiah Berlin, "The Romantic Revolution," in *The Sense of Reality*, ed. Henry Hardy (London: Chatto & Windus, 1996), pp. 169–170.

18. Friedrich Nietzsche, *The Gay Science*, trans. Walter Kaufmann (New York: Vintage, 1974), p. 125.

19. Nietzsche, *Genealogy*, pp. 453, 456.

20. Friedrich Nietzsche, *The Will to Power*, trans. Walter Kaufmann and R. J. Hollingdale (New York: Random House, 1967), p. 353.

21. Nietzsche, *Genealogy*, p. 456.

22. Friedrich Nietzsche, *Beyond Good and Evil*, trans. Walter Kaufmann, in *Basic Writings of Nietzsche*, ed. Walter Kaufmann (New York: Modern Library, 1966), sec. 5.

23. Nietzsche, *Will to Power*, p. 361.

24. Friedrich Nietzsche, *Twilight of the Idols*, trans. Walter Kaufmann, in *The Portable Nietzsche* (Harmondsworth, England: Penguin, 1954), part 5, sec. 6.

25. Friedrich Nietzsche, *Thus Spoke Zarathustra*, trans. R. J. Hollingdale (Harmondsworth, England: Penguin, 1961), part 1, "Of the Afterworldsmen."

26. Nietzsche, *Will to Power*, p. 361.

27. Nietzsche, *Gay Science*, pp. 270, 335, 290.

28. Friedrich Nietzsche, *Untimely Meditations*, trans. R. J. Hollingdale (Cambridge: Cambridge University Press, 1983), essay 2, sec. 9.

Chapter 9. Human Self-Understanding

1. Wilfrid Sellars, "Philosophy and the Scientific Image of Man," in *Science, Perception and Reality* (London: Routledge, 1963).

2. Ibid., p. 6.

3. Carl G. Hempel, "The Function of General Laws in History," in *Theories of History*, ed. Patrick Gardiner (New York: Free Press, 1959); "Reason and Covering Laws in Historical Explanation," in *Philosophy and History*, ed. Sidney Hook (New York: New York University Press, 1963); "Explanation in Science and History," in *Philosophical Analysis and History*, ed. William H. Dray (New York: Harper & Row, 1966); and "Rational Action," *Proceedings and Addresses of the American Philosophical Association* 35 (1962): 5–23.

4. Hempel, "Function of General Laws," p. 351.

5. Ibid., p. 353.

6. These critical responses are usefully sampled in the several anthologies referred to in note 3 above, which also contain bibliographies. But see also Patrick Gardiner, ed., *The Philosophy of History* (London: Oxford University Press, 1974).

7. Alan Donagan, "The Popper-Hempel Theory Reconsidered," in Dray, *Philosophical Analysis and History*, and in Gardiner, *Theories of History;* William H. Dray, *Laws and Explanations in History* (Oxford: Oxford University Press, 1957); William B. Gallie, *Philosophy and the Historical Understanding* (London: Chatto & Windus, 1964); Patrick Gardiner, *The Nature of Historical Explanation* (Oxford: Oxford University Press, 1952); Louis O. Mink, "The Autonomy of Historical Understanding," in Dray, *Philosophical Analysis and History;* Michael Oakeshott, *Experience and Its Modes* (Cambridge: Cambridge University Press, 1933) and *On History* (Oxford: Blackwell, 1983); Frederick Olafson, *The Dialectic of Action* (Chicago: University of Chicago Press, 1979); William H. Walsh, *An Introduction to the Philosophy of History* (London: Hutchinson, 1951), and essays in each of the anthologies referred to in note 3 above; Peter Winch, *The Idea of a Social Science* (London: Routledge, 1958); and Morton White, *Foundations of Historical Knowledge* (New York: Harper & Row, 1965).

8. William H. Dray, "Historical Explanation of Actions Reconsidered," in Gardiner, *Philosophy of History*, pp. 68–69.

9. Ibid., p. 89.

10. On the social aspect of historical explanation, see Olafson, *Dialectic of Action*, pp. 148–152.

11. Hiromichi Yahara, *The Battle for Okinawa*, trans. Roger Pineau and Masatishi Uehara (New York: Wiley, 1995).

Works Cited

Annas, Julia. *The Morality of Happiness*. New York: Oxford University Press, 1993.

Annas, Julia, and Jonathan Barnes. *The Modes of Scepticism*. Cambridge: Cambridge University Press, 1985.

Aristotle. *Nicomachean Ethics*. Translated by W. D. Ross, revised by J. O. Urmson. In *The Complete Works of Aristotle*, edited by Jonathan Barnes. Princeton: Princeton University Press, 1984.

Austen, Jane. *Sense and Sensibility*. Harmondsworth, England: Penguin, 1969.

Baier, Kurt. *The Moral Point of View*. Ithaca: Cornell University Press, 1957.

Barnes, Jonathan. *The Toils of Scepticism*. Cambridge: Cambridge University Press, 1990.

Becker, Lawrence C. *Reciprocity*. London: Routledge, 1986.

Berger, Peter L. *Facing Up to Modernity*. New York: Basic Books, 1977.

Berlin, Isaiah. "John Stuart Mill and the Ends of Life." In *Four Essays on Liberty*. London: Oxford University Press, 1969.

——. "Philosophy and Government Repression." In *The Sense of Reality*, edited by Henry Hardy. London: Chatto & Windus, 1996.

——. "The Romantic Revolution." In *The Sense of Reality*, edited by Henry Hardy. London: Chatto & Windus, 1996.

Berofsky, Bernard. *Liberation from Self*. New York: Cambridge University Press, 1995.

Camus, Albert. *The Myth of Sisyphus*. Translated by Justin O'Brien. London: Hamish Hamilton, 1955.

Cassirer, Ernst. *Philosophy of Symbolic Forms*. Translated by Ralph Mannheim. New Haven: Yale University Press, 1955.

Chisholm, Roderick. *Person and Object*. La Salle, Ill.: Open Court, 1976.

——. *The Problem of the Criterion*. Milwaukee: Marquette University Press, 1973.

Clarke, Stanley G., and Evan Simpson, eds. *Anti-Theory in Ethics and Moral Conservatism*. New York: State University of New York Press, 1989.

Collingwood, Robin G. *Speculum Mentis of the Map of Knowledge*. Oxford: Clarendon Press, 1924.

Cooper, Neil. *The Diversity of Moral Thinking*. Oxford: Clarendon Press, 1981.

Dennett, David C. *Elbow Room*. Cambridge: MIT Press, 1984.

Descartes, René. *Discourse on the Method of Rightly Conducting the Reason and Seeking the Truth in the Sciences*. In *The Philosophical Works of Descartes*, translated by Elizabeth S. Haldane and G. R. F. Ross. Cambridge: Cambridge University Press, 1970.

Donagan, Alan. "The Popper-Hempel Theory Reconsidered." In *Philosophical Analysis and History*, edited by William H. Dray. New York: Harper & Row, 1966.

Double, Richard. "Misdirections in the Free Will Problem." *American Philosophical Quarterly* 34 (1997): 357–366.

Dray, William H. "Historical Explanation of Actions Reconsidered." In *Philosophy of History*, edited by Patrick Gardiner. London: Oxford University Press, 1974.

——. *Laws and Explanations in History*. Oxford: Oxford University Press, 1957.

——, ed. *Philosophical Analysis and History*. New York: Harper & Row, 1966.

Falk, W. David. "Morality, Form, and Content." In *Ought, Reasons, and Morality*. Ithaca: Cornell University Press, 1986.

——. "Morality, Self, and Others." In *Ought, Reasons, and Morality*. Ithaca: Cornell University Press, 1986.

Faulkner, William. *A Fable*. London: Chatto & Windus, 1955.

Fisher, John M. "Freedom and Determinism." In *Encyclopedia of Ethics*, edited by Lawrence C. Becker. New York: Garland, 1992.

——. Introduction to *Moral Responsibility*, edited by John M. Fisher. Ithaca: Cornell University Press, 1986.

Foot, Philippa. "Are Moral Considerations Overriding?" In *Virtues and Vices*. Oxford: Blackwell, 1978.

——. "Morality as a System of Hypothetical Imperatives." In *Virtues and Vices*. Oxford: Blackwell, 1978.

Frankena, William K. "The Concept of Morality." *Journal of Philosophy* 63 (1966): 688–696.

Frankfurt, Harry G. "Freedom of the Will and the Concept of a Person." In *The Importance of What We Care About*. New York: Cambridge University Press, 1988.

——. *The Importance of What We Care About*. New York: Cambridge University Press, 1988.

Frede, Michael. *Essays in Ancient Philosophy*. Minneapolis: University of Minnesota Press, 1987.

Gallie, W. B. *Philosophy and the Historical Understanding*. London: Chatto & Windus, 1964.

Gardiner, Patrick. *The Nature of Historical Explanation*. Oxford: Oxford University Press, 1952.

——, ed. *The Philosophy of History*. London: Oxford University Press, 1974.

——, ed. *Theories of History*. New York: Free Press, 1959.

Gauthier, David. *Morals by Agreement*. Oxford: Clarendon Press, 1986.

Geertz, Clifford. *Local Knowledge*. New York: Basic Books, 1983.

——. "Thick Description: Toward an Interpretive Theory of Culture." In *The Interpretation of Cultures*. New York: Basic Books, 1973.

Gewirth, Alan. *Reason and Morality*. Chicago: University of Chicago Press, 1978.

Goodman, Nelson. *Ways of Worldmaking*. Indianapolis: Hackett, 1978.

Hampshire, Stuart. *Freedom of the Individual*. Expanded edition. Princeton: Princeton University Press, 1975.

——. *Innocence and Experience*. Cambridge: Harvard University Press, 1989.

——. *Morality and Conflict.* Cambridge: Harvard University Press, 1983.

——. *Thought and Action.* London: Chatto & Windus, 1960.

Hare, Richard M. *The Language of Morals.* Oxford: Clarendon Press, 1952.

——. *Moral Thinking.* Oxford: Clarendon Press, 1981.

Hegel, Georg W. F. *The Phenomenology of Mind.* Translated by J. B. Baillie. New York: Harper, 1967.

Hempel, Carl G. "Explanation in Science and History." In *Philosophical Analysis and History,* edited by William H. Dray. New York: Harper & Row, 1966.

——. "The Function of General Laws in History." In *Theories of History,* edited by Patrick Gardiner. New York: Free Press, 1959.

——. "Rational Action." *Proceedings and Addresses of the American Philosophical Association* 35 (1962): 5–23.

——. "Reason and Covering Laws in Historical Explanation." In *Philosophy and History,* edited by Sidney Hook. New York: New York University Press, 1963.

Hiley, David R. *Philosophy in Question.* Chicago: University of Chicago Press, 1988.

Honderich, Ted. *How Free Are You?* Oxford: Oxford University Press, 1983.

Hook, Sidney, ed. *Philosophy and History.* New York: New York University Press, 1963.

Horton, Robin. "African Traditional Thought and Western Science." In *Rationality,* edited by Bryan R. Wilson. Oxford: Blackwell, 1970.

——. "Material-Object Language and Theoretical Language: Towards a Strawsonian Sociology of Thought." In *Philosophical Disputes in the Social Sciences,* edited by Stuart C. Brown. Sussex: Harvester Press, 1977.

——. "Tradition and Modernity Revisited." In *Rationality and Relativism,* edited by Martin Hollis and Steven Lukes. Oxford: Blackwell, 1982.

Hume, David. *Enquiries Concerning the Human Understanding.* 2d ed. Edited by L. A. Selby-Bigge. Oxford: Clarendon Press, 1961.

——. *Enquiries Concerning the Principles of Morals.* Edited by L. A. Selby-Bigge. Oxford: Clarendon Press, 1961.

——. *A Treatise of Human Nature.* Edited by L. A. Selby-Bigge. Oxford: Clarendon Press, 1960.

James, William. *A Pluralistic Universe.* In *William James: Writings 1902–1910,* edited by Bruce Kuklick. New York: Library of America, 1987.

Kane, Robert. *The Significance of Free Will.* New York: Oxford University Press, 1995.

Kant, Immanuel. *Groundwork of the Metaphysics of Morals.* Translated by H. J. Paton. New York: Harper, 1964.

——. *Prolegomena to Any Future Metaphysics.* Revised translation by Lewis White Beck. New York: Liberal Arts, 1950.

Kekes, John. *The Morality of Pluralism.* Princeton: Princeton University Press, 1993.

——. *Moral Wisdom and Good Lives.* Ithaca: Cornell University Press, 1995.

Korsgaard, Christine M. *Creating the Kingdom of Ends.* New York: Cambridge University Press, 1996.

——. *The Sources of Normativity.* New York: Cambridge University Press, 1996.

Kuhn, Thomas S. "Reflections on My Critics." In *Criticism and the Growth of Knowledge,* edited by I. Lakatos and A. Musgrave. Cambridge: Cambridge University Press, 1970.

Kupperman, Joel J. *Value . . . and What Follows.* New York: Oxford University Press, 1999.

Livingstone, Donald W. *Hume's Philosophy of Common Life.* Chicago: University of Chicago Press, 1984.

——. *Philosophical Melancholy and Delirium*. Chicago: University of Chicago Press, 1998.

Machan, Tibor, ed. *The Libertarian Alternative*. Chicago: Nelson-Hall, 1974.

Mates, Benson. *The Skeptic Way*. New York: Oxford University Press, 1996.

McGinn, Colin. *Problems of Philosophy*. Oxford: Blackwell, 1993.

——. *The Subjective View*. Oxford: Clarendon Press, 1983.

Melden, Abraham I. *Free Action*. London: Routledge, 1961.

Mill, John Stuart. *Autobiography*. New York: Columbia University Press, 1924.

——. *On Liberty*. Indianapolis: Hackett, 1978.

——. *A System of Logic*. London: Longmans, 1872.

——. *Utilitarianism*. Indianapolis: Hackett, 1979.

Mink, Louis O. "The Autonomy of Historical Understanding." In *Philosophical Analysis and History*, edited by William H. Dray. New York: Harper & Row, 1966.

Montaigne, Michel de. "Apology for Raymond Sebond." In *Essays*, in *The Complete Works of Montaigne*, translated by Donald M. Frame. Stanford: Stanford University Press, 1948.

Moore, George Edward. "Some Judgments of Perception." In *Philosophical Studies*. London: Routledge, 1922.

Nagel, Thomas. "The Absurd." In *Mortal Questions*. New York: Cambridge University Press, 1979.

——. *Equality and Partiality*. New York: Oxford University Press, 1991.

——. "Subjective and Objective." In *Mortal Questions*. New York: Cambridge University Press, 1979.

——. *The View from Nowhere*. New York: Oxford University Press, 1967.

Nehamas, Alexander. *The Art of Living*. Berkeley: University of California Press, 1998.

Nietzsche, Friedrich. *Beyond Good and Evil*. In *Basic Writings of Nietzsche*, translated and edited by Walter Kaufmann. New York: Modern Library, 1966.

——. *The Gay Science*. Translated by Walter Kaufmann. New York: Vintage Press, 1974.

——. *On the Genealogy of Morals*. In *Basic Writings of Nietzsche*, translated and edited by Walter Kaufmann. New York: The Modern Library, 1966.

——. *Thus Spoke Zarathustra*. Translated by R. J. Hollingdale. Harmondsworth, England: Penguin, 1961.

——. *Twilight of the Idols*. In *The Portable Nietzsche*, translated by Walter Kaufmann. Harmondsworth, England: Penguin, 1954.

——. *Untimely Meditations*. Translated by R. J. Hollingdale. Cambridge: Cambridge University Press, 1983.

——. *The Will to Power*. Translated by Walter Kaufmann and R. J. Hollingdale. New York: Random House, 1967.

Norton, Robert E. *The Beautiful Soul: Aesthetic Morality in the Eighteenth Century*. Ithaca: Cornell University Press, 1995.

Nozick, Robert. *Philosophical Explanations*. Cambridge: Harvard University Press, 1981.

Nussbaum, Martha C. *The Fragility of Goodness*. Cambridge: Cambridge University Press, 1986.

——. *The Therapy of Desire*. Princeton: Princeton University Press, 1994.

Oakeshott, Michael. *Experience and Its Modes*. Cambridge: Cambridge University Press, 1933.

——. *On History*. Oxford: Blackwell, 1983.

——. "Rationalism in Politics." In *Rationalism in Politics*, expanded edition, edited by Timothy Fuller. Indianapolis: Liberty Press, 1991.

———. "The Voice of Poetry in the Conversation of Mankind." In *Rationalism in Politics*, expanded edition, edited by Timothy Fuller. Indianapolis: Liberty Press, 1991.

Olafson, Frederick. *The Dialectic of Action*. Chicago: University of Chicago Press, 1979.

Paton, H. J. *The Categorical Imperative*. London: Hutchinson, 1947.

Plato. *Euthyphro*. Translated by Lane Cooper. In *Plato: The Collected Dialogues*, edited by Edith Hamilton and Huntington Cairns. Princeton: Princeton University Press, 1961.

———. *The Republic*. Translated by Robin Waterfield. New York: Oxford University Press, 1993.

Popper, Karl R. "The Nature of Philosophical Problems and their Roots in Science." In *Conjectures and Refutations*. New York: Harper, 1963.

———. "A Realist View of Logic, Physics, and History." In *Objective Knowledge*. Oxford: Clarendon Press, 1972.

Quine, Willard Van Orman. *Word and Object*. Cambridge: MIT Press, 1960.

Rand, Ayn. *The Virtue of Selfishness*. New York: Signet, 1964.

Rawls, John. *A Theory of Justice*. Cambridge: Harvard University Press, 1971.

Rescher, Nicholas. *Pluralism*. Oxford: Clarendon Press, 1993.

Rorty, Richard. *Consequences of Pragmatism*. Minneapolis: University of Minnesota Press, 1982.

———. *Philosophical Papers*. Vols. 1–2. Cambridge: Cambridge University Press, 1991.

———. *Philosophy and the Mirror of Nature*. Princeton: Princeton University Press, 1979.

Russell, Bertrand. *The Problems of Philosophy*. London: Oxford University Press, 1967.

Ryle, Gilbert. *Dilemmas*. Cambridge: Cambridge University Press, 1956.

———. "Thinking and Reflecting." In *Collected Papers*, vol. 2. London: Hutchinson, 1971.

Scheffler, Samuel. *Human Morality*. New York: Oxford University Press, 1992.

Sellars, Wilfrid. "Philosophy and the Scientific Image of Man." In *Science, Perception and Reality*. London: Routledge, 1963.

Sextus Empiricus. *Outlines of Scepticism*. Translated by Julia Annas and Jonathan Barnes. Cambridge: Cambridge University Press, 1994.

Shusterman, Richard. *Practicing Philosophy*. New York: Routledge, 1997.

———. *Pragmatist Aesthetics*. Oxford: Blackwell, 1992.

Sidgwick, Henry. *The Methods of Ethics*. Indianapolis: Hackett, 1981.

Strawson, Galen. *Freedom and Belief*. Oxford: Clarendon Press, 1986.

Strawson, Peter F. *Individuals: An Essay in Descriptive Metaphysics*. London: Methuen, 1959.

Swanton, Christine. *Freedom*. Indianapolis: Hackett, 1992.

Taylor, Charles. "The Diversity of Goods." In *Philosophy and the Human Sciences*. Cambridge: Cambridge University Press, 1985.

———. "Responsibility for Self." In *The Identities of Persons*, edited by Amelie Rorty. Berkeley: University of California Press, 1976.

———. *Sources of the Self*. Cambridge: Harvard University Press, 1989.

Taylor, Richard. *Action and Purpose*. Englewood Cliffs, N.J.: Prentice-Hall, 1966.

———. "Determinism." In *Encyclopedia of Philosophy*, edited by Paul Edwards. New York: Macmillan, 1967.

———. *Good and Evil*. New York: Macmillan, 1970.

van Inwagen, Peter. *An Essay on Free Will*. Oxford: Oxford University Press, 1983.

Vlastos, Gregory. *Socrates, Ironist and Moral Philosopher*. Ithaca: Cornell University Press, 1991.

Waismann, Friedrich. "Notes on Talks with Wittgenstein." *Philosophical Review* 74 (1965): 15–16.

Waller, Bruce. *Freedom without Responsibility*. Philadelphia: Temple University Press, 1990.

Walsh, William H. *An Introduction to the Philosophy of History*. London: Hutchinson, 1951.

Watson, Gary. "Free Action and Free Will." *Mind* 96 (1987): 145–172.

——. Introduction to *Free Will*, edited by Gary Watson. Oxford: Oxford University Press, 1982.

White, Morton. *Foundations of Historical Knowledge*. New York: Harper & Row, 1965.

Wiggins, David. "Truth, Invention, and the Meaning of Life." *Proceedings of the British Academy* 62 (1976): 331–378.

Williams, Bernard. *Descartes: The Project of Pure Enquiry*. Atlantic Highlands, N.J.: Humanities Press, 1978.

——. *Ethics and the Limits of Philosophy*. London: Collins, 1985.

——. "Moral Luck." In *Moral Luck*. Cambridge: Cambridge University Press, 1981.

——. "Persons, Character and Morality." In *Moral Luck*. Cambridge: Cambridge University Press, 1981.

Winch, Peter. *The Idea of a Social Science*. London: Routledge, 1958.

——. "Understanding a Primitive Society." In *Ethics and Action*. London: Routledge, 1972.

Wittgenstein, Ludwig. *The Blue and Brown Books*. Oxford: Blackwell, 1969.

——. "A Lecture on Ethics." *Philosophical Review* 74 (1965): 3–12.

——. *Philosophical Investigations*. Translated by G. E. M. Anscombe. Oxford: Blackwell, 1968.

——. *Tractatus Logico-Philosophicus*. Translated by D. F. Pears and B. F. Guinness. London: Routledge, 1961.

Wolf, Susan. *Freedom within Reason*. New York: Oxford University Press, 1991.

——. "Moral Saints." *Journal of Philosophy* 79 (1982): 419–439.

Yahara, Hiromichi. *The Battle for Okinawa*. Translated by Roger Pineau and Masatishi Uehara. New York: Wiley, 1995.

Index